A WORLD BANK COUNTRY STUDY

Agriculture in Tanzania Since 1986

Follower or Leader of Growth?

Government of the United Republic of Tanzania

The World Bank
Washington, D.C.

International Food Policy Research Institute
Washington, D.C.

Contents*

* This technical report was prepared by the International Food Policy Research Institute Washington D.C., in November 1999, for the joint United Republic of Tanzania – World Bank Country Economic Memorandum., *Tanzania at the Turn of the Century: From Reforms to Sustained Growth and Poverty Reduction*, 2000. The authors, Dr. C. L. Delgado and Dr. N. W. Minot, based the report on background papers contributed by various Ministries in the Government of Tanzania, University of Dar es Salaam, Institute for Development Management (Morogoro) and IFPRI.

Map of The United Republic of Tanzania

List of Figures

List of Tables

vii

ABSTRACT

Agriculture in Tanzania since 1986: Follower or Leader of Growth is organized in nine parts. In addition to the executive summary which outlines the main findings and key messages, Chapter One addresses the main agricultural controversies in Tanzania's development strategy, outlined earlier. The analysis in the report establishes that agriculture can be an engine rather than a follower of growth in Tanzania and the pivot for poverty reduction. The sector has higher multiplier effects especially through forward linkages than other sectors, the actors in it are responsive to changes in incentives associated with the macroeconomic and policy reforms implemented so far; and with wide variations across crops overall agriculture has posted a modest growth performance after reforms but somewhat less than implied by the national accounts data.

Chapter Two traces the evolution of public policy affecting agriculture and its impact on the sector's performance in Tanzania. It reviews the evolution of sector policy regimes, from unregulated grain and export markets to cooperative-based marketing to centralized crop authorities and back to relatively unregulated markets. On the macroeconomic side the evolution of the exchange rate policy, trade taxes, fiscal stances play a particularly prominent role in shaping agricultural incentives. It is difficult to interpret current policy debates and recent agricultural performance without an understanding of the evolution of these policies. Analysis of government expenditure on agriculture is also included in this chapter.

Chapter Three analyses the impact of the evolving output price incentives for agricultural production since 1986. Specifically it recognizes that the combination of evolving policies towards agriculture and towards the macro economy, the state of infrastructure, the degree of commercialization, weather trends, and shifting world prices have all jointly altered, fundamentally, the structure of output price incentives facing agricultural producers in Tanzania. It also focuses on the effect of these changes on agricultural producers and consumers of different goods. In addition, the chapter assesses the extent to which parts of Tanzania's agriculture are insulated from world price movements, while others are directly linked to world markets. The chapter concludes by a review of trends and issues on the cost side of agricultural production, and brings the evidence together to assess evolving financial profitability and comparative advantage for specific major crops in Tanzania. The report identifies the movement in the real exchange rate to be a prime determinant in the time pattern of the profitability of tradable crops.

Chapter Four analyses the costs and returns to crop production in Tanzania. Relative output prices are only half of the picture regarding incentives; equally important are costs of production. Costs of production depend on the prices of purchased inputs, the cost of primary factors of production such as labor and land, the availability of skills and technology, and the institutions, including functioning markets, to make all these items available to producers. In the absence of technological change, short term changes in the cost of production will be determined essentially by changes in relative prices, actual use of purchased inputs, and by changes in the opportunity costs and use of primary factors. This chapter recognizes that these items changed greatly for different crops over the period in Tanzania. In addition, the costs of marketing outputs and procuring inputs also changed significantly over the period. Even though these changes can be expected to show up in lower producer prices and higher input costs at the farm-gate, the magnitude of marketing costs as a share of prices received and paid by farmers suggests that it is a key factor in influencing the cost formation at the farm level and overall profitability of the sector.

Chapter Five focuses in greater detail on the controversy of what has actually been the performance of Tanzania's agriculture. It is recognized that evaluating the impact of policy reforms on the performance of the agricultural sector in Tanzania is not easy since the mid-1980s when the first economic reforms were implemented because of a number of limitations and inconsistencies in Tanzania agricultural data and the usual problem of absence of a proper counterfactual. As stated earlier, the 1998 OED report had noted that estimates of the annual growth in agricultural output between the mid-1980s and the early 1990s vary between 1 and 5 percent. The study, after reconciling various data sources and using indirect performance indicators, concludes that the sector's growth post reforms averaged 3.3 percent, a modest but considerably better performance than earlier. There were significant differences across crops but generally export crops performing much better than food crops and within food crops those whose demand rises with income level fairing much better than the others. The chapter also assesses performance of the livestock and fisheries sub-sectors since the onset of reforms.

Chapter Six analyses the extent of rural poverty and the status of food security in Tanzania. The study recognizes that progress in reducing poverty, food insecurity, and malnutrition in Tanzania is highly dependent on the performance of the agricultural sector for two reasons. First, poverty is primarily a rural phenomenon. The incidence and severity of poverty is twice as high in rural areas as in urban area, urban incomes are 2-3 times greater than rural incomes, and rural households lag behind urban households in almost every indicator of the standard of living. The study concludes that since 1986 the trends in poverty and nutrition are generally positive or neutral. Household survey data suggest that rural incomes have risen and poverty rates have fallen between 1976 and 1993, the latest year for which national household budget data are available. Furthermore available evidence indicates that nutrition has either improved or has remained unchanged since the mid-1980s when the reforms were implemented. Nutrition surveys reviewed in the study show a decline in the rate of stunting among children (a measure of chronic malnutrition), while wasting (a measure of recent or acute malnutrition) rose slightly. Nonetheless, the chapter concludes that the levels of poverty and malnutrition remain high by international standards and improved agriculture remains a key to reduction of both.

Chapter Seven explores the linkages between agriculture and the rest of the economy. The section applies the method of Domestic Resource Cost Ratio (DRC) in working out the partial equilibrium and the attendant multipliers. Addressing the issues in this section involves defining whether agriculture is the leader of growth, in the sense that it comes first and provides the necessary stimulus to the creation of other economic activities, or whether it is the follower of growth. The study finds the linkage to be particularly strong for export agriculture with a shilling worth of income from this source leading to shillings 1.8 increase in overall GDP. It is also emphasized that for agriculture to be an engine of growth in a small, largely open economy, at least some of its major products must lie within the comparative advantage in production of the country. Furthermore, this chapter reiterates that comparative advantage activities are the only economically sustainable ways to bring in new resource inflows into the country. The chapter confirms Tanzania's strong comparative advantage in traditional export crops and maize as well as paddy among food crops even as the country is diversifying its export base.

Finally, Chapters Eight and Nine summarize the main conclusions and a list of references respectively.

PREFACE

This report was prepared as part of the Tanzania Country Economic Memorandum (CEM), *Tanzania at the Turn of the Century: From Reforms to Sustained Growth and Poverty Reduction*, 2000. It was decided to publish it as a self-standing report in view of its size, comprehensiveness, and prominence as expressed by the various readers and reviewers of its draft. The three-volume CEM incorporates the main findings and the key policy messages flowing from it. This report was prepared by the International Food Policy Research Institute (IFPRI) in collaboration with the World Bank, the Government of Tanzania and local experts. The Government of Denmark and Sweden met most of the costs of the study leading to this report.

The study was launched in April 1999 following agreement on a prospectus for it between the Bank and the Government of Tanzania. A concept paper for the CEM, which included the prospectus for the study, was reviewed and approved in February 1999 in a meeting involving IFPRI, the Government, donors, local experts and other stakeholders. Dr Christopher Delgado and Dr Nicholas Minot, both of IFPRI, led a team of experts from IFPRI and Tanzania in preparing the report. The team collected data, reviewed a wide range of relevant studies and official reports, and interviewed a wide range of actors in the sectors. The study also covered agriculture in Zanzibar. A workshop was held in Dar es Salaam, in September 1999, to review drafts of the report. The participation in the workshop was wide ranging, but it included members of the Technical and Steering Committee for the CEM appointed jointly by the Government and the Bank as peer reviewers and advisors to the study. The Sector Group in the Bank and the Government of Tanzania also presented formal comments on the report.

This study *inter alia* was commissioned partly to shed light on some controversies regarding the performance and the role of the sector in Tanzania's development. Two contrasting views had emerged regarding the performance of Tanzania's agriculture since the onset of reforms. They were perhaps best summarized in a 1998 evaluation report by the World Bank Operations Evaluation Department (OED). The OED report pointed out that the sector's growth performance as reflected in the National Accounts was at serious variance with production estimates from various national and international sources. The National Accounts (prior to revisions) indicated a high growth performance averaging nearly 5 percent annually while production data showed the sector's performance to be at best stagnant. Based also on stagnant food production estimates, there was a concern regarding inconsistency with nutritional status data. This in part led to the OED report to express strong doubts as to whether the policy reforms and investment programs in the sector have had any positive impact and expressed worries about the neglect of this sector, which is so pivotal to poverty reduction and overall development in Tanzania. For credibility of the assessment, and in order to maintain impartiality, it was considered necessary to engage an independent and a reputable institution (IFPRI) to carry out the study.

ACKNOWLEDGMENTS

The authors, Christopher L. Degaldo and Nicholas W. Minot, would especially like to thank Mr. Benno Ndulu of the World Bank Country Office in Dar es Salaam for his vote of confidence in the IFPRI members of the team commissioned to prepare this study, and the Danish foreign assistance agency DANIDA and the Swedish foreign assistance agency SIDA for co-funding the activity. Mrs. Janet Bitegeko very kindly provided liaison to the Ministry of Agriculture and Co-operatives (MAC) of the Government of the United Republic of Tanzania (URT), official cover for the activity, abundant moral support, and quite a bit of time to the team, despite a very busy schedule. Messrs. Albert Ngondo and Rosewald Mlay of MAC also provided a very significant amount of help to the team through insights shared, access to data, and documents. Mrs. S. Kaduma, project coordinator of the Agricultural Sector Management Project (ASMP), MAC, very kindly shared a large number of ASMP project documents with the team.

Grateful acknowledgment is made of the background papers prepared for the report by team members other than the IFPRI group. These consist of: Mrs. J. Bitegeko, Mr. A. Ngondo and Mr. R. Mlay of URT\MAC; Drs. W. Maro, H. Amani, and R. Mabele of the University of Dar-es-Salaam; Dr. E. Wiketye of the Institute for Development Management, Morogoro; Dr. R. Mfungahema, formerly of URT/Planning Commission; and Mr. J. Komba, Consultant. These papers, which have been collected together in the Annex volume, substantially improved the accuracy of team perceptions for Tanzania. The paper by Professor Mabele, on Zanzibar, is virtually the only in-depth source of information available to the team on current agricultural policy issues in Zanzibar.

Thanks are also conveyed to Mr. Rutachozibwa, coordinator of the U.S.A.I.D. Famine Early Warning System (FEWS) project office in Dar-es-Salaam, who facilitated the team's access to food retail price data. Mr. K. Kazungu of the University of Dar-es-Salaam provided very helpful research assistance during field visits in Tanzania. Mr. C. Courbois provided excellent research and editorial assistance at IFPRI. The authors are also very grateful to Mr. P. Wobst of IFPRI's trade and Macroeconomic Division, who performed experiments for the report using a Social Accounting Matrix of the Tanzanian economy constructed for his forthcoming Ph.D. thesis, in support of the section on growth linkages in Tanzania.

Finally, World Bank staff in Dar-es-Salaam and Washington have been uniformly supportive of an activity carried on by an outside agency in an area that is currently the subject of controversy with in the Bank and in Tanzania itself. Besides Mr. Ndulu, the team would also especially like to thank Mr. Ben Tarimo and Mr. Don Sungusia of the Resident Mission, and Ms. Sumana Dhar, and Mr. Tekola Dejene of World Bank headquarters, Washington. Because the subject matter is controversial, because many of the persons cited above may disagree on significant points, and because the IFPRI team felt it important to maintain its independence during writing, Delgado and Minot accept full responsibility for the views expressed and remaining errors, which should not be attributed to any person or institution mentioned above.

EXECUTIVE SUMMARY

1.   Objectives

Is agriculture a lead sector in Tanzania, an engine of growth and poverty alleviation? Or is it merely a follower, extending and distributing benefits from a process started in some other part of the economy? The answer to this question has important implications for Tanzania's long-term development strategy.

In addressing this broader topic, this report investigates four questions concerning the place of agriculture in Tanzania's economy:

- What is the overall effect of agricultural and macroeconomic reforms since 1986 on incentives in the agricultural sector?

- What has been the performance of the agricultural sector in Tanzania since 1986? In particular, how can we reconcile figures showing a high rate of agricultural GDP growth with stagnant food production data?

- What are the trends and patterns in poverty and nutrition in Tanzania? What do they tell us about actual agricultural performance and needed priorities in economic development?

- What is the role of agriculture in overall economic growth in Tanzania? How much priority should the government put on agricultural development compared to other sectors.

2.   Approach of the Report

This report was prepared over the period May-October 1999 by Drs. C. Delgado and N. Minot, with assistance from Mr. C. Courbois. It relies on a thorough bibliographic review, four trips to Tanzania, analysis of agricultural data, econometric analyses of household survey data and price data, social accounting matrix simulations, and nine background papers prepared by Tanzanian researchers for this report. The local collaborators were Mrs. J. Bitegeko, Mr. A. Ngondo, and Mr. R. Mlay of the Ministry of Agriculture and Cooperatives, Dr. H. Amani (assisted by Dr. O. Mashindano), Dr. R. Mabele, and Dr. W. Maro from the University of Dar es Salaam, Dr. E. Wiketye from the Institute for Development Management, Dr. R. Mfungahema, formerly of the Planning Commission, and Mr. J. Komba, formerly with the National Bureau of Statistics. Mr. K. Kazungu provided additional research assistance. Data and insights on Zanzibar were very difficult to obtain. Dr. Mabele provided a special report on Zanzibar reproduced in the annex volume to the main report, from which many of the insights below for Zanzibar are drawn.

3.   Summary of Findings for the Mainland

3.1   Impact of Reforms on Agricultural Prices

EVOLUTION OF POLICY. In the early 1980s, Tanzania was in the midst of a severe economic crisis characterized by 30 percent inflation, unsustainable fiscal and external deficits, shortages of basic consumer goods, the collapse of agricultural exports, and shrinking GDP.

Starting in 1984 and accelerating in 1986, economic reforms were introduced to allow market forces to play a greater role in the economy. From 1986 to 1993, the real exchange rate depreciated significantly, providing better incentives to exporters. Domestic food crop marketing was liberalized, with private traders gradually taking over the role of the cooperatives and crop authorities. From 1991 to 1995, fertilizer subsidies were phased out and markets were opened to private traders. In the mid-1990s, the marketing and export of traditional export crops was liberalized and the commercial role of parastatal crop authorities scaled back.

Since 1993, however, the real exchange rate has appreciated, falling roughly 40 percent. In addition, government expenditure on agriculture has fallen both in absolute real terms and as a percentage of total expenditure. The fiscal savings associated with the elimination of inputs subsidies and loss-making commercial activities have not been redirected to vital public support for the agricultural sector.

IMPACT ON AGRICULTURAL PRICES. The market-determined producer prices of food in the early 1990s were substantially higher in real terms than the official procurement prices of the 1980s. Interpretation of this difference is complicated, however, by the facts that 1) many farmers sold their harvest on parallel markets even in the 1980s, but data for these prices do not exist and 2) market food prices after 1991 were significantly affected by the 1991-92 drought in southern Africa and associated maize exports from Tanzania. Real producer prices of food have fallen 40-60 percent since 1992. These reductions were due to the end of the regional shortages associated with the drought and real exchange rate appreciation since 1993. As a result of the appreciation, the reductions in producer prices for maize, wheat, and rice have been larger (55-60 percent) than those for non-tradable crops.

Export crop prices have been affected by movements in the real exchange rate, world prices, and marketing margins. From 1986 to 1993, successive devaluations increased the shilling value of exports several fold, thus reducing the implicit taxation caused by overvaluation. Real producer prices rose substantially, but less than would be expected given the size of the devaluations. First, the real FOB prices fell for five of the crops, most dramatically for coffee. Second, parastatal crop authorities increased their marketing margins, absorbing part of the benefits of the devaluation.

Since 1993, real producer prices for all the major export crops have fallen between 25 and 70 percent. This has occurred in spite of some reduction in marketing margins due to privatization and in spite of stable world prices. The main explanation for the falling producer prices is the appreciation of the real exchange rate since 1993.

In order to test the tradability of different food crops in Tanzania, we estimate monthly retail prices for maize, rice, and cassava as a function of world prices, the exchange rate, regional supply, national supply, and rainfall. As expected, rice prices are strongly influenced by world prices throughout Tanzania, implying that it is tradable. Cassava prices are unaffected by world prices but strongly affected by domestic supply, implying that it is non-tradable. Maize prices are affected by world prices in the more accessible regions and by domestic supply alone in the more isolated regions.

IMPACT ON INPUT PRICES. Devaluation and input subsidy removal have increased the real price of fertilizer by a factor of 2.5 to 3.9 over 1991-1997. This increase, combined with lower producer prices, has greatly reduced the profitability of fertilizer use, particularly for food crops such as maize and particularly in the Southern Highlands.

IMPACT ON MARKETING COSTS. We also examine the cost of agricultural marketing using monthly retail food prices in 44 markets. The data show that marketing margins for maize, rice, and wheat between Dar and other cities have fallen significantly. These changes presumably reflect the increased efficiency of a competitive private-sector market compared to the previous government regulated markets. The analysis also indicates that the size of the margins reflects the availability of marketing infrastructure such as road distance, ports, and rail lines. Transfer costs on the order of US$0.16 per ton/km were inferred on major trade routes, suggesting the need for urgent action to bring these costs down.

3.2   Performance of the Agricultural Sector Since 1986

DATA PROBLEMS. Agricultural production statistics in Tanzania have suffered from inconsistency among the three main sources of data, but they have improved in recent years. Crop production estimates since 1993 have been largely based on national sample surveys. We concur with the conclusions of Kiregyera et al (1999), Mlay (1999), and Komba (1999) that the food production data used by the National Bureau of Statistics (NBS) in calculating agricultural GDP are seriously flawed and that the data generated by the Agricultural Statistics Unit of the MAC are more accurate. Nonetheless, it should be noted that before 1993 even ASU estimates were based on the subjective reporting of village extension officers, and there is still considerable scope for improvement.

PERFORMANCE OF CROP AGRICULTURE. Replacing the NBS food production data with ASU food production data does not substantially alter the trends in agricultural GDP. However, replacing NBS data for three traditional export crops with data from the ASU results in an upward revision in agricultural GDP growth. Based on these revisions, we estimate that agricultural GDP has grown at 3.3 percent per year since 1985. The six main food crops have grown at 3.5 percent per year, while export crops have grown at 5.4 percent. Other components such as livestock and forestry have lower recorded numbers. Our estimates should be considered very tentative in light of the fact that we have not revised the previous simple projection assumptions used by NBS to estimate growth in minor crops, forestry, and animal products.

Maize production has grown an annual rate of 2.4 percent over 1985-1998. This growth rate is slightly below that of population, but it is fairly respectable given the declining real producer price and the large increase in fertilizer prices. The removal of fertilizer subsidies does not seem to a major factor, as will be seen. Effective demand constraints linked to high marketing costs probably play a larger role in limiting maize output growth.

Since 1985, rice output has expanded three-fold and wheat production has grown by 60 percent. Both commodities have high income elasticities of demand, and both are consumed in greater quantities by urban households. The growth rates of other staple crops such as sorghum/millet, beans, cassava, sweet potatoes, and bananas tend to track population growth, aside from weather-related fluctuations. Limited demand prevents them from expanding any more rapidly.

Export crop production expanded just 1.8 percent per year over the late 1980s. In contrast, the growth rate in the 1990s has been 7.7 percent per year. Strong growth in cashew nuts and tobacco have offset declines in coffee.

PERFORMANCE OF LIVESTOCK AND FISHERIES. Performance in the important beef cattle sector has been mixed. This is hardly surprising given the long-term fall in domestic and world prices, the rising cost and lower access to veterinary and other livestock services over time, and high and arbitrary levels of local and central taxation. Dairy and poultry have performed very well, showing long term growth rates well over 4 percent for dairy and probably higher for poultry and eggs. Animal health remains a major constraint. These intensive occupations are overwhelmingly carried out in small-scale operations within city limits. There are anecdotal reports that pork is also expanding in urban areas. This pattern of development implies a continued high rate of growth in concentrate feed use, and mounting environmental and public health problems in towns.

Aggregate data on fisheries are unreliable, but suggest stagnation in aggregate production. Much more reliable data on fishery exports show explosive growth in exports since the mid to late 1980's. Nile Perch fillets in 1998 from Lake Victoria accounted for more than 75 percent of total fisheries exports, which in turn represented more than 8 percent of total merchandise exports, up from a negligible amount in the mid 1980's.

INPUT USE. The use of fertilizer has fallen by about half as a result of subsidy removal and lower crop prices. The most significant declines were in fertilizer use on maize, particularly in the Southern Highlands. Overall, the impact on national maize production has probably been modest (less than 5 percent). This conclusion is based on: a) low initial use of fertilizer on food crops in a national context; b) calculations using the physical response of maize to fertilizer, c) the absence of measurable reductions in maize yield, and d) the statistical insignificance of fertilizer price in econometric estimation of maize supply. In the case of export crops such as tobacco and coffee, fertilizer remains profitable in many cases, but use may be constrained by lack of credit.

CREDIT. Just 5 percent of Tanzanian farmers obtain credit from non-family sources in a given year. But if the profitability of inputs is the problem, as may be the case for maize in many situations, expanded credit programs will not be successful. In this case, a better strategy would be to focus on reducing marketing and transportation costs. In the case of export crops however, fertilizer is more often profitable and very probably under used. The main problem is how to ensure credit recovery in a liberalized market where farmers have various market outlets. A variety of experiments are underway to develop rules and institutions to facilitate input credit for export crop producers. It would seem that some form of cooperation between state authorities and traders' associations will be necessary to police the repayment of input credit, and to crack down on rogue traders that knowingly buy up crops whose production was financed by other traders, without ensuring repayment of the loan.

SUPPLY RESPONSE. Econometric analysis confirms that farmers are sensitive to prices in their decisions regarding both food and export crop production. Using annual-regional panel data, we estimated the supply response to price for five crops. The short-term supply elasticities of maize, paddy, cotton, and cashew nut were positive and statistically significant. The short-run response of cashew nut production probably reflects farmer decisions regarding sulfur applications and harvesting intensity. There is a three year lag between changes in coffee price and coffee output, reflecting the lag between new tree plantings and the first harvest. The fertilizer price does not have a statistically significant effect for any of the five commodities, either because fertilizer use is determined by other factors (such as availability of credit) or because fertilizer is too low for price changes to make a difference.

3.3   *Poverty, Food Security, and Nutrition*

POVERTY AND AGRICULTURE. Progress in improving poverty, food security, and malnutrition in Tanzania is highly dependent on the performance of the agricultural sector for two reasons. First, poverty is primarily a rural phenomenon. The incidence and severity of poverty is twice as high in rural areas as in urban area, urban incomes are 2-3 times greater than rural incomes, and rural households lag behind urban households in almost every indicator of standard of living. Second, 84 percent of the workforce in Tanzania is involved in agricultural production. Even if farmers were not poorer, no development strategy could expect to improve the lives of the majority of the population without significant investment in agriculture.

Econometric analysis of the HRDS (Human Resource Development Survey 1993/94) household data indicates that incomes are substantially lower in rural areas, and within rural areas farmers are poorer than non-farmers. Among farmers, those who grow cash crops have higher incomes than those who do not, even after holding farm size, education, and other factors constant. Furthermore, income increases going to export crop farmers are associated with increased per capita food consumption among this group.

What do trends in poverty and nutrition tell us about the impact of the reforms and the performance of agriculture since 1986? The trends are generally positive or neutral. Household survey data suggest that rural incomes have risen and poverty rates have fallen between 1976 and 1993, the latest year for which national household budget data are available. Since the period 1976-1984 was one of ever deepening economic crisis, it is safe to assume that the progress was achieved since the reforms were launched in the mid-1980s.

NUTRITION. Available evidence indicates that nutrition has either improved or has remained unchanged since the mid-1980s when the reforms were implemented. Unfortunately, nationally representative nutrition data are only available from the 1991 and 1996 Tanzanian Demographic and Health Survey (TDHS). These surveys show a decline in the rate of stunting among children (a measure of chronic malnutrition), while wasting (a measure of recent or acute malnutrition) rose slightly. Nonetheless, the levels of poverty and malnutrition remain high by international standards. Infant mortality is even higher in Zanzibar than in rural areas of the mainland, mostly because access to health care facilities is so poor.

FOOD DEMAND. In order to get a rough picture of the future trends in food consumption in Tanzania, we conducted an analysis of food demand using the HRDS. The estimated income elasticity for maize is relatively low, while those of wheat, potatoes, animal products, and rice are relatively high. This implies that as per capita income rises, households will shift from maize and other staples toward more expensive sources of calories. Demand analysis also suggests that urbanization will shift demand away from maize, cassava, and sweet potatoes toward wheat, rice, white potatoes, and animal products.

3.4   Role of Agriculture in Tanzanian Economic Development

In order to be a leader or "engine" of growth and economic development, a sector must 1) produce directly exportable items or lower the costs of production of tradables and 2) create large spin-off effects through of intersectoral linkages. We address these in turn.

COMPARATIVE ADVANTAGE. Regarding the production of exportable items, agriculture accounts for half of Tanzanian exports. Furthermore, an analysis of domestic resource cost (DRC) ratios reveals that Tanzania has a strong comparative advantage in maize, paddy, and all the traditional export crops. Non-traditional export crops such as cut flowers may be highly profitable niche activities, but typically cannot provide the overall employment numbers and thus consumption linkages that the traditional export crops can, because of higher capital requirements and more difficult access to markets. Fisheries offer promise, but are subject to some of the same constraints. Livestock products may offer one of the best long run potentials in terms of widespread applicability. In any case, the same policy environment useful for promoting

xvii

traditional exports will also be beneficial for promoting non-traditional exports, and it is not necessary to distinguish them at this point.

INTER-SECTORAL LINKAGES. We find that export agriculture has major growth linkages with the non-farm sector. Backward linkages are negligible because most inputs are imported, and forward linkages are modest because processing is modest. But consumption linkages are significant: based on the HRDS data, we estimate that Tsh 1,000 of new household income from export crop sales can lead to Tsh 2,000 in additional local employment in the production of non-tradable goods and services.

An alternative method for estimating multiplier effects is with a Social Accounting Matrix (SAM). Simulations with a SAM constructed for Tanzania by Wobst (1999) show that a Tsh 1,000 stimulus to the traditional export crop sector leads to a Tsh 1,800 increase in overall GDP. By contrast, a Tsh 1,000 stimulus in light manufacturing adds only Tsh 1,200 to GDP. Not surprisingly, light manufacturing has a smaller effect on incomes in rural areas, where the vast majority of poverty is found. More surprisingly, light manufacturing has a smaller effect on *urban* incomes than does export cash cropping. This is because light manufacturing is less labor-intensive and uses more imported inputs than export agriculture.

URBAN VS. RURAL DEVELOPMENT. A recent World Bank study argues that Tanzania should focus its investment in urban infrastructure, light manufacturing, and peri-urban agriculture. Although surprised, we note the high policy relevance of the empirical finding by the survey underlying the study that intensification of agriculture has not manifested itself in peri-urban areas. Almost everywhere, growing cities are associated with the expansion of poultry, livestock, and horticultural production in peri-urban areas. We conclude that the accumulating evidence of rapidly growing intensive livestock production with the city limits of Dar-es-Salaam and possibly Arusha is in part a response to existing transport cost and taxation barriers to peri-urban-to-urban trade.

At the same time, we are skeptical of the report's conclusions that the absence of intensive peri-urban agriculture in Tanzania is an argument for concentrating resources in urban development. Any public support for one sector (whether through import protection, public investment, or tax preferences) is an implicit tax on other sectors. Agriculture in Tanzania has been severely discriminated against in the past by urban-oriented policies. It is only now beginning to regain some vitality in the vital export sectors, despite heavy taxation, high transport costs, and unfavorable movements in the real exchange rate.

More importantly, agriculture in Tanzania has a proven comparative advantage, strong links with other sectors, and employs the bulk of the poor. By contrast, the comparative advantage of light manufacturing is unknown, the linkages are smaller, and the direct beneficiaries (urban wage earners) are richer than the average Tanzanian. At a minimum, the proponents of a renewal of an urban-oriented strategy need to show how the vast mass of the population, living in areas made into largely non-tradable zones because of poor infrastructure and taxation, will be assisted by such a strategy

4.   Agriculture in Zanzibar

The similarity of issues faced by the agricultural sector of Zanzibar compared to the mainland is striking. The sector presently accounts for roughly 60 percent of the labor force, one-third of GDP, and three-quarters of foreign exchange, despite the fact that at 43 percent, the islands are more urbanized than the mainland. The macroeconomic issues are similar. Yet both food and export agriculture have not done well in the 1990's. Like the mainland, the poor are overwhelming concentrated in agriculture.

Unlike the mainland, Zanzibar has been slow to liberalize the sector, and the legacy of state farms from the former era is only now being dealt with in a new agricultural policy adopted this year. Government investment in agriculture in the 1980's was heavily concentrated in large-scale mechanization and irrigation, which did not leave much over for supporting the needs of small farmers. Food production has fallen by about half in recent years; plant disease and lack of input use remain big problems.

Food trade is now liberalized, and Zanzibar imported about one-quarter of its staple food supply over the 1993-97 period, unlike the mainland for whom a much higher degree of self-sufficiency is a realistic objective. Export crops are still largely in state hands. Traditional export cropping is far more concentrated in Zanzibar in a single crop--cloves--than the mainland (or most places). Cloves have been subject to plummeting international prices since the 1980's, due to significant market entry by Southeast Asian producers, and highly volatile yields.

There has been some success at boosting non-traditional exports, such as seaweed. The latter was as important in value terms as cloves in 1996, which was a poor year for cloves and a good year for seaweed. Diversification out of cloves remains an important policy objective. Zanzibar's island nature boosts the already import role of fishery exports in its diversification drive. High value fishery exports to developed countries have a bright demand future, but one perhaps best served by highly skilled private sector ventures in association with experienced market agents.

5.   Policy Implications

5.1   Long-term Strategy for Agriculture-led Economic Growth

A long-term strategy for agriculture-led growth in Tanzania involves many elements but four are central: macroeconomic balance, research and extension, improved infrastructure, and a tax and regulatory environment that is conducive to investment by both enterprises and individual farmers.

MACROECONOMIC BALANCE. The single most worrisome finding of this report for the agricultural sector is the renewed sharp appreciation of the real exchange rate since 1993. This shift, rather than world prices or export liberalization, is responsible for 25-70 percent reduction in real producer prices of the main export crops since 1993. In addition, the appreciation has reduced the real producer prices of rice, wheat, and maize.

INVESTMENT IN RESEARCH AND EXTENSION. Agricultural research and extension generate high returns on investment, as demonstrated by hundreds of rate-of-return studies. Because of externalities, relying entirely on private-sector research is not an option. In the case of export crops and tradable food crops, almost all the benefits of research accrue to farmers because prices are set by world markets. In the case of nontradable food crops, productivity-increasing research is likely to lower market prices, with benefits shared between producers and consumers.

INVESTMENT IN RURAL INFRASTRUCTURE. Transportation costs are a large share of the cost of agricultural marketing in Tanzania. Improved road and better rail service would 1) raise the producer price of export crops, 2) reduce the farm-level cost of fertilizer and other inputs, and 3) reduce spatial marketing margins in food marketing. It would also allow more rural Tanzanian households to earn income from commercialized agriculture. Similarly, expansion of the phone network (landline or wireless) would facilitate spatial arbitrage and market integration.

A FACILITATING PUBLIC ENVIRONMENT. The incentives to invest are affected not just by interest rates, formal regulations, and codified tax policy but also by intangible aspects of governance such as the attitude of public officials toward the private sector, the certainty and continuity of the business environment, and the risk of exposure to corruption. Tax rates and regulations should be uniform and modest rather than high but negotiable. Regulations should be clear and unambiguous. Furthermore, more progress is needed in creating a reliable and enforceable regulatory environment for internal and external agricultural trade, including measures and standards.

5.2   Short-term Measures to Stimulate Agriculture

There are several measures the government can implement in the short- to medium term to stimulate Tanzanian agriculture and boost rural standards of living. The effectiveness of these measures would be further increased if they were introduced as a package to revitalize agriculture, since they would serve as a public signal of the government's commitment to address the problem of rural poverty and the low returns to agriculture.

LIMIT LOCAL TAXATION OF AGRICULTURE. The central government must take a role in preventing excessive or arbitrary taxation of agricultural production and marketing by local authorities. The decentralization of revenue generation and agricultural support services in Tanzania has led to very different tax regimes being applied in different districts, and also apparently to some arbitrary differences within districts. Agriculture, particularly export agriculture, is an easy target for local revenue collection but should not be asked to support more than its share of local government budgets. Overall tax burdens of 30 to 60 percent on the major traditional export crops are not only inequitable, they have a hidden additional cost in terms of the lost employment creation associated with lower re-spending by households of revenue from the tradable sectors.

LIBERALIZE REGIONAL FOOD TRADE. The government should consider sending a signal to producers by permanently lifting all bans on food exports. This would assist farmers in the border regions, particularly those in the Southern Highlands near Zambia. The effect of export liberalization on poor consumers in deficit areas would be minor and could be offset by direct assistance. It is difficult to justify having poor farmers "pay" for assistance to maize consumers, many of whom are relatively well off. Similarly, the government should adopt and enforce a clear policy banning restrictions or taxation of agricultural trade within Tanzania.

PROMOTE AGRICULTURAL CREDIT. The government should encourage and facilitate systems for providing input credit to farmers. The system will be more sustainable a) if the credit is provided by crop buyers, banks, and cooperatives rather than the government, b) if the interest rates are not subsidized, and c) if it targets producers of commercial crops for which inputs are profitable. The government can facilitate input credit systems by making repayment easier to enforce, by facilitating the creation of groups for group lending schemes, and by generating information on the returns to input use. It can also mediate between buyers and growers to facilitate inter-trader farm loan recovery systems that are transparent and enforceable, particularly in the case of export crops. With adequate government supervision, traders associations can deal with the issue of rogue traders that aggressively buy up crops whose production costs were financed by other traders, without ensuring loan repayment.

Longer term small-scale agricultural investment loans will be facilitated by the new National Microfinance Bank. In this vein, it is to be anticipated that such loans for the foreseeable future will require the type of skills-intensive local servicing, oversight, and technical support that only NGO's or other subsidized organizations can provide. Well-designed subsidies to lending institutions catering to small-scale farmers can be justified in two ways. First, they address the extra financial costs and high overheads raised by the lack of a large number of borrowers in a given location and the lack of collateralizable assets and a culture of repayment. Second, they help create a base of viable borrowers for the future provided that their local presence and close attention to each loan ensures repayment. Direct interest subsidies to borrowers are not necessary. We judge the lack of assurance of reimbursement to be a more important constraint on increased lending to smallholders than the current market price of capital set by large-scale and urban borrowers.

RE-EXAMINE THE IMPACT OF FOOD AID. Food aid is essential for addressing temporary shortages and hunger, but it can also make food markets less predictable and lower returns to farmers. Since the poor are primarily food farmers, it is questionable whether regular annual food aid is really serving the interests of equity. Food aid should be temporary, well-targeted, and used sparingly.

IMPROVE DATA COLLECTION AND ANALYTICAL CAPACITY. The implementation of survey-based estimates of agricultural production is a step forward, but other data gaps need to be addressed. Better or more recent information is needed on production of horticulture, other "minor" crops, intensive small-scale animal agriculture (including aquaculture), the use of fertilizer and other inputs, food consumption patterns, the geographic distribution of poverty, inter-regional marketing flows, and trends in nutrition. Some survey work and analysis could be contracted to local consultants such as the Economic Research Bureau of the University of Dar es Salaam.

INCREASE BUDGETARY SUPPORT FOR AGRICULTURE. In order to implement the recommendations made here, budgetary support for the Ministry of Agriculture and Cooperatives will surely have to be increased. Budgetary support is particularly important in the areas of agricultural research and extension, rural infrastructure, and data collection. The current situation where salaries account for most of actual expenditures is not compatible with a vision of MAC as a public institution facilitating a favorable environment for private investment in agriculture. Prioritization of actions will become increasingly important. MAC will need the kind of staff and procedures that can provide decision-makers with viable options for moving forward. Most importantly, national and donor priorities for public goods creation should be harmonized and financed by both sides, to ensure that they really are priorities.

1. AGRICULTURAL CONTROVERSIES IN TANZANIA'S DEVELOPMENT STRATEGY DEBATE

fol.low.er (fol'o-er) ...An attendant...A machine element moved by another machine element. (Webster's II New Riverside University Dictionary, p. 493 (Soukhanov 1988)).

Lead.er (le'dar) One that leads or guides...The principal performer of an orchestral section or group (Webster's II New Riverside University Dictionary, p. 682 (Soukhanov 1988)).

The juxtaposition of economic sectors as either followers or leaders has a long tradition in economics going back at least 200 years, but most eloquently summed up in Kravis's seminal essay on the role of trade in economic growth (1970). Actors in both Tanzania and the donor community are actively concerned at the present time about at least four interrelated sets of issues pertaining to Tanzanian agriculture and its place in economic development strategy. Although all four have their specific aspects and are discussed below, together they sum to asking whether agriculture in the era of economic reforms is an initiator and engine—a leader--of growth and poverty alleviation, a necessary locomotive to keep the train rolling, or instead is a follower, extending and distributing benefits from a process started in some other sector.

Clearly the answer to this last question is a vital precursor to moving forward with an economic development strategy for the next decade in Tanzania. It is misleading in countries such as Tanzania to discuss "agriculture" as a "sector" comparable in nature, extent, and importance to "health" or "education". As shown in Table 1.1, rural areas in Tanzania in the 1990s still account for three-quarters of the overall population, and agriculture accounts for at least 80 percent of total employment in the country. In value terms, agriculture accounts for only 5 percent of imports (including food imports), but about half of exports. Similarly, it is thought to account for somewhat less than half of GDP, even allowing for controversies in the measurement of the latter.

Zanzibar, though more urbanized than mainland Tanzania (43 percent of households reside in urban areas (World Bank COD 1996c)) also depends a great deal on agriculture for income and employment. Agriculture's share of Zanzibar GDP has fallen recently from over 50 percent in the mid 1980s to 34 percent in 1995-97. Despite this decline, agriculture remains the backbone of the Zanzibar economy, contributing about 75 percent of exchange earnings, employing 60 percent of the labor force, and providing 30 percent of government revenue (Mabele 1999a).

The question then is should agriculture be treated as a "backward" sector, primarily useful for sustaining three-quarters of the population until more remunerative and less onerous non-agricultural employment becomes available in town? Or should agriculture be the focal point of policy for getting a self-sustaining process of economic development moving that will eventually lead to the diversification of the economy? Furthermore, if agriculture is a lead sector, should the focus be on the production of food or on the creation of greater purchasing power?

1

1.1 Four Key Issues Concerning the Place of Agriculture in Tanzania's Economy

The first issue to be explored concerns the overall effect on agricultural incentives of macroeconomic and sectoral agricultural policy reforms undertaken in Tanzania since 1986. This is a complex issue, since some macroeconomic policies that influence the overall level of inflation could unwittingly pull in the opposite direction from sectoral reforms designed to raise producer incomes. Furthermore, sectoral policies such as agricultural output market liberalization that raise producer prices might also have the effect of raising the cost of inputs to farmers. The side effects of institutional changes in agriculture could also be quite different from what was anticipated, as in the drying up of suppliers' credits for inputs when competition was introduced into cotton marketing. Issues of poor implementation, poor governance, and failure to attract significant private investment also suggest incomplete success of policies designed to improve agricultural incentives. Finally, many other influences besides policy impact on agricultural incentives, not the least of which are price trends in world markets.

The second issue is the nature and extent of the actual performance of agriculture in Tanzania since 1986. A recent (1998) World Bank Operations Evaluation Department (OED) evaluation report has seriously questioned whether existing GDP data suggesting a robust contribution of agricultural growth (5 percent per annum over 1985 -1994) to Tanzanian GDP growth is in fact based on real numbers. Household surveys and agricultural production reports compiled by the URT/Ministry of Agriculture and Cooperatives (MAC) suggest much lower growth in food crop agriculture, which accounted for 85 percent of land planted in the 1980s (World Bank OED 1998).

The third issue concerns the relationship between farming and poverty in Tanzania since 1986. The 1998 OED report charges that well-meaning efforts in Tanzania by the government, civil society, and donors (including the World Bank) are not presently focused on the root causes of poverty, but on the symptoms. This issue interacts with agriculture to the extent that in Africa, the poor are typically concentrated in rural areas, and that within the rural areas, relatively better off persons typically get a higher share of income from non-farm sources (Reardon *et al.* 1994). If this also the case in Tanzania, then problems in achieving poverty alleviation are linked to problems in achieving higher agricultural performance.

The fourth and final issue concerns the role of agriculture in overall economic growth in a country such as Tanzania at its present stage of development. The 1998 OED report in particular claims that a failure to recognize traditional export cropping as the engine of growth has led to overall economic distress and is jeopardizing the success of Tanzania's hard-fought and painful structural adjustment effort. On the other hand, a 1999 report on peri-urban development in Tanzania carried out under one of the macroeconomic divisions of the World Bank's Africa Region has actively advocated giving priority in investment to infrastructure in urban areas and to light manufacturing.[1] Observers within the Bank and elsewhere uneasily recall the "urban bias" policies of the 1970s, a generally agreed component of the poor policies leading to the need for structural adjustment in the first place. Favoring one geographic sector, such as light manufacturing and urban infrastructure, *ipso facto* provides a relative disincentive to other geographic sectors. Thus even with in the World Bank, there is considerable controversy as to desirable economic priorities, particularly where the link to the main economic activity of three-quarters of the population is unclear and very possibly negative.

---

[1] This important new study, still in draft, is typically referred to as the "World Bank's Peri-urban Study" in Tanzania (World Bank AFR2M 1999).

1.2   Approach of the Report

There were five aspects of the approach taken to this work. First, available evidence and data was marshaled and synthesized to address the four issues above. Second, to the extent reasonably possible, new empirical research was undertaken on existing on primary and secondary data to generate new insights. Third, an effort was made to separate external (outside Tanzania), policy-mediated, and structural factors that had constrained agricultural performance since 1986. Fourth, findings were documented as clearly as possible for a non-technical audience, but with a level of rigor that is still sufficient for a primarily technical document. Fifth, the findings are translated into a series of policy-relevant findings and recommendations proposed for incorporation into the forthcoming URT/World Bank *Country Economic Memorandum*.

1.3   Outline of the Report

The four key issues will be addressed in turn. The main food crops are dealt with separately from the traditional export crops. Livestock products are stressed, but dealt with in a fashion more limited than the real importance of the sub-sector due to data availability. Fisheries are dealt with peripherally because of their importance in explaining the growth of non-traditional agricultural exports, but the underlying issues for development of this important sector are not explored due to lack to lack of information, and because past experience in Tanzania in this area is largely outside the smallholder sector. Forestry is outside the scope of the issues dealt with in the report for the same reasons.

The next three sections of the report look at "what was net impact of reforms on incentives at farm level?". Section 2 addresses the evolving policy environment for agriculture, separating the influence of macroeconomic and sectoral agricultural policies. Two separate policy reform periods are identified within the 1986 to 1999 window, with very different implications for agriculture within each. Section 2 also explores the evolution of funding priorities within the Ministry of Agriculture and vis-a-vis the rest of the government over the 1990s.

Section 3 examines the separate impacts of policy, world markets, and structural factors on relative output prices faced by farmers. New research results are brought to bear to show that the prices of a significant portion of food crops behave as prices of non-tradable items in the economic sense, and the meaning and implications of this are explored.

Section 4 explores the costs and returns to crop production since 1986, the other side of the incentives scissors. Costs here include marketing margins that depress producer prices, trends in purchased input use and costs, unfavorable trends in the profitability of crop agriculture and the institutional vacuum created by the demise of the parastatals for improving farm incomes.

Section 5 tackles the issue of: "What has been performance of agriculture since 1986?". This involves looking at various assessments of the quality of agricultural data, and examining the relative performance in terms of physical output, value of production and productivity of different parts of agriculture. The issue of the reliability of both new and old agricultural GDP estimates is raised.

Section 6 looks at the issue of: "What is the role of agriculture in poverty alleviation?" It examines the locus of poverty in Tanzania and its relation to farming as an occupation. It then explores the links between agricultural performance and nutrition and food security, and whether export and food crops affect these goals differently. Section 7 then takes up the issue of "What is the link between agricultural growth and overall growth". It will explore the linkages between agriculture and the rest of the economy. The first sub-issue is what has happened to agriculture's comparative advantage over the 1990s. Subsequent sub-issues involve quantification of different sorts of linkages that agriculture in Tanzania has with the rest of the economy. Modeling is used here, involving fixed price multipliers and a national Social Accounting Matrix for 1992 (Wobst 1999). The evolution of rural linkages with towns is explored. The final section, Section 8, synthesizes the main insights and gives a list of policy options and recommendations that follow from this work.

Table 1.1. Agriculture's Contribution to the National Economy
(percent)

Parameter	1970	1975	1980-82	1985-87	1990-92	1997-98
Agriculture share of net exports by value	n/a	n/a	90	85	67	51
Agriculture share of GNP	49	45	49	46	45	50
Agriculture share of imports						
Fertilizer	n/a	n/a	2	4	4	1
Food	n/a	n/a	13	10	3	4
Agriculture share of labor force employment	90	88	86	85	84	82
Population in rural areas	93	90	85	82	79	75

n/a indicates figure not available

Note: Agricultural exports are taken as the six main crop exports: cashew, coffee, cotton, sisal, tea, and tobacco. World Bank COD (1999) estimates that including exports of fish, live animals, horticulture and other non-traditional exports would raise the share of agricultural exports in 1997-98 to 73 percent of total merchandise exports.

Source: Share of exports and GNP through 1992, and imports through 1998 are from World Bank 1998a. Share of labor force employment and share of population rural are from World Bank (1999b). The shares of the main agricultural exports in merchandise exports and GNP for 1997-98 are from World Bank COD (1999).

4

2. EVOLUTION OF PUBLIC POLICY AFFECTING AGRICULTURE

Tanzania has experimented with a wide variety of policy regimes, from unregulated grain markets to cooperative-based marketing to centralized crop authorities and back to relatively unregulated markets. Export marketing has experienced similar changes, as well as dramatic shifts in the real exchange rate. It is difficult to interpret current policy debates and recent agricultural performance without an understanding of this evolution. This section provides a brief overview of economic policy since independence and its impact on the agricultural sector.

2.1 Between Independence and the Arusha Declaration (1961-1966)

At independence in 1961, Tanzania inherited an agricultural sector characterized by a large semi-subsistence smallholder sector and a small number of plantations and estates. Export crops were controlled by marketing boards established by colonial authorities. Grain marketing was largely unregulated, although the colonial government had only recently withdrawn from intervening in this sector. Asian traders played an important role in crop marketing, resulting in some social tension. The cooperative movement had grown quickly in the 1950s, partly in an attempt to circumvent the Asian trading network (Bryceson 1993).

In 1962, the new government implemented the Agricultural Products Control and Marketing Act, which established a three-tier single-channel marketing system for maize, paddy, wheat, oilseeds, cashew nuts, and cotton. Primary cooperative societies supplied the "scheduled" crops to regional cooperative unions who sold them to a national marketing board. The National Agricultural Products Board handled all the "scheduled" crops except cotton. After an unsuccessful attempt to set prices at several levels of the marketing chain, the NAPB began fixing in-store prices, allowing producer prices to vary according with cooperative costs. Movement of more than 360 kg of grain was illegal but enforcement was difficult, leading to the growth of a parallel market (Maro 1999; Sarris and van der Brink 1994).

2.2 From the Arusha Declaration to the Reform Era (1967-1985)

In 1967, the Arusha Declaration announced a development strategy based on the principles of socialism, self-reliance, and egalitarianism. Many large private businesses were nationalized, including plantations, estates, importer/exporters, and food processors. The major milling companies were nationalized and merged to form the National Milling Corporation (NMC). In 1973, the NAPB was abolished and its functions assumed by the NMC. The list of scheduled crops was extended, and pan-territorial prices were introduced at the producer level. In order to facilitate cooperative agricultural production and the delivery of social services, the villagization campaign was launched in 1973. Within four years, millions of farmers were relocated (Maro 1999).

This period saw the nationalization of a wide range of private companies including banks, export-import firms, insurance companies, and other large-scale industries. In the agricultural sector, state enterprises were created from nationalized agricultural processing firms and large-scale estates (e.g. sisal). The number of parastatal organization increased from about 40 in the 1960s to more than 400 in the early 1980s.

The economic strains resulting from these policies began to appear in the early 1970s. The expanded role of the state led to higher government expenditure and fiscal deficits. The monetized deficits in turn resulted in the emergence of inflation, which rose from 3 percent in 1971 to 49 percent in 1975. In spite of the 143 percent increase in domestic prices over 1970-75, the official exchange rate remained at 7.14 Tsh/US$ (Bryceson 1993: 226). The overvaluation of the exchange rate combined with high marketing costs by the parastatal crop boards discouraged agricultural exports, which began a long decline in the early 1970s. Balance of payments problems were compounded by the 1973-74 oil price shock and by food imports associated with the 1973-74 drought.

Reacting to problems of financial mismanagement, high marketing costs, and late payments to farmers, the government dismantled the cooperatives and the three-tiered marketing system in 1976. The village took the role of the primary society, selling directly to marketing parastatals. This complicated the task of the NMC, which was already incurring large losses in its attempt to support pan-territorial prices. Although this system favored the remote surplus regions (notably the Southern Highlands, which provided a large share of the maize purchased by the NMC), it contributed to NMC debts, which reached US$200 million in 1980 (Maro 1999).

The economy improved notably in 1976 in response to a campaign to stimulate agricultural production and good weather. In addition, a frost in Brazil raised world coffee prices four-fold. The coffee tax revenue windfall was devoted to launching a major campaign to improve health, education, and water supply in rural areas, as well as major industrial and infrastructural projects. The improved economic climate was short-lived, however. In 1977, the collapse of the East African Community disrupted trade; the 1978 war against Idi Amin in Uganda further stretched government spending; the second oil shock occurred in 1979; and coffee prices returned to normal by 1981. The early 1980s were characterized by severe import and foreign exchange controls, contracting GDP, and fiscal deficits of 15-20 percent. It has been estimated that 20-30 percent of economic activity was in the parallel market and thus hidden from calculations of national accounts (Bagachwa and Naho 1995).

Food marketing was adversely affected by low producer prices, financial problems at the NMC, shortages of consumer goods necessary to motivate farmers, and lack of fuel and spare parts for the transport sector (Sijm 1997). The adverse effect on exports was even stronger: by the early 1980s, per capita production of agricultural exports had fallen 50 percent from their peak in 1970 (Sarris and van der Brink 1993).

The crisis led to a series of reform programs in the 1980s. The National Economic Survival Program (1981-82) attempted to address the imbalance through redistribution, cutting salaries and raising agricultural producer prices. The Structural Adjustment Program (1982-85) was somewhat more ambitious, involving macroeconomic reforms and a series of devaluations. In 1984, the government devalued the shilling, raised producer prices, raised to 500 kg the amount of grain that could be privately traded, and reduced the number of goods subject to price controls from around 2000 to 75 (Amani *et al.* 1989). In response to problems of financial mismanagement, over-staffing, and high costs in the crop authorities, the cooperative system was reintroduced, restoring the three-tiered marketing channel. Although the SAP did not receive support from the international financial organizations, it demonstrated a commitment to reform and initial signs of improvement paved the way for more fundamental change.

2.3 During the Early Reform Period (1986-1992)

In 1986, the government adopted the three-year Economic Recovery Program (ERP) with support from the International Monetary Fund (IMF), World Bank, and other international donors. This was followed by the second Economic Recovery Program (ERP II), also called the Economic and

Social Action Plan (ESAP), implemented over 1989-1992. The main elements of these programs were reduction in the fiscal deficit, a series of large devaluations, import liberalization, positive real interest rates, and the elimination of most consumer price controls.

Inflation continued at the pre-reform rate of about 30 percent, so that domestic prices (as measured by the national consumer price index) rose by a factor of 5.6 from 1986 to 1993. Yet, repeated devaluation of the Tanzanian shilling raised the nominal exchange rate from an average of 33 Tsh/US$ in 1986 to 425 Tsh/US$ in 1993, or by a factor of 12.9. The net effect on the real exchange rate (RER) was dramatic, as shown in Figure 2.1. The RER, as calculated here, is the nominal exchange rate adjusted for differences in the rates of change in purchasing power of domestic and international currencies. Conceptually, RER is thought of as a proxy for the relative price of tradables to non-tradables (Edwards 1989)[1]. Thus RER tracks the ratio of output prices (tradables whose fundamental value is driven by world markets) to the costs of the non-tradable primary factors used to produce them (labor, land, and capital, whose primary value is given by domestic supply and demand). Depreciation of the RER from 1986 to 1993 reduced the need for import controls and increased the returns to export and import-substitution activities.

In the agricultural sector, domestic food markets were liberalized first. Between 1986-89, private trade in food crops was deregulated, starting with minor crops and eventually including maize and rice. Movement controls were abolished in 1987. The NMC was given more autonomy in management, but was forced to scale back its operations and cover its costs. For example, the Strategic Grain Reserve (SGR) which began operations in 1978 in response to the 1973-74 drought, was transferred from the NMC to the newly created Food Security Department in the Ministry of Agriculture (Amani and Maro 1992).

By 1989, pan-territorial producer prices had effectively been abandoned. The fixed-price single-channel marketing system evolved into a multi-channel one in which the main intervention in grain markets were through purchases by the Strategic Grain Reserve (SGR) to cover emergency food needs. Private traders were able to pay higher prices for maize near the main consumer markets, leaving the NMC and later the SGR to purchase in more remote regions including the Southern Highlands (Maro 1999).

Since its formation in the 1967, the Tanzania Fertilizer Company (TFC) has maintained a monopoly on fertilizer imports[2]. In the late 1980s, private traders were technically allowed to import and distribute fertilizer, but the subsidy (available only to the TFC) and price controls made it unprofitable. The subsidies cost US$5-8 million per year in the early 1980s, rising to US$10-17 million in the late 1980s[3]. This represented 16 to 43 percent of government spending on agriculture in these years (Turuka 1995: 68). Fertilizer subsidies were 70 percent of the total cost of delivering fertilizer in 1990. The subsidy was gradually reduced over the following few years, reaching zero in 1994.

---

[1] Purists would define RER as P (tradables)/P (non-tradables), and call our measure the PPP--or purchasing power parity exchange rate--the usual proxy for true RER.

[2] From 1967 to 1977, the Tanzania Rural Development Bank also imported fertilizer for its credit recipients.

[3] In 1984 and 1985, the government set fertilizer prices at a level allowing full cost-recovery, effectively eliminating the subsidy. However, the price was not adjusted with further devaluations, reintroducing subsidies in 1986 (Turuka 1995: 67).

2.4   The Period Since 1993

The period since 1993 has seen the progressive stabilization of the nominal exchange rate, from 425 Tsh/US$ in 1993 to 670 Tsh/US$ in early 1999. Inflation has also been progressively reduced, falling from an annual rate of nearly 37 percent in 1994 to an estimated rate of 8.5 percent in 1999. These trends are shown as monthly compound growth rates in Table 2.1, which can be compared to the RER in Figure 2.1. It is useful to make the comparison between the outcomes of macroeconomic policies in the three periods.

In the period before 1986, RER went through a long appreciation, because Tanzanian monthly inflation exceeded world monthly inflation by about 1 percentage point on average over the entire period. This led to a dramatic loss of international competitiveness.

Between April 1986 and September 1993, Tanzanian monthly inflation exceeded world monthly inflation by 2 percentage points, twice as bad as the period before 1986. However, the average 2.8 percent per month depreciation of the nominal exchange rate over the period more than made up for this, and RER depreciated 0.8 percent per month over the period, signaling both improving competitiveness and increased austerity for consumers.

Since September 1993, despite progress in controlling inflation, a slowdown in the depreciation of the nominal exchange rate has meant that inflation rate differences over the period exceeded the rate of depreciation of the nominal exchange rate. The result is that the RER has appreciated at an average rate of 1.1 percent per month since October 1993, almost twice the rate that brought on economic ruin in the earlier period. The precise macroeconomic events that stabilized the nominal exchange rate faster than inflation are the subject of other chapters in the current Country Economic Memorandum. However, the impact of these macroeconomic trends on agriculture since 1994 have been severe, as will be demonstrated in following sections.

In the agricultural sector, private traders had begun to distribute fertilizer and other inputs starting in 1992; they began to import them starting in 1994. After 1990, the government no longer fixed the price of seed. As of 1998, there were 13 private seed companies operating in Tanzania (Mfungahema 1999).

Liberalization of traditional exports began in 1993 with the changes in the Coffee, Cotton, Tobacco, and Cashew Acts allowing private traders to buy, process, and export these crops. Private traders began to operate legally in the coffee and cotton sector in 1994-95 and in the tobacco sector the following year. The Pyrethrum Board's factory was closed in 1997 due to financial problems and privatized in 1998. The new owner has restarted operations. Private tea estates already account for 70 percent of production, and the remaining estates and processing plants of the Tanzania Tea Authority are being privatized. The idea was for the government to disengage from direct production and marketing in order to focus on essential public services such as research, extension, sanitary regulations, and quality control. The crop authorities have been restructured as crop boards, responsible for regulation, research, and information services (Bitegeko 1999). The liberalization of other minor and non-traditional export crops was largely completed in 1987 with the dissolution of GAPEX (the General Agricultural Products Export Company).

Unfortunately, the effect of export liberalization and devaluation on producer prices has been muted by a sharp decline in the index of agricultural export prices from a peak in 1986 (Figure 2.2). This decline, however, is largely the result of coffee prices which were unusually high in

1986. As will be shown later, the reforms allowed coffee producer prices to rise moderately over this period in spite of the fall in world prices.

Zanzibar also experienced economic decline from the mid 1970s to mid 1980s. Measured in 1976 Tsh, GDP fell from nearly 1 billion Tsh in 1976 to around 700 million Tsh in the mid 1980s (Mabele1999b). Like on the mainland, the decline was caused by a combination of declining international agricultural commodity prices, increasing energy prices, and macro-economic imbalances that distorted incentives (Mabele 1999b).

Zanzibar trade and agricultural policy began changing in the early 1980s. Zanzibar began experimenting with economic liberalization measures especially in the area of trade. Agricultural policy was changed to try to turn the agricultural sector around after years of either deterioration or stagnation. The policy emphasized mechanisation and irrigation. Success was limited by poor implementation and monitoring (Mabele 1999a), and by a focus on larger-scale activities.

In 1986 these experiments were consolidated and formalised into the First Economic Recovery Programme (ERP I). After ERP I there followed ERP II, which was implemented from 1991 to 1994. The ERP programmes aimed at food, cash, and export crop production, rehabilitating physical infrastructure, increasing capacity utilization in industry, and restoration of external and internal balance through pursuit of appropriate macro-economic policies. Incentives to producers rather than central government directives were intended to achieve the overall objective of increasing the production of goods and services.

Because imports of consumer and other goods were still rigidly controlled on the Mainland, a relatively small market for these imported goods in Zanzibar was quickly saturated with items destined for the mainland. Trade liberalization had a positive impact on the Zanzibar economy. Zanzibar's shops are now fully stocked with consumer goods, much of which are re-exported to the mainland and neighboring countries like Kenya. This raised incomes in the trade sector, including the informal trade sub-sector. These incomes may have had spillover effects to rural people directly through increased investment by rural trading entities and indirectly through remittances from traders to non-traders in rural areas. Increased real incomes, backed by increased physical availability of consumer goods, acted as an incentive for increased agricultural production.

This hypothetical cause and effect is supported by GDP data. Agriculture grew by 7.9 percent in real terms during the first five years of the economic reform programs. While trade in food crops was liberalized, trade in export crops was not. This meant that the all important clove-sub-sector was left out of liberalization and the growth it may have made possible.

2.5   Government Expenditure on Agriculture

No discussion of economic policy affecting agriculture would be complete without looking at public expenditure on agriculture. Table 2.2 shows the real value of budget allocations to the Ministry of Agriculture and Cooperatives (MAC) since the 1990-91 fiscal year. Although there is some fluctuation from year to year, the overall pattern is a sharp decline in budgetary budget support for the MAC. For example, the real allocation in 1997-98 is about one third the average annual value in the 1991-92 to 1993-94 period. There is some recovery of the agriculture budget in the approved 1998-99 budget and the estimated 1999-2000 budgets. Even so, the 1999-2000 estimate is almost one third lower, in real terms, than the average of the allocations in the first three years of the period.

9

The table also presents the allocation of the agriculture budget among different spending categories. Crop and livestock development is the largest item, showing a declining share after 1991-92, the first year in the table to include development budget expenditures along with recurrent expenditures. The declining share of research and development is especially worrisome for future productivity growth in agriculture, falling from 25-30 percent in the early years to an estimated 12 percent in the 1999 -2000 budget.

Table 2.3 shows the sources of funding for the Ministry of Agriculture and Cooperatives. The most striking trend is the drop in the development budget as a share of total over the 1990s. The local development budget went from an average of 17 percent of Ministry expenditures in 1990/92 to 2 percent in 1996/98. Foreign support for the Ministry is all counted in the development budget, and has also fallen significantly since 1994-95. The share of the MAC budget coming from foreign sources declines from 60 to 10-20 percent, implying an even larger drop in absolute funding since the total MAC budget is declining in absolute terms. This trend is exacerbated by a falling share of government spending devoted to the MAC (although there is some recovery in the approved 1998-99 and estimated 1999-2000 budgets).

Subsidies to agriculture have been a major component of agricultural policy in Zanzibar since the revolution. In the 1980s it became clear that subsidies were largely unsustainable. Despite periodic statements about reducing them, they have not been eliminated entirely. Table 2.4 shows recent trends in the provision of subsidies to agriculture. Although Zanzibar Development Budget resources have been declining quite rapidly in nominal as well as real terms, the share going to subsidies to agriculture has increased to more than 6 percent, compared to less than 4 percent in 1994/95. This is because agricultural subsidies tend to be somewhat sticky in nominal terms , with the effect that they have fallen less than overall expenditure. Nonetheless, total agricultural subsidies have declined by more than 20 percent in nominal terms since 1994/95, and by about two-thirds in real terms, due to high inflation.

Ending agricultural subsidies altogether continues to be a stated goal of the Zanzibar government (MALNR FAO 1999). The reduction in the annual inflation rate to single digit terms in the past two years suggests that this past method of real subsidy reduction will be less potent in the future. The current plan is to phase nominal subsidies out gradually while promoting agricultural practices and institutions that will reduce disruption from their removal. These include promoting use of traditional resources and technologies that require little financial input, promoting savings and credit associations, and encouraging formation of farmer associations.

Back on the mainland, it appears that the fiscal savings from eliminating fertilizer subsidies and the loss-making activities of the NMC and other parastatals has not been reallocated to investments in agricultural research, extension, and market development activities. Since a considerable share of MAC activities in earlier years contributed to overall budget deficits, a decision seems to have been made to reallocate savings from MAC retrenchment to deficit reduction, leading to net reductions in government spending on agriculture. It is sobering to note that over the period from 1991/92 to 1998/99, central government spending on the Ministry of Agriculture and Cooperatives (including development spending) averaged just 3.5 percent of total central government expenditures. Other rural development sectors, such as the truly rural (i.e. not urban or central grid infrastructure) components of health, education, water and roads, adds only another 2.6 percent of central government expenditures. This does not include spending by district authorities. However, the combined total of 6.1 percent of central government expenditure on agriculture and rural development is minimal when compared to agriculture's contribution to export revenue (at least 45 percent), to gross domestic product (minimum of 47 percent), and to employment (84 percent).

Figure 2.1. *Index of Tanzania Real Exchange Rate*

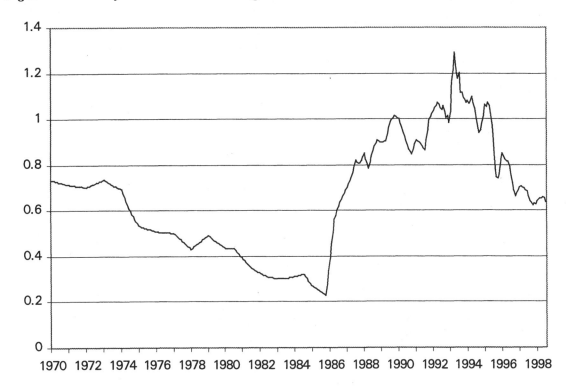

Note: An increase in the index corresponds to depreciation of the Tanzanian Shilling. Calculated as NOER X (MUV/NCPI) where NOER is the nominal official exchange rate, MUV is the World Bank manufacturing unit value, and NCPI is the Tanzania national consumer price index. The NOER is interpolated from annual figures before 1985 and quarterly figures between 1985 and 1992. After 1992 the NOER is from monthly figures. The NCPI is interpolated from annual figures before 1988 and quarterly figures between 1988 and 1994. After 1994 the NCPI is from monthly figures. The MUV is interpolated from annual figures in all years.

Source: Bank of Tanzania (various); World Bank (1999b).

Figure 2.2. *Index of Agricultural Export Prices*
(1990 = 100)

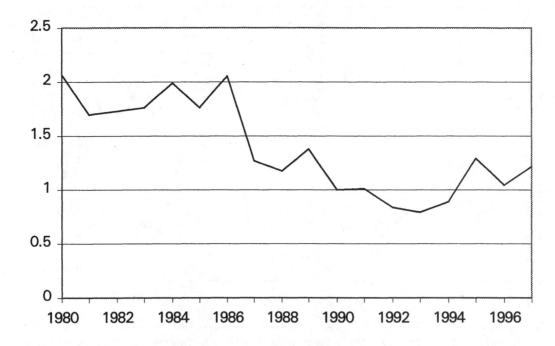

Note: Includes coffee (other mild arabicas ex-dock NY), cotton (US 10 market index), sisal (Tanzanian/Kenyan No. 3 Long, cif London), tea (London daily auction prices—all teas), and tobacco (US all markets) world prices weighted by each commodity's 1997 share of the total Tanzania export value of these 5 crops.

Source: Export quantity data is from Bank of Tanzania (various). Prices are from FAO (various), IMF (1998), and World Bank (1999b).

Table 2.1. Monthly Growth Gates of Tanzania Real Exchange Rate, Nominal Exchange Rate, and Prices
(percent monthly growth)

Index	*January 1970- March 1986*	*April 1986- September 1993*	*October 1993- April 1999*
Real exchange rate	-0.6	0.8	-1.1
Nominal exchange rate	0.4	2.8	0.5
Tanzania CPI minus international MUV	1.0	2.0	1.6

Note: Real exchange rate is nominal exchange rate times the ratio of international inflation (as measured by the World Bank manufactures unit value) to Tanzania inflation (as measured by the Tanzania consumer price index).
Source: Bank of Tanzania (various); World Bank (1999b).

Table 2.2. Real Budget Allocations to Agriculture

Budget item	1990-91[a]	1991-92	1992-93	1993-94	1994-95	1995-96	1996-97	1997-98	1998-99 approved	1999-2000 est.	1991-92-1991-98 total
Total vote	57,293	64,432	71,001	62,696	63,252	40,161	26,420	21,829	37,047	44,421	386,839
Distribution by sector					(million 1998-99 Tsh) (percent)						
Administration	33	10	10	10	5	4	9	13	29	32	13
Crop development	4	47	39	44	47	55	49	48	34	36	42
Research and development	29	25	34	22	30	18	10	15	15	12	20
Cooperative development	0	6	5	6	3	4	5	9	4	4	5
Food security and strategic grain reserve	0	0	0	7	5	6	12	11	3	3	5
Livestock development	33	12	12	12	9	13	16	4	15	13	13
Total	100	100	100	100	100	100	100	100	100	100	100

a 1990/91 distribution by sector includes only recurrent expenditure because development expenditure figures are not allocated by sector.
Note: Total vote includes recurrent and development expenditure. "Administration" includes policy and planning. "Crop development" includes input trust funds. Totals may differ by 1 percent from 100 due to rounding error.
Source: Calculated from figures supplied by the Ministry of Agriculture and Cooperatives (also see World Bank COD 1999).

Table 2.3. Sources of Funding for Government Spending on Agriculture
(percent)

Source of funding	1990-91	1991-92	1992-93	1993-94	1995-95	1995-96	1996-97	1997-98	1998-99 approved	1999-2000 est.	1991-92-1998-99 total
Recurrent	29	51	43	45	37	64	89	74	41	35	49
Development (local)	17	17	13	4	4	7	1	3	3	5	5
Foreign	54	32	44	51	60	29	10	23	56	59	46
Total ministry of agriculture/total government	5.1	4.3	3.6	3.6	4.3	3.6	2.7	2.1	4.1	3.8	3.5
Other rural sector/total government	0.7	3.5	2.2	5.2	3.7	1.3	1.5	2.4	2.9	2.1	2.6

Source: Calculated from figures supplied by the Ministry of Agriculture and Cooperatives (1999).

Table 2.4*. Trends in the Provision of Subsidies to Agriculture in Zanzibar* (thousands of shillings)

Fiscal year	Total available development budget	Agricultural subsidies	%
1994-95	1,		3.9
1995-96	1,		4.6
1996-97			5.2
1997-98			9.7
1998-99	503,000	31,867	6.3

Source: MALNR FAO (1999).

3. EVOLVING OUTPUT PRICE INCENTIVES FOR AGRICULTURAL PRODUCTION SINCE 1986

The combination of evolving policies towards agriculture and towards the macro economy, the state of infrastructure, the degree of commercialization, weather trends, and shifting world prices have all combined to alter fundamentally the structure of output price incentives facing agricultural producers in Tanzania. The present section will focus on the effect of these changes on agricultural producers and consumers of different goods. It will also assess the extent to which parts of domestic agriculture are insulated from world price movements, while others are directly linked to world markets. Section 4 will review trends and issues on the cost side of agricultural production, and bring the evidence together to assess evolving financial profitability and comparative advantage for specific major crops in Tanzania.

3.1 Evolution of Food Prices

Thanks to the many years of work by the Market Development Bureau (MDB) at the Ministry of Agriculture and Cooperatives, Tanzania has an abundance of price data that surpasses that of most other countries in Sub-Saharan Africa. Yet "market-determined" data for food producer prices only began to be collected in 1990/91, with the result that most series show a sudden jump in food producer prices after 1991, even after adjusting for inflation. Export crop producer prices prior to 1991 were largely official prices, but these were probably much closer to what was actually paid to producers than was the case in the food sector. Food retail prices collected by MDB seem to be more realistic before 1991, than do food producer prices. The retail price series are collected using a reasonable protocol (see below) and show seasonal fluctuations and considerable variation across a large sample of markets, as anticipated.

The evolution of real producer prices for the five important staples are shown in Table 3.1, including the official procurement prices for the 1980s and annual market prices since 1991. Market prices after 1991 are 50 to 165 percent greater than the official procurement prices in the 1980s. It should be recalled, however, that some of the harvest in the 1980s was on the parallel market at higher prices. Between 1995 and 1997, the real prices of all five staples began to fall significantly. Wheat and rice fell by 57 and 69 percent, respectively, whereas the other staples fell by substantially less. Food producers as a whole would have had to double or triple output to purchase the same basket of consumer items in April 1999 that they bought with food crop sales income in 1993.

Producer price series for major livestock products are less reliable, but retail prices for milk and beef appear to have been reasonably well collected. Available data, adjusted for inflation, are summarized by the four-year averages in Table 3.2, for seven major urban centers.

Real beef prices fell modestly from 1987/90 to 1991/94 in most markets and stayed roughly constant thereafter. The period of decline saw price falls of the same order of magnitude as those for non-traded food crops, such as cassava and beans. Real milk retail prices barely changed from 1987/90 compared to the average for the next four years, but then fell by about a third through the 1995/99 period. The biggest decline was in Iringa, where milk production has increased rapidly in response to project activity, and the local market appears to have become saturated. Milk retail prices rose slightly relative to beef prices from the late 1980s to the early 1990s, but then fell again through the last four years.

What explains these relative price changes? World prices for cereals, milk, meat, and traditional commodity exports have all trended downwards in real terms over the period in review, which certainly helps explain the general direction of change. Furthermore, world price ratios between cotton and maize closely tracked the evolution of Tanzanian relative prices since 1991 for the same items. However, the relative price movements among major subsets of agricultural goods did not always mimic the relative price movements among commodities in Tanzania. For example, world powdered milk prices moved in the opposite direction, relative to frozen carcass beef, than was the case in Tanzania, falling from the late 1980s through the early 1990s, and then rising since then. Furthermore, as we will see below, Tanzanian food prices behave quite differently across domestic markets while world prices at the Tanzania border apply only at the border.

The answer to the puzzle lies in part in what was happening over the period to the overall structure of incentives in Tanzania due to macroeconomic policy, and in part to the fact that many agricultural products in Tanzania behave as non-tradable goods. The latter fact, as we shall see, does not de-link these prices from world markets or exchange rate effects, but changes the nature of the link substantially.

3.2   Differences Between Tradable and Non-tradable Agricultural Goods

Non-tradable goods are items whose prices are not well-correlated with international prices even in the absence of policy distortions[1]. They are typically not traded across international borders, although small amounts might cross regional borders inland. The prices of non-tradables are set by local supply and demand. Tradable goods, in theory, can always be imported or exported in large amounts at the prevailing world price[2]. The expansion of local production of non-tradables, however, is constrained by effective local demand for the item. An over-supply in the local market leads to rapidly falling prices and producer revenues. Most importantly, non-tradability is a characteristic of the market the good is traded in, not of the good itself. The same good can be a non-tradable in one market (typically in a remote area where local production of the good occurs) and a tradable near the ports.

Simple economic models have typically assumed that physical goods (such as food) are all tradable, while services and factors of production are non-tradable. More sophisticated analysis may allow for the fact that some highly perishable items (liquid milk) or highly elaborated items (dumplings or locally-produced furniture) are non-tradables. However, it is rare that macroeconomic analyses allow for the fact that major raw food staples, such as maize in many markets, might behave as non-tradables (Delgado 1992). It is rarer still that analysts test the tradability assumption for food staples (Kyle and Swinnen 1994).

Yet the issue matters greatly for understanding the evolution of agricultural incentives under economic reform programs. The latter typically are designed to foster a depreciation in the real exchange rate (RER), or the relative price of tradables to non-tradables (Edwards 1989). The implicit assumption is that the agricultural commodities are tradable, while factors of production (labor, land, and capital) are non-tradable. Structural adjustment has at its core the necessary shift

---

[1] Nor are they correlated with the prices of locally-available close substitutes that are well-correlated with international prices.

[2] We assume that Tanzania is a price taker, which is reasonable given the fact that Tanzania does not currently dominate world trade in any single commodity.

in incentives from producers of non-tradables to producers of tradables, in order to restore competitiveness and the trade balance.

Figure 2.1 in the previous section illustrated that economic reform in Tanzania was associated with a sharp and sustained depreciation in the RER after 1986, following a long period of appreciation from the late 1960s. Yet this trend was sharply reversed after 1993, with a strong sustained appreciation of RER. In other words, the impact of macroeconomic reform between 1986 and 1993 was to favor the producers of tradables and producers of non-tradables after 1993.

The transmission mechanism from RER to agriculture is fairly direct. Depreciating RER after 1986 meant, other things equal, that the prices of tradable goods were rising faster than the value of labor and land to produce them; the reverse was the case after 1993. In theory the returns to producers of traditional exports should have risen from 1986 to 1993. Unfortunately, world commodity prices were falling sharply, largely wiping out the gains from depreciating RER (see Figure 2.2). Given the extent of the fall in world prices in the 1990s, the situation of export crop producers would have been disastrous had the RER not been depreciating during at least the early part of the decade.

Conversely, the prices received by producers of non-tradables were declining during the 1986 to 1993 period. The most obvious manifestation of this is the austerity felt by employees in the urban non-tradable industries such as government services where wages did not keep up with the cost of living. But it also applied to producers of non-tradable agricultural goods. After 1993, the price of non-tradables was rising relative to tradables, which would tend to reduce incentives to producers of export crops, but raise the returns of producers of non-tradable goods.

These events are consistent with the price trends seen in Tables 3.1 and 3.2 above. In Table 3.1, the deflator used, NCPI, has a heavy non-tradable component, consisting largely of services, housing costs, locally processed foods, and local manufactures. The real prices of the more tradable crops (wheat, rice, maize) rose from 1991 to 1993, and declined to less than 50 percent of their 1991 level thereafter. This pattern reflects in part the impact of the 1991-92 drought in southern Africa, and associated Tanzanian maize exports. In addition, it mirrors the movement of the real exchange rate, which rose (depreciated) until 1993 and fell (appreciated) after that. The appreciating real exchange rate makes imports of wheat and rice less expensive, driving down domestic prices.

The real prices of the less tradable crops (cassava, sorghum/millet, beans) continued to rise for another two years (except cassava), before falling. Furthermore, their price declines after 1995 were less than those of the tradable crops. In Table 3.2, milk is in fact more of a tradable than meat in the markets considered, because of imported milk powder and tinned concentrated milk, close substitutes for local fresh milk. The milk to beef price ratio rose through 1993 and declined thereafter. The next sub-section will formally test the tradability of three major food staples in Tanzania in both remote and non-remote markets.

3.3   Food Price Behavior and Evidence of Non-tradability of Some Major Staples

In this section we test whether food prices are more affected by domestic supply and demand conditions or by world prices (see Kyle and Swinnen 1994). The analysis is based on data from a monthly survey by the MDB of retail food prices since 1983, further compiled by the FEWS project office in Dar-es-Salaam. The survey collects prices for 15 starchy staples and 23 other food items at the retail level from 44 markets spread over all 20 regions of the country. Each regional capital is included, as well as 24 district markets. Five or six prices are recorded, if possible for each product twice monthly. These are then averaged into a single monthly price. In practice, many observations of less important food items are missing in many months. The series for milled rice, maize grain, and cassava (raw) are relatively complete over the sampling period and were used here; together they account for roughly two-thirds of starchy staple intake.

The markets surveyed are listed in Table 3.3, along with their regional location and approximate distance to Dar-es-Salaam by road or rail. The markets are further sub-divided into 24 "line-of-rail or road (LOR)" markets and 20 "isolated" markets. LOR markets are either located on or near a rail link to Dar-es-Salaam or Tanga (important coastal ports), or on or near a major all-weather road to Dar-es-Salaam or Tanga. Seventeen of the twenty regional capitals are classified as LOR. Isolated markets are all other markets in the survey. As can be seen from Table 3.3, proximity to the capital and the coast are not good indicators of "isolated" status, since many remote markets are LOR, and a number of closer markets are "isolated" because of poor transport connections.

If a staple is tradable and international trade in the staple occurs (i.e. no prohibitive tariffs or quotas), then movements in its domestic price should be largely determined by movements in world prices for the good in question, the price of substitutes, and the free-market exchange rate. Conversely, if the staple in question is non-tradable, and demand is constant, then its price will be determined primarily by the local and national supply of the good.

These assertions are tested formally in a statistical model reported in Table 3.4. Ordinary-least-squares regressions are estimated separately for each of the three crops separately in LOR and isolated markets. Monthly market-level retail prices over the 1983 to 1998 period, deflated by monthly NCPI, are the dependent variables. Explanatory variables consist of twelve monthly fixed effects (to capture seasonal patterns), a monthly time trend, monthly US export prices for wheat, rice, and maize lagged three months[3], national production of the good in question from the most recent harvest, regional production of the good from the most recent harvest, and the real exchange rate (RER)[4]. All prices are adjusted to constant 1998 Tsh or US$.

Results for rice show that this model explains 95 percent of monthly domestic price variation for rice over the 1983 to 1998 period in both LOR and isolated markets. This alone suggests that rice is probably a tradable (Kyle and Swinnen 1994), as common sense would also suggest. World rice prices have a positive influence on Tanzanian rice prices, as would be expected. Local and national rice production are also inversely correlated with domestic rice prices, as would be expected given the importance and inland nature of much of Tanzania rice production. The latter gives a high degree of natural protection to rice in inland areas of Tanzania such as the Lake Victoria region.

The strict interpretation of the world rice price coefficient for domestic rice prices in isolated markets in the table is that for every US$1.00 per kg increase in world rice prices, Tanzanian domestic prices in isolated markets will increase by Tsh 183 per kg three months later, compared to more than Tsh 250 per kg in LOR markets. These are equivalent to a 28 percent pass-through rate for the world price increase in isolated markets and a 38 percent pass-through rate in LOR markets.

---

[3] Lags of 0 and 6 months were also tested. Three months gave the best fit for tradable crops, and none of the lags were statistically significant for any of the non-tradables. Ninety days is a plausible delay between order and international delivery.

[4] The continuous monthly time trend is designed to control for any secular trends in the data.

World wheat and maize relative prices also have significant impact on Tanzanian domestic rice prices. The negative coefficient on world maize prices probably stems from maize and rice being imperfect substitutes in consumption in Tanzania and how import decisions are made. If world maize prices are low, importers and government authorities import more maize and less rice, leaving the (unchanged) domestic supply of rice to satisfy the part of rice demand formally met by imports, putting upwards pressure on domestic rice prices.

Finally, the real exchange rate has a significant negative effect on Tanzanian rice prices, as predicted. The higher the exchange rate (expressed as Tsh/US$), the more it costs to import, and the more valuable import substitutes such as rice become. The bottom line is that rice prices in Tanzania unequivocally behave as prices of a tradable good in both isolated and LOR markets.

The maize story is mixed. In isolated markets, maize prices are influenced only by national and regional production in the harvest immediately prior to the month in question. World prices have no statistically significant effect on prices in these markets, nor does the real exchange rate. In LOR markets, however, maize behaves like a tradable, even more so than rice. A US$1.00 increase in world maize prices translates three months later into a Tsh 586 per kg increase in Tanzanian maize prices, implying a pass-through rate of about 90 percent. Regional maize production decreases maize prices somewhat, but much less so than in the case of isolated markets. National maize production has hardly any impact at all in LOR markets. The bottom line is that maize behaves like a genuine non-tradable in isolated markets and like a highly tradable good in LOR markets. Based on regional production levels, it is estimated that at least one-quarter of all Tanzanian maize production occurs in isolated areas as defined here[5].

For comparison purposes, another set of regressions was run to explain fresh cassava prices in terms of world cereal prices, given that domestic food cassava does not have a comparable world market counterpart. As can be seen in Table 3.4, fresh cassava in both isolated and LOR markets behaves as a non-tradable. As expected, the "goodness of fit" of these regressions (R^2) indicates that the independent variables "explain" a smaller percentage of the variation in the dependent variable than was the case in the regressions for tradable staples.

Although the "t" tests on the own price coefficients in these regressions probably are adequate to make the case for non-tradability, a fuller test is to see whether retail food prices in the isolated markets are driven by the same forces and in the same way as those for LOR markets. More specifically, we test whether the coefficients in the isolated markets are statistically different than the coefficients in the LOR markets. The results shown in Table 3.5 indicate that there are no grounds to distinguish between isolated and LOR markets for rice (as expected), that isolated maize markets fail to resemble the whole sample for maize, and that isolated and LOR cassava markets do not resemble each other, consistent with a high degree of non-tradability.

3.4   Implications of Non-tradability of Food Staples for Incentives

If at least a quarter of locally produced food staple supplies behave as non-tradables, certain simplifying assumptions of conventional economic theory for open economies no longer hold. Instead, Tanzania should be considered what Myint (1975) dubbed the "semi-open" economy, where competitiveness of exports matters to overall growth (as in open economies), but where the competitiveness of tradable sectors generally also depends on what is exogenously occurring in the non-tradable sectors (as in closed economies) (Delgado 1992; Myint 1975). In the purely open economy, producers should follow their comparative advantage in production and trade for their

---

[5] This is clearly a conservative estimate, since it assumes that any region that is largely served by rail or paved road infrastructure is entirely LOR, whereas many villages and towns in such regions clearly are isolated, as suggested by Table 3.3.

preferred consumer goods (such as food). Thus production and consumption decisions are separate. Resources can appropriately be concentrated in specialized growth poles (such as cash cropping zones or urban light manufacturing, depending on comparative advantage) that will pull everyone else along.

In the semi-open economy, however, there is a need for balance between the tradable and non-tradable sectors, as in closed economies. This is fundamentally because producers consume significant amounts non-tradable items (such as food staples) with additional income earned from exports. If the production of these non-tradable consumer items, sometimes called "wages-goods[6]", is inelastic, their prices will be bid up relative to the prices of tradables. For example, an export boom will rapidly increase the demand for food. If food is non-tradable and inelastic in supply, this will increase the price of food, leading to increased wage demands as workers try to protect their standard of living. Higher wages will choke off the export expansion. Under these circumstances, lack of production growth in the non-tradable wages-good sector will promote domestic inflation and a depreciating RER, which eventually will choke off export gains made possible by structural adjustment reforms.

In coastal urban areas, commercially viable imports of cereals are possible because of economies of agglomeration and of lower transport costs to the outside world. Elsewhere, subsidized food aid can temporarily help keep food prices lower than they would be otherwise and thus profit margins in non-food tradable-good activities from evaporating. However, a viable long-run growth strategy will require developing the food sector to the point that a growing supply at a relatively stable price is ensured, whether from technological change in own production or cheaper commercial imports through improved infrastructure, or a mix of the two. The analysis above is critical to understanding the puzzling performance of the traditional export crop sector in Tanzania since 1986.

3.5   Evolution of Output Prices for Traditional Export Crops

Given he long depreciation of Tanzania's RER after 1970 until the beginning of the economic reform program in 1986, it is easy to understand the pressures that led to the decline of traditional export cropping until 1986. The rapid rise of RER from 1986 to 1993, accompanied by increasing liberalization measures, should have increased real producer prices several fold, restoring profitability and economic viability to the sector. In fact, six of the main export producer prices rose substantially (24-68 percent) over this period (robusta producer prices remained unchanged and cotton prices fell). The increase was less than anticipated for two reason. First, real *f.o.b.* prices fell for all but tobacco and pyrethrum. In the case of coffee, world prices fell by about 65 percent, largely eliminating the benefits of the devaluation for producers. For cotton, real world prices were quite favorable in the 1980s, with rapid declines in real terms after 1991 due to China's entry as an exporter into the world market. Second, the crop authorities increased their marketing margins for seven of the eight, absorbing part of the benefits of devaluation. In the case of cotton and flue-cured tobacco, the parastatal shifted from paying farmers 50 percent more than the *f.o.b.* price in 1986 to paying them less than half the *f.o.b.* price in 1993.

Since 1993, real producer prices for the mainland's major export crops have fallen between 25 and 70 percent. Since this corresponds to the period that private traders began to purchase and export many of these crops, it is tempting to attribute the lower producer prices to liberalization and lack of competition among private traders. In fact, producer prices have *risen* as a percent of the *f.o.b.* price for five of the six commodities that have been liberalized (tea and pyrethrum are

---

[6] So called because they are the physical counterpart to returns to labor in low income societies where most income is spend on staples.

not yet fully liberalized). Nor have world prices fallen during this period. Rather the main explanation for the falling producer prices of export crops over 1993-1998 is the appreciation of the real exchange rate during this period.

The prices of Zanzibar's major exports have also not benefited the region. Cloves, traditionally Zanzibar's most important agricultural export, have fallen dramatically in value since the mid 1980s. Export unit values in the 1990s are approximately 10 percent in nominal terms of what they were in an average year in the 1970s and 1980s. Copra prices have been very unstable, with sharp declines alternating with large rises, but have not trended in either direction. The *f.o.b.* price of chilies rose in the mid 1980s, but declined dramatically until the mid 1990s when they rose again but not to the levels of the mid 1980s. Nominal producer prices of cloves fell from near 20 Tsh/kg in 1980 to below 5 Tsh/kg in 1994, even greater than the decline in world market prices in real terms. Producer prices of both copra and chilies, while erratic, have not declined in real terms between the early 1980s and mid 1990s (Mabele 1999a).

The evolution of the ratio of domestic producer prices to *f.o.b.* Tanzania world prices is shown in Table 3.8 over the 1982 to 1999 period, using figures supplied by MAC. These ratios are a little misleading in that they use the nominal exchange rate. This is acceptable with a more market-determined exchange rate after 1988, but makes the ratios before 1988 too high compared to ones after that year. The adjustments to use real exchange rates that would be contained in a nominal protection coefficient were not done in this part of the table. Another issue to consider is that the price ratios only reflect implicit price taxation, and not explicit taxation of the producer after agreeing on a price.

However, if transportation margins are a constant percentage of domestic prices, these price ratios from 1988 onwards are a reasonable proxy of inter-year movements in implicit taxation. The right-hand shaded part of Table 3.8 lists estimates of true nominal and effective protection for the crops in question in 1997/98, based on separate calculations made by the Netherlands Economic Institute Team for the Ministry of Agriculture and Cooperatives (see Mfungahema 1999).

Nominal protection coefficients (NPC) also take into account that export parity prices need to be adjusted (i.e. decreased) to account for transportation from the producing point. This means that NPC will generally be larger than the simple ratio of domestic prices to border prices. Effective protection coefficients further allow for the fact that input subsidies add to protection and input taxes do the reverse. In every case here, EPC was lower than NPC. Even so, the results in Table 3.8 taken together suggest that direct price taxation of export crops would not have been excessive in Tanzania in recent years, if it had been the only taxation of the sector. Rates of the order of 20 percent are not uncommon where few other forms of revenue are available, and are a long way from the 70 to 90 percent implicit taxation rates commonly found in Africa in the late 1970s and early 1980s.

Taking into account the over-estimates before 1988 due to use of an artificial nominal exchange rate, it seems clear that the direct output price taxation of cashews, coffee, cotton, and tobacco have diminished substantially since the late 1980s. This is also borne out in the literature (World Bank AEOD 1994b; MAC NEI 1999d, 1999e). Output price taxation of tea and pyrethrum appears to have been higher in the 1990s than for the other traditional export crops, a fact that may be explained by the fact that these two crops have not yet been liberalized[7].

---

[7] Privatization and liberalization of these two crops was due to begin in 1998-99.

3.6   Explicit Agricultural Taxation

Even as implicit price taxation has declined, explicit taxation of traditional export crops appears to have increased substantially, co-incident with a shift of taxing powers from the central to regional and district authorities. Food crops sold informally are only lightly taxed through the farmer's obligation to pay the Development Levy. However, once small operators attempt to sell through more formal channels in the cash economy, they are liable for paying District, Education, and (sometimes) Village levies that amount in aggregate to as much as 10 percent of sales value (MAC 1999b). These local levies are collected as a cess, which implies that per unit tax rates on small operators are much higher in low-volume years than good ones—the opposite of what is desirable.

Taxation on livestock is multi-sourced, heavy and unevenly applied. Some districts charge annual ownership head tax of up to Tsh 1,000 per head of cattle and Tsh 500 per goat. The Education Levy and Market Fee total up to another Tsh 4,000 per head of cattle and Tsh 1,700 per small ruminant. Some districts also charge for meat inspection and slaughterhouse usage. The Ministry of Agriculture and Cooperatives imposes its own Market Fees, Movement Permit Fees, Grazing Fees, Holding Ground Fees, Consolidation Fees, and Stock Route Fees, often on the same animal, often at the same time (MAC 1999a; MAC 1999b).

Traditional export crops are heavily and unevenly taxed across local districts. One estimate is that for these crops, central taxation is two thirds of the total tax burden and local taxes are one third (MAC 199b). Coffee, cotton, and tobacco have a central tax burden factored in the producer price of 14-20 percent. However, another 7 to 22 percent of producers' gross margins are typically taxed away through other levies. Sometimes district and regional authorities levy the same tax, different districts levy different taxes, and different taxpayers are treated differently. Livestock sales are also heavily and arbitrarily taxed.

Beyond smallholder taxes, export crop estates pay formal sector taxes of different sorts. Profits are taxed at 35 percent, but then additional dividend withholding, capital gains, and payroll taxes may eat up the rest of profit entirely. The Ministry of Agriculture study calculated that the total tax burden on cashew was 90 percent of producer incomes, discouraging further investment despite the worldwide regeneration of the cashew industry in the 1990s (MAC 1999b).

The present system of agricultural taxation is under review. It has a number of structural defects (World Bank AEOD 1999). First, the use of fixed cesses is highly regressive for small farmers. Second, the plethora of different small taxes is hard to administer fairly or efficiently. Third, taxing trade rather than production raises distribution costs and hinders growth and cost-reduction under commercialization. Fourth, differential rates on different commodities distort production and sales incentives arbitrarily. Fifth, unpredictable changes in the administration of taxation at the local level raises risks and thus costs. Sixth, the system is unfair in that different individuals pay very different levels of taxes, and not necessarily in relation to income.

3.7 Relative Profitability for Smallholders of Cash Versus Food Crops

At least 80 percent of export cropping in Tanzania is done by smallholders who grow both export crops and food crops. The evolution of the relative prices for the two kinds of output provides a useful gauge of the evolution of incentives for cash cropping, bearing in mind that the latter are more heavily taxed. Table 3.9 shows changes over time in the ratios of export crop producer prices to food crop producer prices. Cotton has become increasingly less valuable relative to maize over time. In fact the effect is probably underestimated here, since the figures do not include the higher post-pricing taxation of cotton incomes in the later 1990s.

Coffee, on the other hand, became considerably more attractive, because of both liberalization and the 1997 boom in prices. Recently it too has begun to slip. Table 3.9 also illustrates that more tradable food crops (paddy rice, wheat) rose in value compared to less tradable food staples (cassava, beans, maize) from 1985 until 1994, and declined in value after that[8]. In addition, export crops tend to use more tradable inputs than food crops, which suggests that export crops can be expected to decrease in value over time relative to subsistence food crops in the present environment.

Indeed, these movements generally accord with the movements of the RER in Figure 2.1, which are heavily influenced by food price inflation in Tanzania. This and the non-tradability of a significant part of the food sector suggests that the impacts of structure and policy on the unit cost of production side of agriculture are likely to have been as or more important to understanding changes in agricultural incentives in the 1990s than changes in the output price side.

---

[8] Except for wheat/cassava, where wheat experienced a world price spike in 1995-96.

Table 3.1. Real Producer Prices for Food Crops 1981-99

Year	Price index[a]	Maize	Paddy	Wheat	Millet	Beans	Cassava
			Official procurement prices				
			(constant 1998-99 Tsh/kg)				
1981-85	1.4	140	232	195	117	334	n/a
1986-90	5.6	149	250	170	109	369	n/a
			Market prices				
			(constant 1998-99 Tsh/kg)				
1990-91	12.3	106	212	473	279	471	n/a
1991-92	14.7	279	370	495	289	508	73
1992-93	18.6	298	491	525	365	533	91
1993-94	25.2	256	424	497	376	712	84
1994/95	32.7	181	254	452	484	797	76
1995-96	43.3	165	216	423	538	571	75
1996-97	58.3	138	245	362	245	475	67
1997-98	77.3	117	195	272	175	431	61
1998-99[b]	100.0	118	151	228	175	317	53

a National Consumer Price Index where 1998-99 = 100.
b To April 1999.
Source: Figures supplied by MAC.

Table 3.2. Deflated Livestock Product Retail Prices in Major Urban

Region	Commodity	1987-90	1991-94	1995-98
		(1998-99 Tsh/kg)		
Dar-es-Salaam	Milk	656	774	505
	Beef, mixed cut	2,312	1,918	1,480
	Milk/beef	0.28	0.40	0.37
Arusha	Milk	624	546	342
	Beef, mixed cut	1,926	1,484	1,422
	Milk/beef	0.33	0.37	0.24
Mwanza	Milk	716	521	370
	Beef, mixed cut	1,664	1,174	1,089
	Milk/beef	0.43	0.45	0.38
Tabora	Milk	550	483	322
	Beef, mixed cut	1,527	1,135	1,242
	Milk/beef	0.36	0.43	0.29
Lindi	Milk	562	n/a	365
	Beef, mixed cut	2,144	1,135	1,663
	Milk/beef	0.26	n/a	0.22
Tanga	Milk	561	571	371
	Beef, mixed cut	1,835	1,525	1,551
	Milk/beef	0.31	0.37	0.23
Iringa	Milk	488	490	188
	Beef, mixed cut	1,510	1,303	759
	Milk/beef	0.32	0.38	0.27

Source: Annual averages of retail prices collected by Market Development Bureau/MAC and deflated by NCPI base 1998-99.

Table 3.3. Market Coverage of MDB Price Survey, Main Food Staples, 1983-98

Market classification	Region	Market	Distance to Dar (Km)
Markets classified as line of rail or major road	Arusha	Arusha	647
	Kilimanjaro	Moshi	562
	Kilimanjaro	Gonja (Same)	472
	Dar-es-Salaam	Dar-es-Salaam	0
	Coast	Mafia	140
	Coast	Bagamoyo	60
	Coast	Kisarawe	20
	Morogoro	Morogoro	196
	Tanga	Tanga	354
	Tanga	Lushoto	363
	Mwanza	Mwanza	1,164
	Mwanza	Magu	1,224
	Mwanza	Kwimba	1,075
	Mara	Musoma	1,369
	Mara	Tarime	1,429
	Shinyanga	Shinyanga	1,001
	Kigoma	Kigoma	1,442
	Dodoma	Mpwapwa	435
	Dodoma	Dodoma	479
	Tabora	Tabora	1,039
	Tabora	Urambo	1,139
	Mbeya	Mbeya	851
	Iringa	Iringa	501
	Iringa	Mafinga	581

Source: MDB

28

Table 3.3. Market Coverage of MDB Price Survey, Main Food Staples, 1983-98 (cont'd)

Market classification	Region	Market	Distance to Dar (Km)
Markets classified as isolated	Arusha	Mbulu	700
	Kagera	Bukoba	1,425
	Mwanza	Geita	1,284
	Mwanza	Sangerema	1,200
	Mara	Ukerewe	1,400
	Shinyanga	Maswa	1,075
	Shinyanga	Kahama	1,000
	Kigoma	Kasulu	1,352
	Kigoma	KIbondo	1,222
	Rukwa	Mpanda	1,400
	Rukwa	Sumbawanga	1,186
	Singida	Singida	709
	Iringa	Njombe	791
	Ruvuma	Songea	992
	Ruvuma	Mbinga	1,082
	Ruvuma	Tonduru	720
	Mtwara	Mtwara	558
	Mtwara	Newala	680
	Mtwara	Masasi	600
	Lindi	Lindi	459

Source: MDB

Table 3.4. Evidence of Non-tradability of Maize (isolated markets) and Cassava in Tanzania

Estimated parameter	Rice		Maize		Cassava	
	Isolated market	Line of rail market	Isolated market	Line of rail market	Isolated market	Line of rail market
Average base price over period (Tsh/kg)	528	532	148	168	164	205
Continuous monthly time trend	-1.00	-1.11	-0.36	-0.53	-0.35	-0.29
Deflated US export prices in US dollars lagged 3 months:						
Wheat	871	707	n.s.	-703	n.s.	n.s.
Maize	-579	-378	n.s.	586	n.s.	n.s.
Rice	183	250	n.s.	47	n.s.	n.s.
Production at start harvest year:						
All Tanzania	-0.25	-0.30	-0.02	-0.02	n.s.	0.10
Local administrative region	-0.75	-0.68	-0.19	-0.13	0.05	n.s.
Real exchange rate (Tsh/$)	-0.19	-0.18	n.s.	-0.05	-0.20	n.s.
Seasonal low:						
Lowest 3 of 12 month dummies (in lieu of intercept)	July-Sept.	July-Sept.	June-Aug.	Aug.-Oct.	June, July, and Nov.	Jan., Aug. and Nov.
Number of observations	2,230	3,096	2,184	2,976	1,204	1,805
Adjusted R^2	0.95	0.95	0.89	0.92	0.82	0.78

n.s. Not statistically different from zero at the 5 percent level.

Note: Effect on monthly local price in regional markets deflated by national CPI. OLS regressions on monthly price (constant 1998 Tsh) per kg; data are reported for 44 markets across Tanzania, where market price data were collected by the Market Development Bureau and compiled by FEWS, January 1983-December 1998, deflated by monthly national CPI. Monthly observations are matched with explanatory variables from multiple sources; the base margin is the mean of the dependent variable; production data pertain to the June period preceding the month in question. All non-zero coefficients shown are significant at 5 percent or better.

Table 3.5. *Tests of Whether Prices are Determined in Isolated Markets the Same Way That They are in "Line of Rail" Markets*

Commodity	F-statistic	Degrees of freedom of F	Conclusion about H_0 at 5%	Comment
Rice	0.969	(3,096; 2,211)	Fail to reject	H_0 cannot be rejected at 20%
Maize	1.005	(2,976; 2,165)	Reject	H_0 narrowly fails
Cassava	2.103	(1,805; 1,185)	Reject	H_0 rejected

Note: $F = \dfrac{(e'e - e_1'e_1)/m}{e_1'e_1/(n-k)}$

Where e'e is the sum of the squared residuals from regressions pooling isolated and line of rail markets as defined in Table 3.1, m is the number of line of rail observations, n is the number of isolated observations, k is the number of parameters estimated, and $e_1'e_1$ is the sum of squared residuals in the isolated markets regressions.

Table 3.6. *Evolution of Real World Commodity Prices*
(1990 US$/MT)

Year	Coffee, arabica	Coffee, robusta	Cotton	Tea	Tobacco
1981	5,678	3,135	2,194	2,790	3,211
1982	4,445	3,435	1,857	2,711	3,601
1983	4,524	3,934	1,852	3,342	3,822
1984	4,840	4,469	2,205	5,071	4,092
1985	4,782	3,893	1,884	2,889	3,807
1986	6,295	4,038	1,435	2,382	3,287
1987	2,638	2,538	1,574	1,921	3,092
1988	2,816	2,198	1,326	1,876	2,590
1989	2,297	1,760	1,493	2,122	3,345
1990	1,846	1,211	1,582	2,030	3,392
1991	1,571	1,074	1,523	1,801	3,425
1992	1,162	902	1,131	1,872	3,227
1993	1,380	1,109	1,157	1,745	2,536
1994	2,865	2,395	1,474	1,662	2,397
1995	2,697	2,344	1,754	1,376	2,218
1996	2,324	1,601	1,526	1,553	2,682
1997	3,396	1,643	1,442	2,190	3,264
1998	2,577	1,776	1,080	2,289	3,202
1999	1,964	1,544	921	2,169	3,013
1981-85	4,854	3,773	1,999	3,361	3,707
1986-90	3,178	2,349	1,482	2,066	3,141
1991-95	1,935	1,565	1,408	1,691	2,760
1996-99	2,565	1,641	1,242	2,051	3,040

Source: International Monetary Fund 1999.

Table 3.7. Evolution of Real Export Crop Producer Prices
(1998-99 Tsh/kg)

Year	Cashew nuts, raw	Coffee, mild arabica	Coffee, robusta	Cotton, seed	Tea, green	Tobacco, flue	Tobacco, fire	Pyrethrum
1981	366	1,097	427	390	183	1,280	762	914
1982	489	880	342	362	147	1,231	753	977
1983	365	875	459	343	146	1,313	839	729
1984	421	1,011	530	361	169	1,084	692	843
1985	424	1,017	558	363	177	1,090	696	848
1986	396	951	543	438	165	1,278	786	792
1987	463	1,292	738	430	194	1,254	772	835
1988	584	1,286	734	379	193	1,227	760	768
1989	572	1,287	729	320	192	1,081	697	761
1990	910	1,365	596	303	184	975	758	650
1991	881	1,263	493	334	228	953	741	978
1992	917	1,567	477	477	273	1,670	1,145	1,567
1993	665	1,343	537	322	215	1,585	1,182	1,236
1994	1,073	1,590	358	318	179	1,526	966	914
1995	1,070	2,846	929	367	153	1,725	1,079	764
1996	762	2,279	808	462	115	1,312	1,052	693
1997	540	1,286	489	291	94	1,172	946	514
1998	388	1,294	388	259	65	924	617	388
1999	500	1,000	250	185	65	621	539	320
1981-85	413	976	463	364	164	1,200	748	862
1986-90	585	1,236	668	374	185	1,163	754	761
1991-95	921	1,722	559	364	209	1,492	1,023	1,092
1996-99	547	1,465	484	299	85	1,007	788	479

Sources: Annual producer prices and national consumer price index deflator supplied by MAC.

Table 3.8. *Evolution of Producer Prices as a Percent of F.O.B. Prices 1981-99, Compared to 1997-98 Nominal and Effective Protection Coefficients* (percent)

| Crop | Producer prices as a percentage of f.o.b. prices at nominal exchange rates | | | | | | | Nominal protection coefficient 1997-98 | Effective protection coefficient 1997-98 |
	1982-85	1985-88	1988-91	1991-94	1994-97	1997-98	1998-99		
Cashews	81	40	59	62	64	56	83	78	72
Coffee	75	57	55	73	72	56	68	82	81
Cotton	90	119	37	45	51	64	68	83	81
Tobacco	94	101	47	56	66	52	52	87	84
Tea	34	58	48	60	37	27	35	70	67
Pyrethrum	80	58	24	31	23	22	22	n/a	n/a

n/a means not available

Source: Price ratios are calculated from annual estimates of domestic producer to *f.o.b.* export border prices by the Market Development Bureau, Ministry of Agriculture and Cooperatives. Ratios before 1988 may be misleading because of use of a non-market exchange rate. The 1997-98 nominal protection coefficients use social prices and real exchange rates, are taken from the MAC NEI 1999d and figures supplied by MAC. They assume the following locations and level 2 improved maintenance; cotton, Shinyanga, mixed soils, ox plow, line sowing, medium technology; tobacco, flue cured, Tabora, medium input level; tea, Iringa, smallholder, medium input level.

Table 3.9. Evolution of Relative Producer Prices for Different Crops, 1985–89 to 1995–98

Crop	1985-89	1990-94	1995-98	1998
Export crop price/food crop price				
Cotton (B)/maize	3.08	2.78	2.61	2.23
Coffee (Ar)/maize	7.65	13.98	20.98	15.85
Cotton (B)/paddy	1.90	1.59	1.73	1.34
Tradable food price/non-tradable food price				
Wheat/cassava	1.81	4.08	4.52	3.91
Paddy/cassava	2.62	3.20	2.78	2.81
Paddy/maize	1.65	1.67	1.54	1.67
Maize/beans	0.42	0.42	0.27	0.27
Paddy/beans	0.69	0.68	0.42	0.45

Source: Crop producer prices supplied by MAC.

4. COSTS AND RETURNS TO CROP PRODUCTION

The previous section examined the trends and determinants of agricultural output prices. Relative output prices are only half of the picture regarding incentives; equally important are costs of production. Costs of production depend on the prices of purchased inputs, the cost of primary factors of production such as labor and land, the availability of skills and technology, and the institutions (including functioning markets) to make all these items available to producers. In the absence of technological change, short term changes in the cost of production will be determined essentially by changes in relative prices, actual use of purchased inputs, and by changes in the opportunity costs and use of primary factors.

These items changed greatly for different crops over the period. In addition, the costs of marketing outputs and procuring inputs also changed significantly over the period. Even though these changes can be expected to show up in lower producer prices and higher input costs at the farm-gate, the magnitude of marketing costs as a share of prices received and paid by farmers suggests analyzing this area in conjunction with other elements of cost formation at the farm level.

4.1   Inter-regional Food Crop Marketing Costs

The period since 1986 has seen rapid growth in market flows of food crops within Tanzania, due to both liberalization of distribution systems and the phenomenal growth in the population of Dar-es-Salaam relative to the rest of the country. A large proportion of food crops are still consumed within the household or locality that produced them. Maro (1999) reports MAC estimates that between 1992/93 and 1997/98, only 26 percent of maize and 50 percent of rice produced was sold. Dar-es-Salaam is by far the main destination for sales.

MAC estimates that over the 1992/93 to 1997/98 period Dar-es-Salaam was the destination of 13 percent of the maize marketed surplus, 70 percent of marketed domestic rice, and 95 percent of marketed beans (Maro 1999). Maro convincingly argues that the rapid increase in quantity of food marketed to Dar following liberalization--as well as improvement in quality (fruits, vegetables, animal products)--is the unheralded success story of Tanzanian agriculture, at least for the first half of the 1990s. Four areas are listed as supplying 90 percent of maize to Dar-es-Salaam: Dodoma (46%), Iringa (19%), Mbeya (16%) and Songea (10%), although much of the Dodoma grain is undoubtedly transiting through from further inland. Dar-es-Salaam's rice supply comes from Mbeya (43%), Morogoro (29%), Shinyanga (19%) and Tanga (8%). Ninety-five percent of the marketed surplus of beans are sold to Dar-es-Salaam, and 6 regions (Mbeya, Arusha, Tanga, Morogoro, Iringa, and Songea) account for 95 percent of Dar-es-Salaam's supply.

Poor road and communications infrastructure greatly increase the cost of agricultural trade within Tanzania, as does arbitrary official taxation at the local level discussed in the previous section, not to mention unofficial levies. Maro (1999) reports MAC estimates that the total costs of marketing 40 bags of maize from wholesalers in Morogoro to wholesalers in Dar-es-Salaam in the 1995/96 season--excluding returns to traders--were 27 percent of the final wholesale value in Dar-es-Salaam. Sixty percent of the marketing cost was attributable to transportation, 19 percent to packing materials, 9 percent to local taxes and the remainder to a variety of storage and handling charges. At US$0.18 per ton/km (1995/96 prices), these transport costs may seem to be similar to the costs on unpaved highways in inland West Africa in the late 1980s (Delgado 1992), until it is recalled that Morogoro is the first major town on the main paved road inland from the capital city, in the Tanzanian case!

Since traders, like parastatals, cannot be expected to continue to work without return, trader profits need to be factored into marketing costs. Maro (1999) shows that the liberalization of food crop marketing after 1988 led to a lower cost private distribution system compared to the previous distribution operated by the National Milling Corporation. In the maize example above, the total return to traders, as inferred from the difference between total revenue and total cost, was 7.6 percent of the final wholesale price in Dar-es-Salaam.

Although studies of actual marketing costs are hard to come by, it is possible to track with some accuracy the evolution of spreads between food prices in different parts of the country and Dar-es-Salaam. Assuming that wholesale-to-retail markups do not differ greatly in percentage terms across markets, the difference in retail prices between two locations between which trade is actually occurring is a good indicator of total marketing costs, including the trader's margin. The abundance and quality of price data from the Market Development Bureau of the MAC (see previous section) permits statistical analysis of the evolution of monthly price spreads between outlying markets and Dar-es-Salaam between January 1986 and December 1998.

The dependent variable in this analysis is the difference between the deflated monthly retail price in Dar-es-Salaam and those of 43 other markets. The explanatory variables include a monthly time trend, road distance from Dar-es-Salaam, road distance squared (to allow for a non-linear relationship), and twelve monthly dummy variables, to control for seasonal effects. We also include a dummy variable for isolated markets (defined as in Section 3 above), for markets physically situated on a railroad (a little more restrictive than "line-of-rail or road" in Section 3), and for markets in port towns. The purpose of these dummy variables is to partially control for the fact that not all markets actually trade with Dar-es-Salaam, in which case price differences may be less than the marketing cost. All price differences are expressed in constant December 1998 Tsh/kg.

Results for wheat, rice, maize and cassava are shown in Table 4.1. The first row shows the mean price spread (in December 1998 Tsh) for the crop in question between all markets and Dar-es-Salaam in all months over the 1986 to 1998 period. Spreads are highest for wheat (93 Tsh) and rice (less liberalized); next comes fresh cassava root, a perishable. Spreads are lowest for maize (24 Tsh/kg).

The time trend coefficient indicates that wheat spreads have declined at an average monthly rate of Tsh 1.35 over the period, mostly because of liberalization towards the end of the period. Rice and maize spreads declined moderately at about 1 Tsh/kg per annum (Tsh 0.06 to 0.08 per month). Cassava spreads, which involved a smaller number of markets due to missing observations, increased significantly over the period (0.6 Tsh/kg per month). Unlike the grains, cassava was not previously marketed by a parastatal, so there is no compelling reason why liberalization would have caused margins to decrease. However, the lack of statistical significance of the other explanatory variables raises questions as to whether this crop is actually being actively traded to Dar most of the time.

Distance to Dar has a positive effect on spreads for wheat rice and maize, as expected. For rice, for example, an extra km of distance from Dar adds 0.11 Tsh/kg to the spread (or US$0.16 per ton/km), in between Maro's estimated spreads per km for rice and maize shipments to Dar from Morogoro. The presence of statistically significant but very small negative coefficients for distance squared is interpreted as evidence of unit economies of distance, as expected.

If a market is on a rail line, other things being equal, the spread for wheat and maize will be reduced by 12 Tsh/kg and 4 Tsh/kg respectively. However, it increases the spread for rice significantly, perhaps because the main rice producing regions of the country are all on railroads, and Dar is in a part supplied by imports. If the supplying market is a port city, the spread is much lower for wheat and rice, both importable crops, although this is much less important for maize, as expected. Finally, spreads can be expected to be lowest when inland prices are high. This is the case at the start of the cropping season for the three cereals, and right after the cereals harvest for cassava, and is shown in Table 4.1.

In sum, there is solid evidence from both point studies and broad-based statistically-significant trends that spatial marketing margins have decreased over time for previously regulated tradable food crops like wheat, rice and maize. However, transport costs remain very high, and thus absolute spatial margins are still quite high in Tanzania. This, combined with occasional prohibitions on cross-border trade, is a fundamental reason why a quarter of the country's maize supply was seen to behave as a non-tradable crop in Section 3. Market-mediated structural reforms will continue to be difficult to implement until spatial marketing margins can be brought down further, through infrastructure improvements and rural transportation policies that reduce transportation costs.

4.2   Export Crop Marketing Costs

Unlike food crops, the effect of liberalization here cannot be measured by comparing retail prices in different locations over time. However, the available literature seems quite clear that the increased competition from the entry of private marketing agents has greatly reduced marketing margins in cotton, cashew nuts, and coffee (MAC NEI 1999d; Maro, 1999). This is further supported in the previous section by rising relative producer prices for export crops (relative to world prices) after the mid to late 1980's, and before 1995/96. However, liberalization has also affected the farm purchase prices of inputs such as fertilizers and chemicals. This effect may not be major on food crops, which in many cases made relatively little use of purchased inputs (see sub-section 4.4 below), but was quite important in the case of export crops.

4.3   Use of Agricultural Inputs

Purchased inputs are not widely used in Tanzanian agriculture. According to the 1994-95 National Sample Census of Agriculture (NSCA), 15 percent of Tanzanian farmers use chemical fertilizer, 27 percent use improved seed, and 18 percent use pesticides. This section briefly describes the evolution of input markets and patterns of input use.

Fertilizer

During the 1970s and 1980s, fertilizer in Tanzania was imported and distributed almost exclusively by the Tanzania Fertilizer Company (TFC), a parastatal enterprise, and the Tanganyika Farmers' Association (TFA). Most of the fertilizer imports were in the form of aid-in-kind rather than being commercial imports. Fertilizer was provided to farmers either free or at heavily subsidized prices in an attempt to stimulate agricultural production. Fertilizer use rose from 80 thousand tons in the 1970s to over 100 thousand tons in the late 1980s (MAC, 1997). Similarly, the proportion of farmers using fertilizer rose from 7 percent in 1971-72 to 14 percent in 1986-87[1]. Pan-territorial prices provided heavy subsidies to users in remote areas. More than half the fertilizer was used farmers in three Southern Highlands regions (Iringa, Mbeya, and Ruvuma), most of whom applied it to maize, These regions benefited from the policy of pan-territorial pricing. Another 10-20 percent was consumed by farmers in Tabora, mainly on tobacco (MAC 1997a).

In addition to the fiscal burden of the fertilizer subsidy (US$5-15 million per year), there were chronic problems of late delivery and insufficient supplies. These problems led the government to liberalize the fertilizer market as part of the reform process. As discussed in Section 2, private enterprises were allowed to import fertilizer in the late 1980s, but price controls and subsidies to the TFC made it unprofitable. The fertilizer subsidy was phased out over the period 1990-91 to 1994-95. In 1993-94, the subsidy was made available to private importers, resulting in a massive over-supply of fertilizer. Eight importers, some of them with little experience and no storage facilities, imported a total of 227 thousand tons, equivalent to a 2-3 year's supply. This overhang resulted in unsold stocks, large losses, and reduced orders in subsequent years. It is estimated that current fertilizer consumption is about 67 thousand tons, almost all of which is supplied by commercial imports. Fertilizer use on maize and in the Southern Highlands has fallen significantly, while Tabora now accounts for half of all fertilizer use (MAC 1997a).

The proportion of farmers using fertilizer reached 27 percent in 1991-92 according to the Cornell-ERB household survey (Ferreira, 1994). By 1994-95, when the subsidies had been phased out, the National Sample Census of Agriculture (NSCA) estimated that 15 percent of Tanzanian farmers used fertilizer. According to the NSCA, the proportion is highest in the Southern Highlands (24-55 percent), the northern highlands (10-39 percent), and Tabora (35 percent (United Republic of Tanzania, 1996). The highland regions enjoy relatively good rainfall, and fertilizer is used to grow maize and coffee. Tabora is the main tobacco growing area in Tanzania.

An important issue is whether fertilizer use has fallen because relative price changes have made it unprofitable in many situations or because the institutional arrangements for providing agricultural inputs on credit have collapsed. In the former case, fertilizer use may have simply fallen to its low level given prevailing unfavorable crop and fertilizer prices, so government efforts should focus on improving the price ratio faced by farmers. The problem then would be that for a variety of reasons the farm-gate price ratios of outputs to inputs were too low. Policy remedies would then involve addressing the underlying distortion or structural problem. For example, improved transportation infrastructure, which raises the farm-level price of export crops and lowers the farm-level cost of fertilizer.

Alternatively, farmers may wish to use fertilizer, but do not have the liquidity to pay for it when needed. The problem then is lack of credit; government efforts should focus on facilitating the creation of institutions to overcome market failures associated with credit. Essentially, this means helping traders and agricultural processors enforce credit agreements with farmers (see Poulton, Dorward, and Kydd 1998). The major problem here is that when the output market is no longer controlled by a single entity such as a parastatals, giving suppliers credits to farmers becomes risky since they are free to sell their crops to a third party without having to reimburse the loan. Such problems are in fact not limited to fertilizer use and are most apparent in the case of cash cropping, as will be seen below.

---

[1] The first figure is based on the 1971-72 Household Budget Survey, while the second comes from the 1986-87 Agricultural Sample Survey (AGASU), both cited in Sarris and van den Brink (1993: 143).

Improved Seed

The experience of the seed market has some parallels with that of the fertilizer market. In the 1980s, a parastatal, TANSEED, monopolized seed production and imports. TANSEED produced 4-7 thousand tons of seed and imported 1-2 thousand tons of hybrid maize seed from Kenya. This system was characterized by poor seed quality, inadequate supply, and persistent losses by TANSEED. With liberalization in the early 1990s, seven seed companies entered the market, marginalizing TANSEED. The competition resulted in greater choices in seed varieties, although at the cost of some confusion on the part of farmers (MAC, 1997a). According to the National Sample Census of Agriculture, 27 percent of Tanzanian farmers use improved seed of one crop or another. The proportions are highest in Kilimanjaro, Tanga, Dodoma, and Singida. This regional pattern may be partly caused by the proximity to Kenya, with its relatively well-developed seed system and hybrid maize varieties.

Pesticides

Pesticides (including insecticides, herbicides, and fungicides) are subject to more health and safety regulations than fertilizer and seed, of course, but the pesticide market was more liberalized. For example, the government did not establish a parastatal enterprise with monopoly powers. Private firms imported pesticides through the Agricultural and Industrial Supply Company (AISCO). Often the imports were carried out on the basis of tied-credit from a donor country. In 1987, pesticide imports were liberalized, but they continued to be distributed to farmers free or at heavily subsidized prices by the primary societies. Private sector involvement in distribution grew only after the subsidies were removed and prices decontrolled. Initially, there were problems with adulteration and counterfeit products. These problems are less serious now that importers and distributors have established reputations to protect and buyers are more cautious.

Around 1990, cotton and coffee were said to account for 70 percent of pesticide use. However, various problems in the coffee industry have led to declining use of pesticides. At the same time, the rehabilitation of the tobacco and cashew nut sectors has generated increasing demand from these sectors. Input use in tobacco is facilitated by a system to distribute inputs on credit (MAC, 1997a). In the case of cashew nut production, sulfur dusting is expensive, costing as much as half of the value of the harvest, but it increases yields several fold (Misanga, 1998).

Pesticide imports have declined by roughly 40 percent since the late 1980s, according data compiled by MAC (1997a). Comparing the results of the 1991 Cornell-ERB survey and the 1994-95 NCSA, it appears that the proportion of farmers using pesticides did not change over this period. The proportion is highest in Kilimanjaro, probably related to coffee production, and Iringa, where pesticides are used in maize storage (see Ferreira, 1994 and United Republic of Tanzania, 1996).

4.4 Input and Small-Scale Agricultural Investment Credit

In the 1980s, inputs were provided free or on credit by the primary society or the relevant crop authority. Repayment could, in theory, be enforced because these institutions also monopolized the marketing of agricultural commodities, allowing them to deduct the cost of the inputs at harvest. In practice, the credit was not always repaid, either because of weather-related crop failure, corruption, or political pressure. The mounting debts of the cooperatives and the crop authorities stem in part from the problems of recovering agricultural credit from farmers.

The task of recovering credit has, if anything, become more difficult with output market liberalization. When several buyers are competing to purchase the harvest, it is easier for the farmer to avoid repaying inputs received on credit. Since the enforcement of credit agreements is difficult, traders and cooperatives are less willing to provide inputs on credit. This problem has surfaced in a number of African countries (see Poulton, Dorward, and Kydd 1998).

Although data on the proportion of farmers receiving credit during the 1980s is not available, the NSCA reveals that barely 5 percent of farmers received credit in 1994-95, although this does not cover informal sources such as friends, neighbors (other than established moneylenders), and extended family, where non-financial obligations are important and the expectation of financial reimbursement is low from the start. The proportion of identified true financial credit was highest in Ruvuma and Tabora. There is evidence of a gender bias in that the percentage of female-headed farms obtaining credit was just 3 percent, compared to almost 6 percent among male-headed farms (alternatively, the gap may reflect gender differences in the crops grown, which in turn could also be a reflection of a gender gap in access to inputs). The vast majority of the credit was received from a cooperative union (50 percent) or a moneylender (40 percent).

In the tobacco sector, the credit system continues to function: private buyers provide inputs on credit and deduct the repayment from the crop payment at harvest. However, some conflicts have arisen between buyers and growers concerning different estimates of the size of the debts. In the case of coffee, buyers are experimenting with a system in which part of the harvest payment is given in the form of a voucher, worth about 4 percent of the farm-gate value of the coffee sold, that can be used to purchase inputs for the next year. A secondary market for the vouchers has developed, threatening the viability of the system from the strict standpoint of financing input use on coffee (Ngondo, 1999).

In the case of cashew nuts, credit is needed to purchase sulfur dust and blower services to fight powdery mildew disease. Private firms began importing sulfur in 1991-92. Importers sold sulfur to stockist on credit, allowing them to extend credit to farmers. In a competitive marketing system, it is difficult to enforce repayment, so stockists have become very selective in giving credit. In 1994-95, an input fund was started using a Tsh 10/kg levy, but the fund has been criticized for mismanaging the revenues (Misanga, 1998; Poulton, Dorward, and Kydd 1998).

Cashew provides one of the few examples where use of ago-chemicals has increased over time. The use of sulphur dust increased from 100 MT in 1990/91 to over 900 MT in 1995/96 in the Ruvuma region, during a period of rapid rise in producer output prices for cashew, yet most of the increase could be ascribed to the activities of the Cashew Input Development Fund, an NGO started with trader participation in 1996 that is allowed to levy from traders 2 percent on the value of cashew nut exported and provides credit for sulphur imports (by traders) and use (by farmers) (World Bank COD 1999).

Kilimanjaro Cooperative Bank was started in 1995 using levy funds from coffee sales, and has rapidly expanded its loan clientele among primary cooperative societies in the Arabica coffee producing region. Initial results from a widespread Arabica coffee producer input financing in 1999 through primary cooperative societies seem quite promising. Thirty-day loans for inputs were made by the primary cooperative to farmers, allowing them to purchase inputs from an approved list.

Small-scale investment credit is different from input credit in that it is less reasonable to suppose that traders will fund it, although this does happen once land can be used as collateral, as in

Southeast Asia. The new National Microfinance Bank may help in Tanzania. In the absence of collateralizable assets, subsidized organizations present in local areas (not direct credit subsidies) will continue to be necessary to screen loans, monitor progress, provide technical support, and ensure repayment. NGO's may continue to have a big role here. As an example from the livestock sector, acquiring a grade heifer was typically a major constraint on the expansion of smallholder dairy output. NGO-operated schemes such as Heifer-in-Trust were effective at channeling inputs to farmers in rural areas and ensuring that loans were repaid. Where effective demand for milk has also grown strongly, such as in the smallholder urban production system of Dar-es-Salaam, private credit systems linked to the collateral offered by urban salaries and land titles have managed investment finance quite effectively (MAC NEI 1999f).

4.5   Unfavorable Trends in the Ratio of Crop to Input Prices

The story of input use cannot be divorced from that of profitability, even if the latter is not a sufficient condition for growth in input use. Over time, it is clear that on the whole, purchased inputs such as fertilizer have become progressively more expensive to farmers relative to the value of their produce. Figures in the Agricultural Inputs Study (MAC 1997a) show that the aggregate price of the four main types of fertilizer used in Tanzania increased three times faster than the rapid rate of domestic inflation over the 1983/84 to 1996/97 period. Fertilizer use dropped from 124,000 tons annually in 1985/89 to 65,000 tons in 1996/97, mostly because of decreased use on maize (MAC 1997a).

Free-market fertilizer prices are a good proxy of all agricultural chemical prices. Diminishing profitability of input use in both food and export crops is shown in Table 4.2. The table, which compares crop to fertilizer prices, may actually underestimate the extent of the shift in relative prices between the late 1980s and early 1990s, since food producer prices recorded before 1991 tended to under-estimate actual market prices, as discussed in Section 3 above. The elimination of fertilizer subsidies after 1995 shows up clearly in the table.

The relative price effect is more evident for the main food crops (maize, cassava, rice) and for cotton than it is for the other main export crops and wheat. The difference between these commodity groups is probably not because of world prices. World cotton prices were lower in 1990/94 than in 1995/98. World wheat prices were relatively high during the mid 1990s, but so were maize and rice prices. A likely explanation for the difference is that the prices of the more fully tradable commodities (wheat and export crops) were more responsive to nominal exchange depreciation than was the case for the imperfectly tradable food sector.

Cotton prices may also have behaved differently than the other major export crops for two reasons. First, cotton faced problems maintaining export quality grades during the later part of the 1990s, depressing the average producer price. Second, cotton exports incur high transportation costs because the producing areas are far from the coast and because cotton has a low value-to-bulk ratio.

Rapidly escalating fuel prices in the 1990s would reduce the producer price of cotton more than the other export commodities that have higher value-to-bulk ratios such as coffee and flue-cured tobacco, and more than commodities with shorter internal shipping distances, such as cashew nuts. Fertilizer prices delivered to the farm that rise with distance from the coast would compound the problem.

4.6   Impact of Rising Input Prices on the Profitability of Crop Agriculture

Extension agents and others interviewed by the authors of this report consistently state that farmers make the claim that fertilizer has become too expensive to use on maize in recent years. Claims are also made that the decline of input use on food crops explains falling yields and production of food crops. Yet as Section 5 will demonstrate, fertilizer use on maize was quite low even when fertilizer was subsidized, and its decline in use on food crops cannot explain their performance, or lack thereof. That said, it is clear that it has become much less profitable to use purchased inputs on maize over the 1990s. This is demonstrated in detail in Table 4.3.

Table 4.3 assumes that the exact package of inputs (seed, fertilizer, and pesticide) deemed to be profitable for maize in 1991 is used every year up through 1998, at current prices. According to these calculations the returns to labor and land in maize cultivation have been reduced by 75 percent. The real return per man-day falls to 500 Tsh in 1998, or significantly less that the poverty norm of US$1.00/day.

It should be noted that these calculations overestimate the decline of incentives to grow maize. First, farmers generally use less fertilizer and other inputs than is recommended by extension agents so they are less adversely affected by input price increases. Second, farmers respond to higher input prices by reducing input use, further dampening the decrease in returns.

Interestingly in Table 4.2 above, the producer price ratio of maize to fertilizer has stabilized at 0.36 since 1995. This suggests the physical response to fertilizer must be at least 3 bags of maize per bag of raw fertilizer in order to be profitable.

Typical physical returns to fertilizer use on grain in East Africa are 3 to 5 bags of maize per bag of nitrogen, equivalent to 1.0-1.7 bags of maize per bag of fertilizer (Heisey and Mwangi 1997). The ratio of maize to raw fertilizer prices would need to increase to about 1990-94 average levels (0.83) before fertilizer use on maize would be profitable. This abstracts from the longer run issue of resource degradation from soil mining. Yet when use is so unprofitable in the short run, it seems unlikely that farmers will do much about the long run concern.

The impact of rising input costs on returns to farmers' labor and land in producing the four main traditional export crops is shown in Table 4.4. Using mid-range extension recommendations for 1992/93, the table traces out the changes from 1992/93 to 1995/96 in terms of the cost of the recommended package of purchased inputs and the value of output. The last row of the table shows the returns per man-day, whereas the two preceding rows show the percent change in costs and the percent change in returns to labor and land, once inflation is removed. For cotton, the real rise in input costs was 81 percent, whereas the real change in returns to labor was 4 percent over the period.

The decline in the profitability of input use was particularly severe for cotton, which primarily uses imported inputs. Overall profitability declined most for flue-cured tobacco and cashew, because of output price factors. The returns to coffee were fairly stable, although the returns to input use on coffee fell by 27 percent. Even so, the returns to coffee remain very high on a per man day basis. It is anticipated that growers with good coffee land will continue to hire labor and to use purchased inputs. Again, it is important to recognize that, to the extent that these calculations overstate input use and to the extent that farmers respond to higher input prices, the reduction in returns to land and labor will be less than reported here.

4.7   The Difficult Institutional Transition Under Liberalization

The changes in output/input price ratios tell a story of declining profitability of purchased input use that is in some ways adequate to explain the observed reduction in input use. More importantly, declining price ratios help explain why alternative institutions have not been quick to emerge to take up the input supply roles of the former parastatals. Such institutions may not be a major issue for food crops, at least not until the output/input price ratio rises substantially. At the present time, however, they are an important issue for export crops, where quality is a major issue in the market and highly dependent on input use.

Credit to secure necessary purchased inputs is critical to all fully commercial enterprises; in export cropping, it is a central issue for the survival of the activity. Provided that the country retains a comparative advantage in the activity, input use on export crops should be able to pay for itself in terms of foreign exchange, provided that the institutional environment is up to the task of supplying inputs and marketing outputs. Compared to other African countries, Tanzania has had a particularly difficult time in the 1990s moving from a parastatal-led input supply/output marketing set of institutions to a set of private banking, trading, and regulatory institutions compatible with free-market principles (Shepherd and Farolfi 1999).

There is a voluminous recent literature on the reasons for this difficult transition and possible solutions (Havnevik and Harsmar 1999; World Bank COD 1999; Wiketye 1999). This report cannot do justice to all the issues here, but several points stand out. First, it will not be possible to increase input use even where financially profitable until some form of rural credit system is established. In cotton areas, for example, the Tanzania Cotton Marketing Board (TCMB) used to be the only outlet for sales. On the output marketing side, this meant that farmers were in a poor bargaining position and received low and late payments. On the input side, it meant that the parastatal could freely provide suppliers credits, in the certainty that loans would be recovered at harvest.

Presently, in the absence of enforceable contracts, traders are reluctant to lend to farmers because the farmer can always sell the crop to a trader's competitor. It is also harder to enforce quality standards. The return of suppliers credits in the situation will require probably "rules of the game" set by TCMB and enforced by an association of buyers and ginners on the one hand, and farmers associations and the marketing board on the other.

It will be important to monitor the success of the case of 30 day suppliers' credits mentioned above for Arabica coffee in Arusha/Kilimanjaro. Returns remain relatively good for coffee and the trees represent a sizeable fixed investment for farmers. If this program, initiated by the Kilimanjaro Cooperative Bank, works well, it could be a model for cases where farmers have much to gain by playing by the rules.

One somber possibility hinted at in some recent policy literature, but not explicitly investigated, is that the structural changes of recent years in Tanzania and world price changes have led to fundamental changes in the country's comparative advantage away from agriculture (see the conclusions to World Bank AFR2M (1999), for example). If this were true, it would not be advisable to invest foreign exchange or policy resources into improving the institutional environment for agricultural export crop competitiveness. Instead, scarce resources should be invested some other sector, such as urban infrastructure to promote labor intensive light manufacturing. The issue of comparative advantage will be examined in the next section, and then the implications of findings will be analyzed in an economy-wide context.

Table 4.1. Determinants of Spreads Between Dar-es-Salaam Monthly Retail Prices for Food Staples and Interior Market Retail Prices 1986-98

Result	Wheat	Rice	Maize	Cassava
	(December 1998 Tsh)			
Mean real spread over period	174.09	135.30	45.88	101.90
Continuous time trend	-1.35	-0.06	-0.09	0.60
Road distance from Dar (km)	0.11	0.11	0.05	n.s.
Road distance squared	-0.00	-0.00	-0.00	n.s.
Markets on a rail line	-12.41	21.32	-3.71	n.s.
Market is isolated	n.s.	n.s.	10.87	n.s.
Market is a port city	-20.25	-32.04	-5.53	n.s.
Lowest two of twelve monthly dummies	Nov. Jan.	Dec. Jan.	Oct. Nov.	Jul. Aug.
	(units)			
Number of observations	3,504	4,861	4,721	1,220
Adjusted R^2	0.67	0.68	0.71	0.60

Source: From OLS regressions by crop using data from MAC FEWS (1999); the dependent variable is the local price minus the Dar price; prices are in December 1998 Tsh per kg. All coefficients are statistically significant at 5 percent or better unless shown as n.s. N.s. indicates not statistically significant at 5 percent.

Table 4.2. *Ratios of Average Crop Producer Prices to Farmgate Fertilizer Prices 1985-98*

Crop	1985-89	1990-94	1995-98	1998
Food crops				
Maize	1.40	0.83	0.37	0.36
Paddy	2.23	1.39	0.56	0.60
Wheat	1.58	1.87	0.92	0.84
Millet/sorghum	1.05	1.15	0.85	0.54
Cassava	0.86	0.50	0.20	0.21
Beans	3.23	2.25	1.39	1.33
Export crops				
Cotton Grade B	4.37	2.47	0.98	0.81
Coffee, Mild Arabica	10.01	11.79	8.03	5.73
Cashew, High Quality	4.02	6.09	2.80	2.91
Tobacco, Flue cured	10.18	12.11	5.90	6.56

Source: Crop producer prices supplied by MAC/Market Development Bureau. Fertilizer price series constructed for aggregate of four main types from data in MAC 1997a.

Table 4.3. Hypothetical Change in Returns to Maize Cultivation Under Constant Input Levels and Yields 1988-98

Production year	Nominal cost of seed, fertilizer, pesticides	Nominal price per kg	Nominal gross revenue per ha	Nominal gross margin per ha	Nominal return per man-day	Real return per man-day
			(current Tsh)			(1998-99 Tsh)
1991	20,582	41	61,500	40,918	333	2,218
1992	24,966	56	83,295	58,329	474	2,496
1993	31,507	64	96,630	65,123	529	2,118
1994	43,134	59	88,650	45,516	370	1,121
1995	56,246	72	107,400	51,154	416	967
1996	75,651	81	120,750	45,099	367	632
1997	89,495	90	135,600	46,105	375	487
1998	115,717	118	177,300	61,583	501	501

Source: A maize budget for 1988 was calculated in detail in 1991 by MDB/MAC. Assumptions are: hand-hoe technology, involving 123 man-days of family labor, with a yield of 1,500 kg/ha. Cash costs for inputs are assumed to grow at the same rate as national CPI in order to maintain a constant level of input use each year.

Table 4.4. Evolution of Costs and Returns in Smallholder Cash Cropping Under Liberalization

Statistic	Cotton	Tobacco	Arabica coffee	Cashew
Output technology assumptions (per ha)	Mwanza-Shinyanga, improved hand cultivation, 159 man-days	Tabora, flue-cured, 700 kg/ha, 533 man days	Kilimanjaro-Arusha, coffee-banana intercropping, family labor, 370 kg coffee/500 bunches of bananas	Mtwara, "typical" smallholder, chemical disease control, 650 kg/ha, 91 man-days
Input package per ha assumptions	7.5 kg Thiodan, 8 batteries, cloth, tools. All inputs tradable.	650 kg NPK, 12.5 kg Thiodan, misc. tools, supplies, barn, firewood. 14% of inputs are non-tradable.	13 bags SA fertilizer, 20 kg manure per tree, assorted chemicals, sacks. 40% of inputs are non-tradable.	Pesticides, sulfur, rental of blower, bags. All inputs tradable.
		(total percent change 1992-93-1995-96)		
Change in producer prices	183	87	100	-10
Change in farm-gate cost of input package	253	142	102	23
Change in returns to factors or production (labor, land)	146	26	138	-61
Real (deflated) change in input costs[a]	81	1	-27	-69
Real (deflated) change in returns to labor and land[a]	4	-81	-1	-78
		(1995-96 current Tsh/man-day)		
Returns to labor and land	390	285	1,364	376

a Deflated by Tanzania national CPI.
Source: Calculated from farm budgets supplied by Market Development Bureau/MAC.

5. PERFORMANCE OF AGRICULTURE

Evaluating the performance of the agricultural sector in Tanzania since the mid-1980s when the first economic reforms were implemented is not easy because of a number of limitations and inconsistencies in Tanzania agricultural data. An evaluation by the World Bank OED (1998) noted that estimates of the annual growth in agricultural output between the mid-1980s and the early 1990s vary between 1 and 5 percent. In particular, the study highlighted a discrepancy between high growth rates in agricultural GDP over this period and low growth rates in food production, particularly maize.

Most of the concern regarding agricultural statistics has been focused on the production of the six "main" food crops[1]. As shown in Table 5.1, these six crops account for about 46 percent of agricultural GDP, other food crops about 20 percent, and cash crops 9 percent. Livestock production is about 13 percent of GDP, while forestry, hunting, and fishing account for the remaining 12 percent. Although maize is the largest single item in agricultural GDP, it accounts for less than a quarter of the total. One implication of these figures is that stagnation in maize production is not necessarily inconsistent with growth in agricultural GDP.

It is important to note that the problems with agricultural statistics are not new. For example, Temu (1975) used data from the 1969 Household Budget Survey and the 1971 Agricultural Census to argue that actual maize production in 1970 was twice the official figure. Similarly, Sarris and van den Brink (1993) argued that the 10 percent annual growth in official estimates of per capita food production between 1971 and 1976 is implausible in light of other data. In particular, they point out that the mid-1970s was characterized by rising real food prices, increasing maize imports, a drought, and disruption associated with villagization. They also pointed out that Household Budget Surveys of 1969 and 1976-77 suggest a slower rate of growth in food production. Most recently, the World Bank OED (1998) gives numerous examples of the variety of estimates of growth in agricultural production. As mentioned above, the OED report argued that the high rates of growth in agricultural GDP were being used as the basis for positive assessments of the impact of economic reforms, in spite of the fact that food production data showed little growth.

At the same time, significant progress has been made in identifying the problems with agricultural statistics and developing methods to improve the quality and consistency of the data (see Kiregyera et al. 1999; Komba 1999; and Mlay 1999). In particular, the quality of agricultural data in Tanzania has improved since the early 1990s and objective survey-based estimates have largely replaced the use of subjective estimates by village extension officers.

In order to assess the performance of Tanzanian agriculture since the mid-1980s, we begin with an assessment of the problems associated with estimates of Tanzanian agricultural production. Then we discuss the likely performance of the food, cash crop, and livestock sectors. Finally, we show how estimates of agricultural GDP vary depending on which food production estimates are used.

---

[1] By convention, the six "main" food crops in Tanzania are considered to be maize, rice, wheat, sorghum/millet, cassava, and beans. These six crops do not, however, correspond to the most important ones in value terms. For example, the value of cooking banana output is eight times that of wheat production (and only somewhat smaller than that of sorghum/millet and cassava production). In fact, the value of wheat production is surpassed by that of a number of "minor" crops: sweet potatoes, groundnuts, onions, tomatoes, and dry peas.

5.1   Assessment of Agricultural Production Data

The most obvious problem with Tanzanian agricultural production statistics is that there are multiple and conflicting statistics issued by different government agencies. National estimates of food crop production, for example, are produced by the Crop Monitoring and Early Warning Unit (CMEWU) of the Ministry of Agriculture and Cooperatives (MAC), the Agricultural Statistical Unit (ASU) of the MAC, and the National Accounts section of the National Bureau of Statistics (NBS). The estimates vary, sometimes significantly. To evaluate the credibility of each source, we need to examine the data collection methods.

Crop Monitoring and Early Warning Unit (CMEWU)

Before 1993/94, CMEWU production statistics were based on area estimates produced by the agricultural reporting system of the MAC. Under this system, village extension officers made subjective estimates of area and yield based on direct observation, weather, input availability, and their knowledge of local farming systems. These estimates were compiled and adjusted first at the district level, then at the regional level, and finally at MAC headquarters. Yields were estimated separately using a agro-meteorological model that predicts yield as a function of climatic variables. This system produced highly disaggregated estimates at relatively low cost, but the methodology is weak and subject to error.

Recognizing the limitations of this system, the CMEWU adopted a survey-based system for generating crop production forecasts in 1993-94. Since that year, the CMEWU uses farm surveys in 540 villages to produce regional estimates of production. Two sets of estimates are released each year: a pre-harvest forecast in April/May and a final forecast in June/July[2].

Agricultural Statistical Unit

The Agricultural Statistical Unit (ASU) of the MAC has relied on a variety of sources, including the agricultural reporting system and surveys. Before 1994-95, the ASU relied largely on the agricultural reporting system for national production estimates. Although the ASU and CMEWU both used data from the agricultural reporting system, their estimates differ, possibly due to different methods of measuring yields.

Since 1993-94, the ASU has collaborated with the National Bureau of Statistics on a series of national surveys to measure crop production, as described in Table 5.2. The sample size of these surveys has increased over time, allowing regional estimates of production since 1994-95 and district estimates starting in 1998-99. Since 1994-95, these surveys have been the basis for ASU estimates of regional and national production.

National Bureau of Statistics

The National Bureau of Statistics carried out Agricultural Sample Surveys (AGASU) from 1987 to 1990. The survey was based on a sample of 100 villages selected from the National Master Sample. As such, it generated national production estimates but not regional estimates. More recently, the NBS collaborated with the Statistical Unit of the MAC in the implementation of the

---

[2] This second forecast is sometimes called the post-harvest estimate, but it is more appropriate to call it a forecast since it is calculated before the end of the main (masika) harvest.

National Agricultural Sample Census, the Expanded Agricultural Survey, and the Integrated Agricultural Survey (see Table 5.2).

The NBS uses agricultural production estimates to calculate the agricultural component of gross domestic product (GDP). Roughly every ten years the base prices used to calculate constant GDP are updated. The GDP series with base years 1966, 1976, and 1985 used production data on the six main food crops from the CMEWU and producer price data collected by the Market Development Bureau (MDB/MAC) of the MAC. The latest series, using 1992 prices, adopted a different approach and relied heavily on the 1991-92 Household Budget Survey (HBS). Crop production for years before and after 1992 have been calculated based on subjective growth rates taking into account weather conditions and speeches of the Ministry of Agriculture and the Prime Minister. The producer prices are also derived from the HBS[3].

Other Sources of Agricultural Production Data

Data on production on large-scale farms cannot be accurately measured from a nationally representative sample survey because these farms are rare and few appear in the sample. The NBS attempted to collect information on large-farm production in 1986-97 using a mail survey, but the response was not good. Better response was obtained with surveys implemented in 1994-95 and 1997-98 by the Ministry of Agricultural and Cooperatives (Mlay 1999).

Data on export crop production were collected by the respective marketing boards in the 1980s and early 1990s. At this time, their legal monopoly on purchasing and export simplified the process of data collection. Even so, different sources report different estimates (see Table 5.3). With export liberalization in the early 1990s, purchasing and export are carried out by private traders, complicating the task of collecting accurate data (Mlay 1999).

The production of animal products is estimated by the Livestock Department of the MAC based on estimates of herd size and yield rates. These figures are not used by NBS in the calculation of the GDP of the livestock sector. Instead, the estimates from the 1990-91 Household Budget Survey are projected forward and backward using subjective growth rates for each year. The CDP data on livestock appear particularly fragile, as will be seen below.

Assessment of Food Production Data

The wide variation in estimates of food production is shown in Table 5.4. It is not uncommon for the highest estimate to be double the lowest estimate. In Table 5.5, we calculate the average gap between the highest and lowest estimates from the three main data sources, expressed as a percentage of the lowest estimate. Over the period 1982-1998, the average gap is about 20 percent for maize and over 50 percent for wheat, cassava, and sorghum/millet. The table also shows that the average gap has declined substantially from the 1980s to the 1990s, probably reflecting the adoption of survey-based sampling methods for CMEWU and ASU/MAC production estimates.

---

[3] Kiregyera *et al.* (1999) reports that the producer prices used to value agricultural production are calculated "by dividing the value of non-monetary consumption by the quantity consumed" (p 7). However, the value of non-monetary consumption must have been imputed using observed prices, probably either purchase prices or sale prices from the HBS. If producer prices were used, the result would be at least as valid as the use of producer price data from the Market Development Bureau.

Table 5.5 also reveals that the percentage gap between CMEWU and ASU/MAC figures is smaller than the three-way gap, particularly in the 1990s. Since 1990, the average gap between CMEWU and ASU/MAC estimates has ranged from 1 to 23 percent, depending on the crop. This is a reasonable gap given that the CMEWU figures are pre-harvest forecasts and ASU/MAC figures are post-harvest estimates.

The annual growth rates are given in Table 5.6. It is notable that the National Accounts growth rates show remarkably little variation and are always positive[4]. This is highly implausible considering that Tanzanian agriculture is predominantly rainfed and that rainfall is quite variable. Furthermore, in a given year, the almost-identical growth rates for paddy, cassava, beans, and sorghum/millet suggest that National Accounts section uses the same subjective estimates of annual growth for various crops.

The average growth rates derived from the CMEWU and Statistical Unit estimates tend to be positively correlated, as shown in Table 5.7. In contrast, neither the CMEWU growth rates nor those of the ASU are strongly correlated with those of the National Accounts section of the NBS (wheat is the only exception). In fact, the National Accounts growth rates are negatively correlated with CMEWU growth rates for two of the six crops.

Table 5.7 examines growth in food production since the mid-1980s according to the three data sources and using different periods. The National Accounts growth rates are strikingly similar, reflecting the very simple assumptions used to obtain them. In addition, the growth rates from the ASU and the CMEWU are quite sensitive to the choice of period, with the highest rates coming from a comparison of 1985 and 1998. This is presumably due to the fact that the 1996 and 1997 harvests were poor due to El Nino and La Nina climate conditions, respectively. Thus, including these years in the endpoint average reduces the growth rate.

Overall, we agree with the conclusions of Kiregyera et al. (1999), Komba (1999) and Mlay (1999) that the National Accounts production estimates are unreliable, being based on crude assumptions about crop production growth rates with little empirical support. We also agree that current ASU estimates should be considered the "official" government estimates for purposes of planning and analysis of long-term trends. The case for adopting ASU production estimates for the 1980s is plausible but less persuasive since both ASU and CMEWU relied on the agricultural reporting system until 1994-95. The CMEWU data continue to be useful for early warning of production shortfalls and resulting food insecurity.

Finally, it should be noted that agricultural GDP is conceptually distinct from agricultural production. First, agricultural GDP values production at market prices, a process that gives greater weight to the trends in high-value crops (including most commercial and export crops). Second, agricultural GDP measures the value of output *net* of the cost of agricultural inputs, while production data are gross values. Third, agricultural GDP includes investment. For example, the value of newly planted coffee trees and the purchases of agricultural equipment are counted in agricultural GDP but not in production data.

Thus, it is not surprising that production and agricultural GDP growth rates are not the same, even in the absence of data inconsistencies. In some years, such as the period after 1996 in the

---

[4] The coefficient of variation of the annual growth rates based on the National Accounts production data is less than 2 for all but one crop (bananas), whereas the coefficient of variation for the other two data sources is greater than 70 for every crop.

Arabica-producing areas of the north, the difference between the two can be quite substantial because of heavy investment in new plantings after the boom in prices in 1996/97.

5.2   Food Crop Production Performance

Based on the conclusions from the previous section, this section uses the ASU production data to discuss the performance of the food crop sector. We focus on the most important crops in terms of their contribution to caloric intake, with less attention to other food crops.

Maize

Maize is the main staple crop in Tanzania, being grown on about 41 percent of the cultivated land during the *masika* (main) season and 47 percent of the cultivated land during the *vuli* (second) season (United Republic of Tanzania 1996: 15). According to the 1993 Human Resource Development Survey (HRDS), 82 percent of rural households grow maize and, of these, 26 percent sell maize (HRDS 1996). The largest surpluses are generated by the "big four" maize producers: Iringa, Mbeya, Ruvuma, and Rukwa.

The annual growth in maize production has been 2.4 percent over 1985-1998[5] and 2.7 percent since 1990. On the one hand, it is an matter of concern that maize production has not kept up with population growth, generally assumed to be 2.8 percent[6]. On the other hand, it is impressive that maize output has almost kept up with population growth during a period in which real producer prices have fallen and fertilizer prices have more than doubled.

Possible explanations for the slow growth of maize output relative to population growth include: 1) the end of pan-territorial pricing of crops, 2) the higher cost of fertilizer due to input market, 3) expansion of export crops due to export liberalization, 4) shifts in demand toward other staples, and 5) insufficient rain in recent years.

Pan-territorial pricing effectively subsidized the movement of maize from the southern highlands to Dar-es-Salaam, thus subsidizing production in this high-potential zone and urban consumers. The regional composition of maize production shows that between 1987-89 and 1996-98 maize output has declined by 13-19 percent in the three more remote regions of the southern highlands (Mbeya, Ruvuma, and Rukwa), while expanding in Iringa, Dodoma, and other regions closer to Dar. Since this is a one-time policy change, it should have a one-time effect on maize output and future growth should not be affected.

Although the higher price of fertilizer is often cited as a factor in constraining maize output, this is not likely to be a major factor. According to FAO data, fertilizer use in Tanzania fell from 44 thousand tons of nutrient per year in 1985-89 to 33 thousand tons over 1995-96. Attributing all of the decrease to maize production, this implies a reduction of 11 thousand tons of nutrient. Turuka (1995) estimates that the marginal product of fertilizer use in two Tanzanian districts is 5-7 kg of maize per kg of nutrient. This implies that the fertilizer reforms might be responsible for a one-time reduction in maize output of 77 thousand tons or 2.8 percent of current production.

---

[5] As discussed in Section 5.2, the growth rate is sensitive to the choice of period. Using 1985 and 1998 as endpoints probably gives a good idea of the general pattern. Neither are drought years nor bumper crop years, and the trend line for maize production passes quite near both points (see Figure 5.1).

[6] It is worth noting that this figure is apparently based on the growth in population between the 1976 census and the one in 1988. We are not aware of more recent estimates of population growth, so there is some question how accurate this figure is.

Expressed another way, if the fertilizer subsidies had been maintained, the annual growth rate over 1990-98 would have been 3.0 percent instead of 2.8 percent. Now that the subsidy removal is complete, future growth rates in maize output will not be affected.

Similarly, changes in export crop production are likely to have only modest effects on national maize production. According to the 1994-95 National Sample Census of Agriculture, the cotton area in Tanzania is 196 thousand hectares, while maize area is 1.8-2.0 million hectares. Thus, even if all cotton expansion came from substitution from maize area to cotton area, a 10 percent expansion in cotton output could be achieved with a 1 percent reduction in maize output. This is a maximum figure since 1) cotton production could also be increased through yield improvements, 2) the total cropped area could expand, and 3) the cotton area could expand at the expense of crops other than maize. The result of this calculation would be similar for coffee, which is grown on 235 thousand acres.

It seems likely that demand constraints play an important role in limiting the growth of maize production. Formal exports through Dar are not economical unless the domestic price falls below the export parity price, an event that is fairly rare. Maize exports to Zambia and other neighboring countries have been banned in recent years due to food security concerns. Thus, maize growth is limited by domestic demand. The relatively low income elasticity of maize (see Section 6) indicates that maize demand growth will be modest even with per capita income growth.

In order to examine more systematically the factors that influence maize production, we use data for the 20 regions of Tanzania over 1986-1997 to estimate maize supply as a function of prices and rainfall. The following regression equation was used to estimate regional maize supply:

$$QMZ_{r,t} = a + bPMZ_{r,t-1} + cQMZ_{r,t-1} + dPF_{t-1} + ePC_{t-1} + fRAIN_{r,t} + gRAINSQ_{r,t}$$

where QMZ_t is maize production in region r in year t, PMZ_{t-1} is the average retail price of maize in region r over the 12 months before the planting season for the harvest in year t, PF_{t-1} is the national average price of fertilizer for the year t-1, PC_{t-1} is the average producer price of cotton for the year t-1, $RAIN_t$ is the rainfall in region r over the 12 months prior to the harvest in year t, $RAINSQ_t$ is the rainfall squared in region r over the 12 months prior to the harvest in year t.

As shown in Table 5.9, the results indicate that the previous year's maize price[7] as a statistically significant effect on maize production. The implicit short-run price elasticity of supply is 0.25[8]. The lagged production variable is also significant, meaning that either farmers do not fully respond to new prices in the first year or that they form expectations about prices based on several years of prices. In either case, the implication is that maize farmers are more responsive to prices in the long run than they are in the short run. Specifically, the coefficients suggest that the long-run supply elasticity is 1.96[9].

---

[7] The producer price series collected by the Market Development Bureau records official government procurement prices until 1990. Since these prices did not reflect market prices and hence the opportunity cost facing farmers, we use the retail maize price in the regression.

[8] The price elasticity of supply is calculated as $\beta(P/Q)$, where β is the price coefficient obtained from Table 5.9, P is the mean price of maize, and Q is the mean national quantity produced. The supply elasticities for other crops are calculated in a similar manner.

[9] The long-run supply elasticity is calculated as $\varepsilon/(1-\theta)$, where ε is the short-run supply elasticity and θ is the coefficient on the lagged dependent variable.

The coefficient on fertilizer price is not significant. This means that the removal of fertilizer subsidies over 1992-95 and the consequent higher fertilizer prices have not had a statistically significant effect on maize production. As noted above, even a dramatic reduction in fertilizer use would have only modest effects on maize production because application rates were already so low before liberalization.

The coefficient on the cotton price indicates that higher cotton prices reduce maize output. The cross-price elasticity is -0.43, meaning that a 10 percent increase in cotton prices reduces maize output by 4.3 percent. This is somewhat surprising given the small area planted to cotton relative to the area with maize. It may be that cotton prices tend to move with other export crop prices (such as through changes in the exchange rate), so that this coefficient is picking up the effect of an increase in various export crops.

Both rainfall variables are statistically significant. Higher rainfall is associated with higher maize production, but beyond a certain point very high rainfall reduces maize production. A year in which rainfall is 10 percent above average (1,100 mm) will produce a maize harvest that is 12.7 percent above average, other factors being equal.

Paddy

Between 1985 and 1998, paddy production increased almost four fold. This represents an annual growth rate of almost 11 percent, making paddy the fastest growing food crop. Three factors have contributed to this expansion. First, paddy is a tradable good, as Tanzania has imported 50-100 thousand tons of rice in most years since 1990. As a tradable good, the domestic price is influenced by the exchange rate and international prices. The economic reforms have resulted in exchange rate depreciation, making imports more costly and stimulating domestic production of tradable goods including rice.

Second, the income elasticity of rice is quite high. As will be shown in Section 6, data from the Human Resource Development Survey of 1993 (HRDS 1996) indicate that the income elasticity of rice is 1.25 in rural areas and 0.84 in urban areas, relatively high for a food commodity. As a result, we expect per capita demand for rice to increase at approximately the same rate as per capita income growth.

Third, exceptionally high and well-distributed rainfall in 1997-98 contributed to a bumper crop in 1997-98. Even the poorer crop of 1996-97 was more than double the average paddy output in the early and mid-1980s.

We used regression analysis to identify the determinants of rice supply. The results indicate that the short-run supply elasticity is 0.68 (Table 5.10). The coefficient on lagged rice output variable suggests that farmers have completed about half of their adjustment in the first year, so the long-run supply elasticity is 1.33. Maize prices, fertilizer prices, and annual rainfall were not statistically significant. Although rainfall clearly has an influence on paddy production, this effect is not picked up by a crude measure such as annual total rainfall.

Wheat

The case of wheat is similar to that of paddy. Wheat production has grown at about 4 percent per year over 1985-1998. Like paddy, wheat is a tradable good, with imports running at 30 to 70 thousand tons per year (roughly 40 percent of national consumption). Thus, the policy of a market-based exchange rate has favored domestic wheat producers by making imported wheat more costly in local-currency terms. This has been offset somewhat by the very low world wheat prices currently prevailing.

Also like paddy, wheat has a relatively high income elasticity. Our analysis of the HRDS data (HRDS 1996) in Section 6 below indicates that the income elasticity of wheat products is 1.25 in urban areas and 1.92 in rural areas. Thus, we expect the per capita demand for wheat products to rise more quickly than per capita income. These two factors help to explain the relatively rapid growth in wheat production.

Cassava

Cassava grows well in poor soils, requires little rainfall, and can be "stored" in the ground until needed. These attributes make it useful as a famine crop. Kagera, Mtwara, and Mwanza are the main producing areas, accounting for 40 percent of the total. The perishability of the fresh cassava root (once harvested) and the low value-to-bulk ratio limit the long-distance marketing of cassava root. Cassava is mainly produced for home consumption or marketed locally. Long-distance trade and urban consumption is usually in the form of cassava flour. Cassava production is around 1,500 thousand tons and has grown 3.8 percent over 1985-1998, although the selection of endpoints probably overstates its growth (see Figure 5.4). Cassava production statistics should be interpreted with caution, however, since the pattern intermittent harvesting makes data collection difficult. This problem is underscored by the large discrepancy between MAC and FAO data on cassava production in Tanzania.

Sorghum/Millet

Sorghum and millet are grown in the low-rainfall areas of Tanzania. Current production is around 900 thousand tons, 60 percent of which is grown in Dodoma, Singida, Shinyanga, and Mwanza. Outside traditional sorghum areas such as Dodoma, consumers prefer maize so the market price is low. Low prices and low yields imply that average returns are below those of maize, but the drought-resistance of sorghum/millet means that returns are less subject to weather-related variation. Thus, it is grown as a famine crop, particularly in years when rainfall is expected to be below average. Most sorghum/millet is grown for own consumption, either as grain or in the form of traditional beer. As a result, the market is thin and there are wide variations in prices across markets and over time. According to data from the Agricultural Statistics Unit of the MAC, sorghum/millet production was stagnant in the late 1980s, but appears to have increased (though erratically) in the 1990s. This may be associated with the adoption of a new high-yielding variety (Tegemeo) in Dodoma (MAC NEI 1999b).

Other Staples

Cooking bananas are grown in somewhat cooler, wetter areas. Production is around 650 thousand tons, two-thirds of which comes from Kagera and Kilimanjaro. Output has been stagnant since 1985, although the harvest in 1997-98 was substantially higher than average. Like cassava, cooking bananas have a low value-to-bulk ratio and are generally retained for home consumption.

Sweet potato is also a less preferred drought-resistant crop with a low value-to-bulk ratio. Tanzania produces 400 thousand tons, of which over half is grown in Shinyanga and Mwanza. Output has increased since the mid-1980s, roughly keeping pace with population growth.

Pulses are grown throughout Tanzania, with Arusha and Kagera having the largest harvests. Pulses are often inter-cropped with maize and production is currently around 400 thousand tons. Since the mid-1980s, production has followed a gradual upward trend with considerable fluctuation (see Figure 5.6). Pulses tend to have a somewhat higher value-to-bulk ratio, implying greater commercialization than cassava, sweet potatoes, and cooking bananas.

Zanzibar

Zanzibar food crop production decreased from 510,983 to 243,030 metric tons between 1984/85 and 1993/94, a 52 percent decrease (Mabele 1999a). Yields appear to have fallen because output decreased by more than acreage. The major problem facing food crop production in Zanzibar is the prevalence of low-yielding varieties and disease and pest infestation. Research and extension efforts need to be directed towards food production in order to help attain higher levels of production.

5.3 Performance of Export Crops

As mentioned above, export crops account for 9 percent of the value of agricultural output or 12 percent of the value of crop production. Overall, export crops have done well, but there is considerable variation from crop to crop.

Coffee

Coffee is one of the two largest agricultural exports, earning about US$100 million per year. The main producing areas are Kilimanjaro and Kagera, accounting for over half of Tanzanian coffee production. Ruvuma, Mbeya, Arusha, and several other regions also produce coffee. In the late 1980s, successive devaluations of the Tanzanian shilling increased the average producer price for Arabica, but the sharpest increase was in 1994 following the export liberalization and the entry of private buyers. This increase in producer prices resulted in an increase in harvests, presumably due to greater input use and harvesting effort. Producer prices fell in 1996, dragging production down the following year. Yields are low because of the limited use of fertilizer, but part of the declining trend in coffee production is due to a reduction in planted area, a phenomenon that began to be reversed after the boom in 1997.

One of the main problems with the coffee sector is the absence of a stable system for providing inputs on credit. It is risky for a buyer to extend credit to farmers without being sure that he will be able to buy the harvest and thus recover the loan. A system of input vouchers is currently being tried in which farmers are paid for their harvest part in cash and part with vouchers that are redeemable for fertilizer and other inputs. Unfortunately, some farmers have resorted to selling the vouchers for less than face-value to "divert" the money to other purchases.

We used regression analysis to study the determinants of coffee production. As shown in Table 5.11, the one- and two-year lagged producer prices of coffee are not statistically significant. However, the three-year lagged producer price is highly significant. This pattern is not surprising given the fact that coffee requires three years from planting to the first harvest. Thus, there is a three-year lag between changes in the producer price and changes in output. The long-run (three year) elasticity is 1.19, indicating that coffee farmers are quite sensitive to price changes, even if the production cycle creates a delay in supply response[10]. Maize prices, fertilizer prices, and rainfall variables were not statistically significant.

Cotton

Cotton is the other main export crop, generating about US$ 100 million per year. Shinyanga and Mwanza produce over 80 percent of Tanzanian cotton. The producer prices for cotton have been erratic, with peaks in 1986, 1992, and 1996. Cotton production has followed an equally volatile pattern, with peaks occurring one or two years after the price increase.

Regression analysis was used to examine the determinants of cotton output (Table 5.12). The cotton producer price from the year before has a positive and significant effect on cotton output. The coefficient suggests that the price elasticity of cotton supply is 1.00. In addition, the price of maize in the previous year was found to have a negative and significant effect on cotton output. An increase of 10 percent in the maize price is associated with a decrease of 4.2 percent in cotton production the following year. Annual rainfall and fertilizer price did not have a significant effect on cotton output after controlling for the other variables. This is somewhat surprising given the general presumption that high rainfall reduces the cotton harvest. High rainfall is said to have reduced the 1997-98 harvest, for example.

Cashew Nut

Cashew nut is one of the success stories of Tanzanian agricultural exports. Production had fallen below 20 thousand tons in the late 1980s. Exchange rate reform increased the shilling returns of exports, while export liberalization introduced strong competition among cashew nut buyers. These factors resulted in doubling of real producer prices between the mid-1980s and the mid-1990s. Although the effect on production was delayed because cashew nut is a tree crop, output eventually responded, rising to 100 thousand tons in 1998.

Since 1996, real producer prices have fallen both in absolute terms and as a percentage of the *f.o.b.* price. Some argue that buyers have become organized enough to restrain competition in cashew nut purchasing. Whatever the reason, the real producer price has now fallen to the level it was in the mid-1980s , suggesting that production may decline in the coming years.

We use regression analysis to study the factors influencing cashew nut performance. The lagged producer price has a positive and significant effect on cashew nut production, as shown in Table 5.13. The coefficient corresponds to a short-run supply elasticity of 0.84. It may be surprising to find cashew nut output responding to prices within the year given that cashew is a tree crop that requires 4-5 years to begin bearing fruit. The apparent explanation is that, while the number of trees is fixed in the short-run, the application of chemicals and the harvesting effort vary with the producer price. In particular, cashew trees require sulfur spraying to avoid mildew damage. These factors create a short-term supply response to price changes. The long-term supply elasticity is fairly elastic, 1.69.

---

[10] The long-run supply elasticity for coffee is calculated as $(\beta_1+\beta_2+\beta_3)/(P/Q)$, where the βs are the three lagged coefficients for coffee price, P is the average price, and Q is the average coffee production.

Tobacco

Tobacco is grown in areas with low rainfall (600-900 mm) and sandy soils. Cultural practices required for tobacco production are labor- and skill-intensive, making it a profitable small-farmer crop. At the same time, the tobacco plant is sensitive to various diseases implying the need for pesticide and/or crop rotation. Fertilizer applications are also required, since sandy soils have little nutrient.

Tobacco production stagnated in the late 1980s. Although devaluation increased the shilling value of exports several fold, the producer price did not increase in real terms. Since 1990, however, tobacco production has increased four-fold, growing at 21 percent per year.

Private tobacco buyers have assumed the role of buying and exporting the crop, paying producer prices that are a higher share of the *f.o.b.* price. In addition, the buyers provide fertilizer and other inputs to farmers on credit. Fertilizer use in Tabora, the main tobacco-growing area, has almost doubled since 1992 in spite of the removal of fertilizer subsidies (MAC NEI 1999d).

Tea

Tea is grown in Iringa, Tanga, and Kagera. Slightly more than half is grown on large-scale estates (54 percent), the remainder being grown by smallholders (44 percent). Tea production grew at 3.8 percent in the late 1980s and 3.3 percent since 1990. Looking at the annual data reveals, however, that much of the "growth" in second period is due to unusually good harvest in 1998. The process of liberalizing tea marketing and export is complicated by the rehabilitation of tea estates (see Faber 1995). While most of the traditional export crops were liberalized starting in 1994-95, tea marketing is being liberalized this year.

Zanzibar's Agricultural Exports

Zanzibar's three important most agricultural exports traditionally have been cloves, copra and chilies, with cloves occupying first place by a wide margin. In recent years, several fish species and seaweed have also become important. The international clove market has been bleak for sometime, with recent prices being only a tenth in nominal terms of the high prices in 1980, when Zanzibar still enjoyed a virtual monopoly on clove exports (Mabele 1999a). While inherently volatile due to fluctuations in yields, prices have fallen dramatically since the early 1980s with changing sources of supply in South East Asia. Annual production in Zanzibar between 1985 and 1997 fluctuated in the 1,000-2,000 metric ton range, interspersed with occasional years with over 10,000 metric tons production.

Clove yields are low, particularly because of the old age of many of the trees. Replanting has not proceeded at a pace fast enough to increase the proportion of young trees. Husbandry practices are also said to be poor. Although declining in output and value, cloves are still very important to Zanzibar for foreign exchange and as a source of income to many rural people. In the new agricultural policy currently being debated in Zanzibar's political institutions, it is intended to improve extension services for cloves and to create incentives for replanting (Mabele 1999a).

Production of chilies has not fared much better. Output reached a peak of 4.2 metric tons in 1990. When prices have been good, producers have responded positively by increasing production. However prices have at times been discouraging and production was negatively affected. Zanzibar has at times failed to adapt export production to changes in the preferred varieties and qualities, with a consequent fall in average prices received. The new agricultural policy intends to encourage the production of the preferred varieties and to help improve yields through extension services.

Copra comes from processed coconuts. Like cloves, the age of the trees and slow replanting rates have contributed to low yields, in addition to poor husbandry which is responsible for heavy pest and disease infestation of coconut trees. Production of copra has fallen steadily in the 1990s.

In recent years, following the liberalization programs, non-traditional exports have grown in importance. While cloves are still the dominant export in most years, accounting for over 90 percent of the value of total exports on average, some non-traditional exports have shown that they can contribute significantly to export earnings. Seaweed in particular has great potential. While seaweed is not bought and exported by a state monopoly, oligopolistic private buyers reportedly at present pay only 10% percent of the export price to producers (Mabele 1999a). The government of Zanzibar is exploring ways to facilitate a more competitive environment that can pass on a higher return to the producer.

5.4   Performance of Agricultural GDP on the Crop Side

Current estimates from the National Accounts section of the National Bureau of Statistics (NBS) for the mainland show agricultural gross domestic product (GDP) growing 2.2 percent per year over the period 1985-1996. This is lower than earlier estimates of 5 percent growth cited in the 1994 Agricultural Sector Memorandum (World Bank AEOD 1994b) and criticized in the evaluation report cited earlier (World Bank OED 1998). This downward revision apparently took place when the 1992-base GDP series was generated. Since population growth is believed to be 2.8 percent, based on the 1988 census, the NBS estimates suggest that agricultural GDP declined in real per capita terms over the period 1985-1998.

Table 5.14 decomposes this growth rate into several components. According to the NBS, forestry and hunting have grown 2.6 percent per year over 1985-1998, while fishing output has risen 3.4 percent per year. But these two categories have little effect on the overall trend, as they account for less than 15 percent of agricultural GDP. The dominant component of agricultural GDP is the value added from crop and animal production, estimated to have grown just 2.1 percent per year.

Table 5.15 provides a further disaggregation of the gross value of crop production. According to this table, crop production grew 3.3 percent per year, mainly because of strong growth (3.6 percent) in the six main food crops. Two aspects of this table raise questions about the quality of the estimates. First, the uniformity of growth rates in food production is striking. It reveals that the NBS is calculating agricultural GDP by making strong simplifying assumptions. One assumption is that all the main food crops other than maize grow at the same rate each year. Another assumption is that all the "minor" food crops grow at the same rate each year. The second notable feature of this table is the discrepancy between the healthy rate of the growth in the gross output of crop production (3.3 percent over 1985-1997) in Table 5.15 and the poor rate of growth in the value added of crop and animal production in Table 5.14.

Kiregyera (1998), Mlay (1999), and Komba (1999) argue that production statistics from the Agricultural Statistics Unit of the MAC should be used rather than the NBS estimates. Tables 5.16 and 5.17 give preliminary estimates of agricultural GDP that would be obtained from using ASU data for production of the six main food crops, cotton, coffee, and cashew nuts. Table 5.17 reveals that using ASU production data would not change the performance of the main food crops. The growth rate is actually 0.1 percent points lower in each period with ASU data compared to the original NBS data. The output of cash crops, however, is revised upward by using ASU data. Annual growth in export crop production is 1.8 percent in the late 1980s (compared to -2.2 percent using the NBS figures), rising to 7.7 percent in the 1990s (compared to 6.4 percent in the NBS data), for an average growth rate of 5.4 percent over 1985-1997. Overall, crop production grows at a healthy 3.5 percent per year using the ASU data.

Table 5.16 summarizes the crop output growth (now expressed as value added rather than gross output) and combines it with other components of agricultural GDP. Slower growth in livestock output (2.7 percent) and forestry and hunting (2.6) pull down the overall growth in agricultural GDP to 3.3 percent.

5.5   Performance of the Livestock Sector

Data uncertainties in the livestock sector are especially acute. The NBS data used in GDP estimates suggest that the sector as a whole has declined in importance between 1985/86 and 1998/99, going from 14.1 percent of agricultural GDP to 12.9 percent, respectively, when re-evaluating agricultural GDP using ASU data for crops. But comparing three year weighted averages from 1985/86-88/9 to 1996/97 to 1998/99 from the same data suggests that the share has remained constant at just over 13.5 percent. (Table 5.15).

Furthermore, a recent study calculates that per capita livestock consumption is going down in the long-term, based on extrapolation of the results of the 1991/92 household budget survey (MAC NEI 1999f). While possibly true in the short-run, this is unlikely to be true in the long-term. It also contradicts the implications of our analysis in Section 6 below of the 1993/94 Household Rural Development Survey.

It is clear in Tanzania, as in the rest of Africa, that animal products are income responsive in consumption patterns. Given falling livestock prices and increasing livestock supply, livestock product consumption per capita would only decline if real per capita incomes declined, especially in rural areas where income responsiveness is generally thought to be higher given lower average income levels. However, rapid population growth rates (circa 2.8 % p.a.) more than make up in aggregate for any decline in per capita consumption (0.1 % p.a. at most), strongly suggesting that aggregate consumption of livestock products has increased sharply.

The long-term performance figures chosen by the recent MAC review of the livestock sector using the NBS data (MAC NEI 1999f) are annual rates of increase in animal numbers between 1971 and 1995 as follows: 2.1 percent for traditional cattle, 4 percent for dairy cattle, and 3.9 percent for goats. As is often the case, 95 percent of the attention in recent reviews of the "livestock" sector in Tanzania has been directed to ruminant livestock, especially cattle. The NBS estimates indigenous cattle population of 15.3 million head in 1995, compared to 246,000 grade dairy cattle. The former are kept by over one million households, whereas the latter are thought to be kept by 60,000 households, primarily in and around urban areas. Tanzania is judged to have a comparative advantage in cattle production on the range, but cannot legally export due to recurring problems with Foot-and-Mouth Disease (FMD). Export on the hoof to Kenya is estimated to involve up to 300,000 animals per year (MAC NEI 1999f).

The star on the ruminant side is dairy development. Traditional cows produce on average 100 liters of milk per annum, whereas cross-bred dairy cows produce on average 1,000 liters per annum. Although the rise in smallholder dairy development in Tanzania has been rapid, it is still considerably less so than in Kenya and Uganda. Even so, the numbers of grade dairy cattle more than doubled between 1984 and 1995 (MAC Sokoine ILRI 1998). Processing and marketing are

61

major issues, in that milk prices have risen considerably in the main consumption areas, but have fallen quite low in the surplus production regions such as the Southern Highlands. Anecdotal evidence from mid 1999 in Dar-es-Salaam would also suggest the potential of an imminent big fall in local dairy prices as supply increases rapidly within the metropolitan area.

Time series data on chickens and swine are not reported in MAC NEI (1999f), and are probably not reliable. Approximately 60 percent of chickens are thought to be kept in small-scale extensive systems in rural areas. The 1994/95 National Sample Census of Agriculture gives a point estimate of nearly 4 million households raising an average of 7 chickens at any one time. MAC NEI (1999f) estimates that less than 2 percent of chicken production is under industrial systems. Newcastle's disease is the major constraint in small-scale systems, as elsewhere in Africa. Feed cost is the immediate issue in the large-scale systems, although it is doubtful that the full social cost of waste disposal has been taken into account in past evaluations.

According to NBS, swine are less than one-half million; 90 percent are kept by peasant farmers under subsistence conditions in rural areas. Disease problems, including African Swine Fever, and the cost of high energy feeds, are the major issues in increasing production.

Critics have pointed out that the NBS 1995 figures underestimate the true importance of poultry and swine herd growth in recent years, but they do not provide alternative figures. The World Bank's draft "Peri-Urban Study" (World Bank AFR2M 1999) did not find evidence of extra-normal livestock development in peri-urban rural areas, but did not survey urban areas. A MAC-Sokoine-ILRI (1998) rapid appraisal of dairy in Tanzania in 1997 found evidence of at least 20,000 dairy cattle kept within the city limits of Dar-es-Salaam.

A casual stroll into the capital city on the main northern road shows hardly any sales points for feed items outside the city limits (and police post). Beginning one hundred feet inside the city limits, kiosks advertising high energy feeds are to be found every few hundred feet for several miles. Indeed, MAC NEI (1999f) reports that in 1993, 580,000 tons of industrial crop by-products were used by 15 private feed mills in the country. This is too low an estimate of high energy feed production even in 1993; it does not include grain used directly as feed, either mixed in or separately. It also does not include the Napier grass and other forages typically fed to dairy cattle.

Although most of the industrial by-products are probably used as a supplement for grade dairy cattle, likely annual feed production seems larger than both the dairy cattle and the recorded small number of chickens would use. It seems quite plausible that the current poultry and swine numbers around and in Dar-es-Salaam, Arusha, and Mwanza are much higher than previously thought, although this remains to be established.

5.6   Performance of the Fisheries Sector

Fisheries have long been an important source of food in Tanzania, with 90 percent of the recorded catch at the present time being attributable to artisanal fishers. Overall production statistics in this sector are especially unreliable, as they are in most countries in the world. What is available shows that freshwater fisheries in mainland Tanzania have always dominated marine fisheries (at roughly 6 to 1 in volume terms), and that there has been little discernable change between the mid 1980's and present in the estimated level of production, even though the recorded marine catch fluctuates quite a bit from year to year (World Bank COD 1999).

The main commercial species caught from the different lakes are Nile Perch (*Lates niloticus*) in Lake Victoria and "sardines " in Lake Tanganyika (*Stolothrissa tanganicae* and *Limnothrissa miodon*). A variety of fish from the *Chichlid family are found in Lake Nyasa, in the south.* Tilapia and catfishes are found in these and other inland bodies of water. Nile Perch and Tilapia are the main freshwater fish with export potential. Marine waters provide shrimp for export and various local small pelagic fish for food. Sixteen commercial vessels are presently involved in the shrimp fishery (World Bank COD 1999).

The big change in fisheries is the very rapid rise in the export of Nile Perch fillets to Europe and Asia since the second half of the 1980's. As shown in Table 5.18, the average annual value of total fisheries exports from Tanzania went from U.S.$ 3 to 62 million from 1986-88 to 1996-98. While shrimp has contributed modestly to this, more than 82 percent of mainland fisheries exports by value were from freshwater; more than 90 percent of freshwater fisheries exports were from Lake Victoria Nile Perch fillets alone. Fisheries amounted to more than 8 percent of total merchandise exports from the mainland in 1998. This parallels similar rises in fishery exports from the Kenyan and Ugandan sides of the lake.

Table 5.18 also shows that the average export unit value of marine fisheries actually increased in nominal terms over the last decade, due to the increasing share of shrimp in marine production. Shrimp is both a relatively high-value commodity and one that has succeeded in maintaining its value relatively well in the last ten years. The average freshwater export unit value has fallen noticeably, even in nominal terms. This is because the very high prices earned in a tiny niche fishery in the 1980's could not survive the rapid expansion of Nile Perch production in East Africa since then. This illustrates a peril of non-traditional exports: their domestic markets are small and their international markets thin. A good chunk of the high initial profit disappears if many countries start doing the same thing. While some see considerable room for further fisheries expansion, a number of the environmental, distributional and regulatory issues remain to be resolved in this sector.

5.7   Summary

Agricultural GDP calculated by the NBS uses estimates of food production that are based on assumed growth rates that vary little across crops. We concur with the conclusions of Kiregyera *et al.* (1999) and Komba (1999) that agricultural GDP should be recalculated using measured estimates of agricultural production. In choosing between CMEWU and ASU figures, the data are equally plausible in our view, but the preferred source depends on the selected purpose. CMEWU estimates are forecasts of the new crop; ASU figures are the authoritative statistical record. ASU food production data are more reliable for assessing past developments.

Recalculating agricultural GDP with ASU production data does not appear to affect growth rates in food production. On the other hand, using ASU data for export crops results in a significant upward revision. The livestock figures used for grade dairy cattle, poultry and swine are probably too low, especially in the case of poultry in and around urban areas.

Overall, agricultural performance in the post-reform period has been respectable but not outstanding. We estimate that agricultural GDP grew 3.5 percent per year over 1985-90 and 3.3 percent over 1990-1998, for an average rate of 3.3 percent over the entire period, without adjusting the livestock figures. In the early period, food crop production grew quickly in response to domestic market liberalization, while export production was stagnant. Since 1990, food crop production growth has slowed to approximately the rate of population growth, while export crops posted an impressive 7.7 percent rate of growth. Export liberalization and exchange rate depreciation have improved the incentives for export crop production, and Tanzanian farmers have responded well in spite of continuing institutional and credit problems in the sector.

Performance in the important beef cattle sector has been mixed. Dairy and poultry have performed very well, showing long-term growth rates well over 4 percent for dairy and probably higher for poultry and eggs. Animal health remains a major constraint. These intensive occupations are overwhelmingly carried out in small-scale operations within city limits. The urban concentration of intensive livestock production appears to result from high transportation costs and possibly from high taxation outside city limits.

Aggregate data on fisheries are unreliable, but suggest stagnation in aggregate production. Much more reliable data on fishery exports show explosive growth in exports since the mid to late 1980's. Nile Perch fillets in 1998 from Lake Victoria accounted for more than 75 percent of total fisheries exports, which in turn represented more than 8 percent of total merchandise exports.

Figure 5.1. Maize Production and Real Producer Price

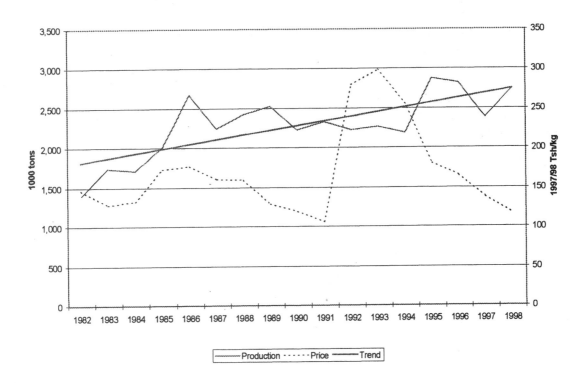

Note: Until 1991 official prices, after 1991 market prices.
Source: Production data from ASU/MAC. Prices from MDB.

Figure 5.2. *Paddy Production and Real Producer Price*

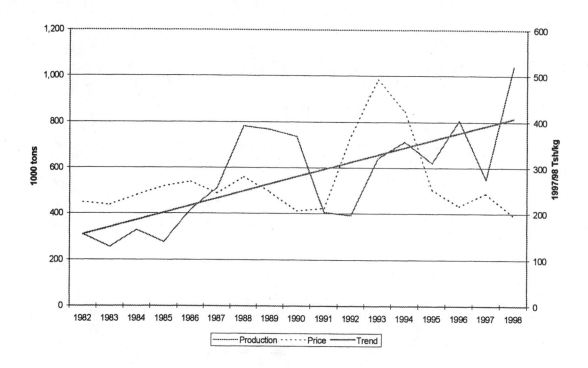

Source: Production data from ASU/MAC. Price data from MDB.

Figure 5.3. *Wheat Production and Real Producer Price*

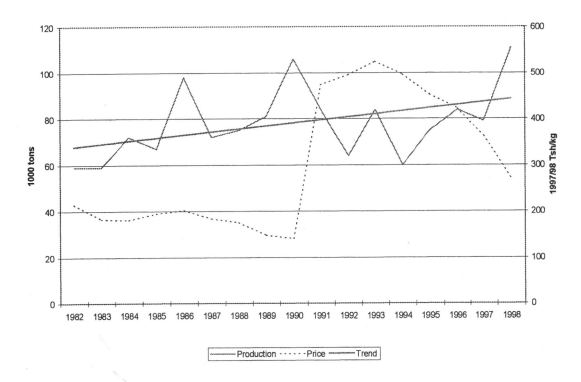

Note: Until 1990 official prices, after 1990 market prices.
Source: Production data from ASU/MAC. Prices from MDB.

Figure 5.4. Cassava Production

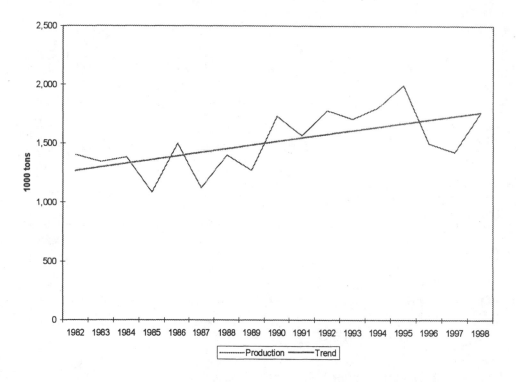

Source: Production data from ASU/MAC. Price data from MDB.

Figure 5.5. Sorghum/Millet Production and Real Producer Price

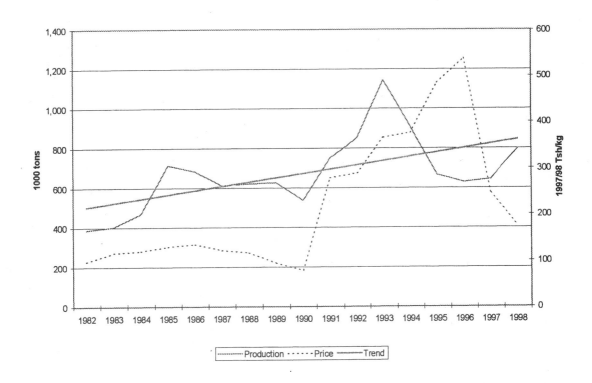

Note: Until 1990 official prices, after 1990 market prices.
Source: Production data from ASU/MAC. Prices from MDB.

Figure 5.6. *Bean Production and Real Producer Price*

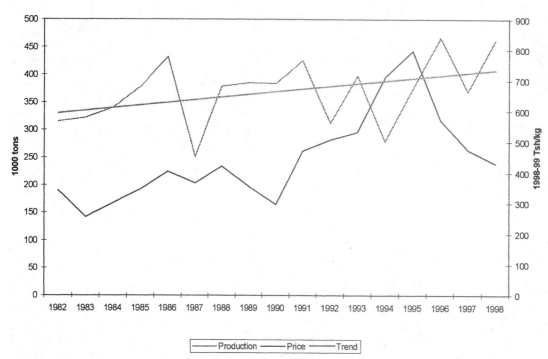

Source: Production data from ASU/MAC. Price data from MDB.

Figure 5.7. Coffee Production and Real Producer Price

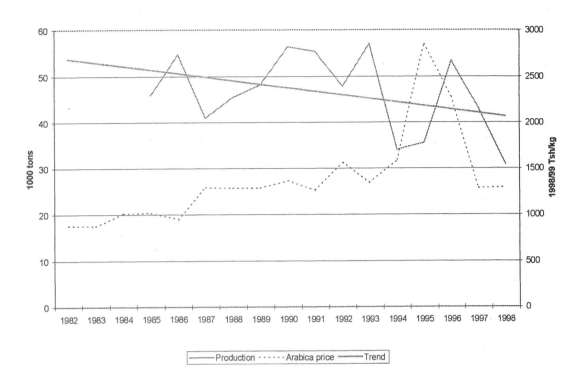

Source: Production from ASU/MAC. Prices from MDB.

Figure 5.8. *Cotton Production and Real Producer Price*

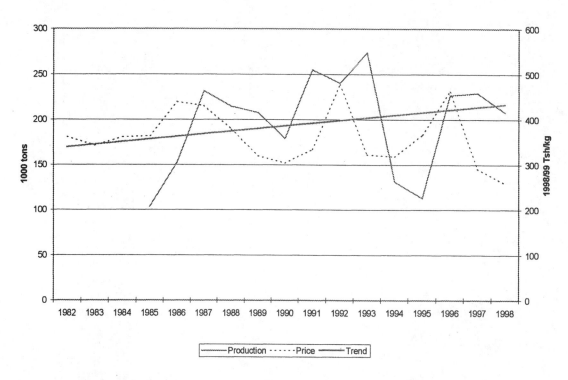

Source: Production from ASU/MAC. Prices from MDB.

Figure 5.9. *Cashew Production and Real Producer Price*

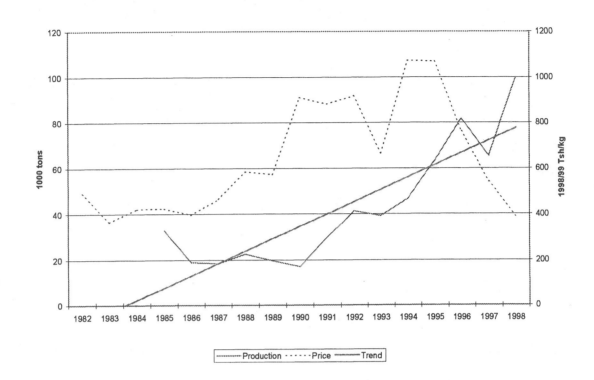

Source: Production from ASU/MAC. Prices from MDB.

Table 5.1. Composition of Agricultural Output

Commodity	Gross domestic product	Percentage of agricultural GDP
	(million Tsh at 1992 prices)	(percent)
Crop production	549,569	74.3
Maize	168,492	22.8
Paddy	59,333	8.0
Wheat	3,487	0.5
Millet/sorghum	33,780	4.6
Cassava	33,602	4.5
Beans	38,673	5.2
Other food crops	144,212	19.5
Cash crops	67,991	9.2
Livestock	98,680	13.3
Forestry, hunting, & fishing	91,691	12.4
Total	739,940	100.0

Source: National Bureau of Statistics, National Accounts Section files, compiled by Komba (1999).

Table 5.2. Characteristics of Selected Agricultural Surveys in Tanzania

Name of survey	Year(s)	Institutions	Coverage	Number of villages	Method to estimate area and yield	Comments
Current Agricultural Sample Survey	1984-91	ASU/MAC	3-5 regions	around 100	Direct measurement	Generated estimates for several regions only
Agricultural Sample Survey (AGASU)	1987-91	NBS, ASU/MAC	National	100	Direct measurement	Generated national but not regional estimates, first to use National Master Sample from 88 Census
Food crop forecasting survey	1993	CMEWU, NBS, ASU/MAC	4 regions		Farmer interviews	Pilot test of survey to provide early warning of food shortages
	1994-present	CMEWU, NBS, ASU/MAC	National	540	Farmer interviews	Carried out twice per year, generates preliminary and final crop forecasts by region
National Sample Census of Agriculture	1994	NBS, ASU/MAC	National	100 for crop data, 540 for livestock data	Direct measurement	Logistical problems limited sample, generated national estimates of crop production
Expanded Agricultural Survey	1995	NBS, ASU/MAC	National	540	Direct measurement	Generated regional estimates
	1996-97	NBS, ASU/MAC	National	540	Direct measurement	Generated regional estimates, similar to NSCA but only current data
Integrated Agricultural Survey	1998	NBS, ASU/MAC	National	540	Farmer interviews	Generated regional estimates
	1999	NBS, ASU/MAC	National	3064	Farmer interviews	Generated district estimates

Note: Year refers to the second part of the agricultural year (1995 = 1994-95). ASU/MAC refers to the Agricultural Statistics Unit of the Ministry of Agriculture and Cooperatives. NBS refers to the National Bureau of Statistics, formerly the Bureau of Statistics. CMEWU refers to the Crop Monitoring and Early Warning Unit of the Ministry of Agriculture and Cooperatives.
Source: Komba (1999); Mlay (1999).

Table 5.3. *Purchases of Coffee, Cotton, and Cashew Nuts by Data Source*

Commodity and source	1985	1986	1987	1988	1989	1990	1991	1992	1993	1994	1995	1996	1997	1998
Coffee														
AES	49.08	55.15	58.74	45.71	55.13	53.07	44.12	47.99	51.25	36.39	35.84	46.95	43.49	30.85
ASU/MAC	45.90	54.70	41.00	45.40	48.20	56.40	55.40	47.90	57.10	34.10	35.60	53.50	43.20	..
NA	49.00	56.00	53.00	49.00	51.00	56.00	54.00	48.00	57.00	35.00	41.00	54.00	43.00	37.00
Cotton														
AES	156.84	105.90	214.57	254.92	189.24	112.90	149.14	268.73	303.98	145.22	123.66	245.91	249.44	207.75
ASU/MAC	103.50	152.60	231.40	214.30	207.60	179.00	255.00	240.30	273.80	131.30	113.10	226.70	229.20	..
NA	217.00	254.00	192.00	113.00	148.00	141.00	267.00	308.00	149.00	124.00	251.00	253.00	201.00	107.00
Cashew nuts														
AES	32.53	18.90	16.55	24.29	19.28	17.06	28.87	41.24	39.32	46.60	63.40	81.73	63.03	99.92
ASU/MAC	32.80	19.00	18.40	22.50	19.60	17.00	29.70	41.30	39.20	46.70	63.40	81.80	65.40	..
NA	33.00	33.00	18.00	27.00	20.00	17.00	30.00	41.00	39.00	47.00	63.00	82.00	67.00	75.00

.. represents missing data

Note: AES is the Annual Economic Survey. ASU is the Agricultural Statistics Unit of the Ministry of Agriculture. NA is the National Accounts Section of the National Bureau of Statistics. The ASU/MAC series are only slightly different from the crop board and Market Development Bureau figures reported in World Bank COD (1999).

Source: Annual Economic Survey 1998 Tables 36, 38 & 42. Basic Data Agriculture and Livestock Sector 1983/84-1987/88, 1984/85-1988/89, 1991/92-1997/98. National Accounts Files. Compiled by Komba (1999).

Table 5.4. *Food Crop Production According to Different Sources*

Crop and source	1984	1985	1986	1987	1988	1989	1990	1991	1992	1993	1994	1995	1996	1997	1998
Maize															
CMEWU	2,113	2,125	2,211	2,359	2,339	3,126	2,445	2,332	2,226	2,282	2,159	2,564	2,663	1,835	2,685
Statistics Units	1,712	2,013	2,671	2,244	2,423	2,528	2,227	2,331	2,226	2,267	2,188	2,875	2,822	2,387	2,685
National Accounts	2,113	1,857	1,929	2,009	2,091	2,193	2,302	2,367	2,409	2,494	2,522	2,659	2,761	2,886	2,863
AGSASU	..	..	..	2,003	1,710	..	1,860	..	..	..	..	..	..	..	..
Paddy															
CMEWU	387	427	547	644	629	718	481	624	370	641	614	705	734	550	676
Statistics Units	328	276	418	511	782	767	736	406	392	641	714	622	807	550	1,040
National Accounts	387	483	502	523	544	571	599	616	627	649	656	692	719	751	788
AGSASU	..	..	..	337	434		698	..	..	..	..	..	..	..	..
Cassava															
CMEWU	416	1,923	2,052	1,709	1,736	1,948	1,731	1,566	1,778	1,802	1,802	1,802	1,498	1,426	1,758
Statistics Units	1,385	1,086	1,499	1,125	1,399	1,272	1,731	1,566	1,778	1,708	1,802	1,992	1,498	1,426	1,758
National Accounts	..	1,249	1,297	1,352	1,407	1,475	1,548	1,592	1,621	1,678	1,697	1,789	1,857	1,941	2,036
Beans															
CMEWU	517	441	318	424	386	503	388	425	425	508	385	407	475	374	462
Statistics Units	340	378	432	251	379	385	384	425	312	398	279	374	467	369	462
National Accounts	..	311	322	336	350	367	385	396	403	417	422	445	462	483	506

Table 5.4. Food Crop Production According to Different Sources (Cont'd)

Crop and source	1984	1985	1986	1987	1988	1989	1990	1991	1992	1993	1994	1995	1996	1997	1998
Wheat															
CMEWU	84	83	72	72	76	97	106	84	80	79	59	63	84	78	111
Statistics Units	72	67	98	72	75	81	106	84	64	84	60	75	84	79	111
National Accounts	..	33	34	35	37	39	41	42	42	44	44	47	49	51	53
Sorghum/millet															
CMEWU	562	1,024	941	954	700	804	568	750	850	857	681	647	1,237	835	799
Statistics Units	469	714	685	613	622	627	537	750	850	1,143	908	665	629	645	799
National Accounts	..	431	447	466	485	509	534	549	559	578	585	617	640	669	702
Banana															
CMEWU	..	..	..	792	812	743	823	750	794	800	834	834	641	603	836
Statistics Units	..	..	777	792	792		823	750	794	798	733	651	641	604	836
National Accounts	..	780	805	831	857	881	906	931	357	984	1,012	1,040	1,069	1,099	1,130

.. represents missing data

Source: Basic Data Agriculture and Livestock Sector 1983/84-1987/88, 1984/85-1988/89, 1991/92-1997/98, National Accounts Files, AGSASU Reports. Compiled by Komba (1999).

Table 5.5. Average Percentage Difference Between Highest and Lowest Production Estimates

Sources and crops	1980s (1984-89)	1990s (1990-98)	Overall (1984-98)
Among CMEWU, ASU, and NA			
Maize	27.5	14.3	20.5
Paddy	33.9	34.4	34.2
Cassava	123.6	13.8	65.5
Beans	45.9	20.6	32.5
Wheat	94.0	85.7	89.6
Sorghum/millet	68.4	44.0	55.5
Banana	8.8	51.3	38.3
Between CMEWU and ASU			
Maize	18.7	6.7	12.3
Paddy	25.5	22.9	24.1
Cassava	121.0	1.8	57.9
Beans	40.9	12.8	26.0
Wheat	16.7	5.9	11.0
Sorghum/millet	33.7	22.4	27.7
Banana	0.8	4.7	3.7

Note: The difference is calculated as a percentage of the lowest estimate.
Source: Calculated from Table 5.3.

Table 5.6. Annual Growth in Food Crop Production According to Different Sources

Crop and source	1986	1987	1988	1989	1990	1991	1992	1993	1994	1995	1996	1997	1998
Maize													
CMEWU	4.0	6.7	-0.8	33.6	-21.8	-4.6	-4.5	2.5	-5.4	18.8	3.9	-31.1	46.3
Statistics Units	32.7	-16.0	8.0	4.3	-11.9	4.7	-4.5	1.8	-3.5	31.4	-1.8	-15.4	12.5
National Accounts	3.9	4.1	4.1	4.9	5.0	2.8	1.8	3.5	1.1	5.4	3.8	4.5	-0.8
Paddy													
CMEWU	28.1	17.7	-2.3	14.1	-33.0	29.7	-40.7	73.2	-4.2	14.8	4.1	-25.1	22.9
Statistics Units	51.4	22.2	53.0	-1.9	-4.0	-44.8	-3.4	63.5	11.4	-12.9	29.7	-31.8	89.1
National Accounts	3.9	4.2	4.0	5.0	4.9	2.8	1.8	3.5	1.1	5.5	3.9	4.5	4.9
Cassava													
CMEWU	6.7	-16.7	1.6	12.2	-11.1	-9.5	13.5	1.3	0.0	0.0	-16.9	-4.8	23.3
Statistics Units	38.0	-24.9	24.4	-9.1	36.1	-9.5	13.5	-3.9	5.5	10.5	-24.8	-4.8	23.3
National Accounts	3.8	4.2	4.1	4.8	4.9	2.8	1.8	3.5	1.1	5.4	3.8	4.5	4.9
Beans													
CMEWU	-27.9	33.3	-9.0	30.3	-22.9	9.5	0.0	19.5	-24.2	5.7	16.7	-21.3	23.5
Statistics Units	14.3	-41.9	51.0	1.6	-0.3	10.7	-26.6	27.6	-29.9	34.1	24.9	-21.0	25.2
National Accounts	3.5	4.3	4.2	4.9	4.9	2.9	1.8	3.5	1.2	5.5	3.8	4.5	4.8
Wheat													
CMEWU	-13.3	0.0	5.6	27.6	9.3	-20.8	-4.8	-1.3	-25.3	6.8	33.3	-7.1	42.3
Statistics Units	46.3	-26.5	4.2	8.0	30.9	-20.8	-23.8	31.3	-28.6	25.0	12.0	-6.0	40.5
National Accounts	3.0	2.9	5.7	5.4	5.1	2.4	0.0	4.8	0.0	6.8	4.3	4.1	3.9

Table 5.6. Annual Growth in Food Crop Production According to Different Sources (Cont'd)

Crop and source	1986	1987	1988	1989	1990	1991	1992	1993	1994	1995	1996	1997	1998
Sorghum/millet													
CMEWU	-8.1	1.4	-26.6	14.9	-29.4	32.0	13.3	0.8	-20.5	-5.0	91.2	-32.5	-4.3
Statistics Units	-4.1	-10.5	1.5	0.8	-14.4	39.7	13.3	34.5	-20.6	-26.8	-5.4	2.5	23.9
National Accounts	3.7	4.3	4.1	4.9	4.9	2.8	1.8	3.4	1.2	5.5	3.7	4.5	4.9
Banana													
CMEWU			2.5	-8.5	10.8	-8.9	5.9	0.8	4.3	0.0	-23.1	-5.9	38.6
Statistics Units		1.9				-8.9	5.9	0.5	-8.1	-11.2	-1.5	-5.8	38.4
National Accounts	3.2	3.2	3.1	2.8	2.8	2.8	-61.7	175.6	2.8	2.8	2.8	2.8	2.8

Note: Growth rate refers to the percentage difference between production in the stated year and production the year before.
Source: Calculated from Table 5.3

Table 5.7. Average Annual Growth in Food Production According to Different Sources

Crop	Data source	Annual growth rate (percent)		
		From 1985 to 1998	Two-year average from 1985-86 to 1997-98	Three-year average from 1985-87 to 1996-98
Maize	CMEWU	1.8	0.3	0.6
	Ag. Statistical Unit	2.2	0.7	1.2
	National Accounts	3.4	3.5	3.6
Paddy	CMEWU	3.6	1.9	1.8
	Ag. Statistical Unit	10.7	7.2	6.5
	National Accounts	3.8	3.8	3.7
Cassava	CMEWU	-0.7	-1.8	-1.7
	Ag. Statistical Unit	3.8	1.8	2.1
	National Accounts	3.8	3.8	3.7
Beans	CMEWU	0.4	0.8	0.9
	Ag. Statistical Unit	1.6	0.2	1.8
	National Accounts	3.8	3.8	3.7
Wheat	CMEWU	2.3	1.7	1.7
	Ag. Statistical Unit	4.0	1.2	1.3
	National Accounts	3.7	3.7	3.8
Sorghum/millet	CMEWU	-1.9	-1.5	-0.2
	Ag. Statistical Unit	0.9	0.3	0.3
	National Accounts	3.8	3.8	3.7

Source: Calculated from Table 5.3.

Table 5.8. *Correlation of Annual Growth in Food Crop Production Estimates From Different Sources*

| Crop | Correlation of annual growth rates from 1984-85 to 1997-98 | | |
	CMEWU and statistical unit	*Statistical unit and national accounts*	*CMEWU and national accounts*
Maize	0.51	0.01	-0.33
Paddy	0.44	0.12	0.12
Cassava	0.48	0.11	-0.02
Beans	0.09	0.40	0.28
Wheat	0.48	0.61	0.42
Sorghum/millet	0.21	-0.20	-0.14

Source: Calculated from Table 5.5.

Table 5.9. Regression Analysis of Maize Supply in Tanzania
Dependent Variable: Maize Production

Analysis of Variance

Source	DF	Sum of squares	Mean square	F Value	Prob > F
Model	6	1707274.7979	284545.79965	88.528	0.0001
Error	207	665340.22737	3214.20400		
C Total	213	2372615.0253			

Root MSE	56.69395
Dep Mean	128.18925
C.V.	44.22676
R-square	0.7196
Adj R-sq	0.7114

Parameter Estimates

Variable	DF	Parameter estimate	Standard error	T for HO: parameter = 0	Prob > |T|	Variable label
INTERCEP	1	-0.091492	37.39640451	-0.002	0.9981	Intercept
DMZPRICE	1	0.018568	0.00882255	2.105	0.0365	Real maize price
LAGQTY	1	0.873064	0.04023979	21.697	0.0001	Lagged maize output
FERTREAL	1	0.000104	0.00152316	0.068	0.9458	Real fertilizer price
COTTON	1	-0.446999	0.21340421	-2.095	0.0374	Real producer price of cotton
RAINFALL	1	0.077260	0.04097885	1.885	0.0608	Rainfall(mm)
RAINSQ	1	-0.000032209	0.00001709	-1.884	0.0609	Rainfall squared

Table 5.10. *Regression Analysis of Rice Supply in Tanzania*
Dependent Variable: Rice Production

Analysis of Variance

Source	DF	Sum of squares	Mean square	F Value	Prob > F
Model	15	253278.62822	16885.24188	15.148	0.0001
Error	75	83600.86167	1114.67816		
C Total	90	336879.48989			

Root MSE	33.38680
Dep Mean	59.10110
C.V.	56.49099
R-square	0.7518
Adj R-sq	0.7022

Parameter Estimates

Variable	DF	Parameter estimate	Standard error	T for HO: parameter = 0	Prob > |T|
INTERCEP	1	6.295112	67.46636212	-0.093	0.9259
RICEPRIC	1	0.041126	0.02455856	1.675	0.0982
DMZPRICE	1	-0.000929	0.01388531	-0.067	0.9469
LAGQTY	1	0.503634	0.09376486	5.371	0.0001
FERTREAL	1	0.001428	0.00155723	0.917	0.3622
COTTON	1	0.315188	0.19499345	1.616	0.1102
RAINFALL	1	-0.159016	0.11698551	-1.359	0.1781
RAINSQ	1	0.000086030	0.00005360	1.605	0.1127
MOROGORO	1	46.741297	15.70610691	2.976	0.0039
MWANZA	1	40.882165	16.81210782	2.432	0.0174
SHINYANG	1	72.928296	20.93285731	3.484	0.0008
DODOMA	1	16.867605	25.23479524	-0.668	0.5059
MBEYA	1	50.980335	16.66221931	3.060	0.0031
IRINGA	1	-1.357375	15.09013138	-0.090	0.9286
MTWARA	1	4.669082	15.09926198	0.309	0.7580
LINDI	1	-7.587470	14.75997022	-0.514	0.6087

Table 5.11. Regression Analysis of Coffee Supply in Tanzania
Dependent Variable: Coffee Production

Analysis of Variance

Source	DF	Sum of squares	Mean square	F Value	Prob > F
Model	16	2408.57019	150.53564	48.634	0.0001
Error	93	287.86081	3.09528		
C Total	109	2696.43100			

Root MSE	1.75934
Dep Mean	4.47000
C.V.	39.35884
R-square	0.8932
Adj R-sq	0.8749

Parameter Estimates

Variable	DF	Parameter estimate	Standard error	T for HO: parameter = 0	Prob > |T|
INTERCEP	1	5.239859	3.02200722	1.734	0.0862
RCOFFEE	1	0.005983	0.00386997	1.546	0.1255
RCOFF_2	1	0.002106	0.00408101	0.516	0.6071
RCOFF_3	1	0.018746	0.00554202	3.382	0.0011
DMZPRICE	1	-0.000270	0.00061572	-0.439	0.6615
FERTREAL	1	0.000104	0.00008737	1.187	0.2381
RAINFALL	1	0.001008	0.00227879	0.442	0.6593
RAINSQ	1	-0.000000806	0.00000093	-0.864	0.3900
ARUSHA	1	-5.944700	0.75699829	-7.853	0.0001
TANGA	1	-9.483347	1.00530424	-9.433	0.0001
MOROGORO	1	-10.547811	0.76780043	-13.738	0.0001
RUVUMA	1	-3.712452	0.84416172	-4.398	0.0001
IRINGA	1	-10.614567	0.75641384	-14.033	0.0001
MBEYA	1	-2.910715	0.77323339	-3.764	0.0003
KIGOMA	1	-10.386496	0.75644225	-13.731	0.0001
KAGERA	1	3.412463	1.27808355	2.670	0.0090
MARA	1	-10.041685	0.83694860	-11.998	0.0001

Table 5.12. *Regression Analysis of Cotton Supply in Tanzania*
Dependent Variable: Cotton Production

Analysis of Variance

Source	DF	Sum of squares	Mean square	F Value	Prob > F
Model	10	88243.67586	8824.36759	50.272	0.0001
Error	66	11585.23868	175.53392		
C Total	76	99828.91455			

Root MSE	13.24892
Dep Mean	33.21818
C.V.	39.88455
R-square	0.8839
Adj R-sq	0.8664

Parameter Estimates

Variable	DF	Parameter estimate	Standard error	T for HO: parameter = 0	Prob > |T|
INTERCEP	1	-14.448924	17.39580744	-0.831	0.4092
COTTON	1	0.273866	0.08661079	3.162	0.0024
DMZPRICE	1	-0.006826	0.00202637	-3.368	0.0013
FERTREAL	1	-0.000618	0.00064156	-0.963	0.3391
RAINFALL	1	0.005961	0.01768082	0.337	0.7371
RAINSQ	1	-0.000000250	0.00000660	-0.038	0.9699
KIGOMA	1	-6.868775	5.59716518	-1.227	0.2241
SHINYANG	1	74.938412	5.23671272	14.310	0.0001
KAGERA	1	-3.249376	8.74033099	-0.372	0.7113
MWANZA	1	63.872592	5.25916852	12.145	0.0001
MARA	1	13.270856	5.26869741	2.519	0.0142

Table 5.13. *Regression Analysis of Cashew Nut Supply in Tanzania*
Dependent Variable: Cashew Nut Production

Analysis of Variance

Source	DF	Sum of squares	Mean square	F Value	Prob > F
Model	9	3375.78976	375.08775	22.503	0.0001
Error	48	816.76651	16.66870		
C Total	58	4192.55627			

Root MSE	4.08273
Dep Mean	6.78475
C.V.	60.17517
R-square	0.8052
Adj R-sq	0.7694

Parameter Estimates

Variable	DF	Parameter estimate	Standard error	T for HO: parameter = 0	Prob > |T|
INTERCEP	1	7.151722	7.30998710	0.978	0.3327
CASHEWS	1	0.024226	0.01053035	2.301	0.0257
LAGQTY	1	0.502916	0.11776556	4.270	0.0001
DMZPRICE	1	-0.001198	0.00170624	-0.702	0.4858
FERTREAL	1	0.000048463	0.00030796	0.157	0.8756
RAINFALL	1	-0.014029	0.01059596	-1.324	0.1917
RAINSQ	1	0.000004831	0.00000413	1.170	0.2475
LINDI	1	0.850668	1.52863152	0.556	0.5804
MTWARA	1	8.468254	2.38814298	3.546	0.0009
RUVUMA	1	-1.083138	2.02266465	-0.536	0.5947

Table 5.14. Agricultural GDP According to NBS/NA

Crops	Agricultural GDP														Growth rates		
	1985	1986	1987	1988	1989	1990	1991	1992	1993	1994	1995	1996	1997	1998	1985-90	1990-98	1985-98
	(millions of shillings at 1992 prices)														(percent per year)		
Crop & animal	493,715	506,706	455,638	465,206	483,879	512,171	530,993	536,374	552,677	563,390	598,302	621,886	636,487	648,251	0.7	3.0	2.1
Forestry & hunting	33,891	34,812	35,750	36,720	37,710	38,758	39,820	40,909	42,077	43,223	44,404	45,615	46,846	47,429	2.7	2.6	2.6
Fishing	28,572	29,441	30,336	31,257	32,217	33,141	34,108	35,119	36,668	38,106	39,633	41,240	42,764	44,262	3.0	3.7	3.4
Agricultural GDP	556,178	570,959	521,724	533,183	553,806	584,070	604,921	612,402	631,422	644,719	682,339	708,741	726,097	739,942	1.0	3.0	2.2

Note: Crop and animal production data presented here differ from the sum of NBS/NA estimates of crop and animal production in Table 5.15 for unknown reasons.

Source: National Bureau of Statistics, National Accounts Section, compiled by Komba (1999).

Table 5.15. Gross Value of Crop Output According to NBS/NA

Crops	Gross value of agricultural output (millions of shillings at 1992 prices)														Growth rates (percent per year)		
	1985	1986	1987	1988	1989	1990	1991	1992	1993	1994	1995	1996	1997	1998	1985-90	1990-98	1985-98
Main food crops																	
Maize	113,871	118,246	123,190	128,202	134,431	141,115	145,101	147,725	152,900	154,627	163,014	169,277	176,929	175,513	4.4	2.8	3.4
Paddy	37,935	39,392	41,039	42,709	44,784	47,011	48,339	49,213	50,936	51,512	54,306	56,392	58,941	61,805	4.4	3.5	3.8
Wheat	2,229	2,315	2,411	2,509	2,631	2,762	2,840	2,892	2,993	3,027	3,191	3,314	3,463	3,632	4.4	3.5	3.8
Millet/Sorg.	21,597	22,427	23,364	24,315	25,496	26,764	27,520	28,018	28,999	29,327	30,918	32,105	33,557	35,187	4.4	3.5	3.8
Cassava	21,483	22,309	23,241	24,187	25,362	26,623	27,375	27,870	28,846	29,172	30,755	31,936	33,380	35,002	4.4	3.5	3.8
Beans	24,725	25,675	26,749	27,837	29,189	30,641	31,506	32,076	33,199	33,575	35,396	36,756	38,417	40,284	4.4	3.5	3.8
Subtotal	221,840	230,364	239,994	249,759	261,893	274,916	282,681	287,794	297,873	301,240	317,580	329,780	344,687	351,423	4.4	3.1	3.6
Other food crops																	
Oth starches	2,638	2,722	2,809	2,899	2,980	3,064	3,150	3,238	3,328	3,422	3,517	3,616	3,717	3,821	3.0	2.8	2.9
Groundnuts	6,506	6,716	6,930	7,152	7,352	7,558	7,770	7,986	8,211	8,440	8,677	8,920	9,170	9,426	3.0	2.8	2.9
Onions	2,637	2,721	2,808	2,898	2,979	3,063	3,147	3,237	3,327	3,420	3,516	3,615	3,716	3,820	3.0	2.8	2.9
Tomatoes	7,753	7,994	8,250	8,521	8,754	9,002	9,250	9,513	9,777	10,056	10,335	10,622	10,920	11,225	3.0	2.8	2.9
Potatoes	2,406	2,483	2,563	2,645	2,719	2,795	2,873	2,954	3,036	3,121	3,209	3,299	3,391	3,486	3.0	2.8	2.9
Sw. potatoes	10,596	10,935	11,285	11,646	11,972	12,308	12,652	13,006	13,371	13,745	14,130	14,525	14,932	15,350	3.0	2.8	2.9
Fruits	8,394	8,662	8,939	9,225	9,484	9,749	10,022	10,303	10,592	10,888	11,193	11,506	11,828	12,159	3.0	2.8	2.9
Barley etc.	5,992	6,183	6,382	6,586	6,770	6,960	7,155	7,355	7,561	7,773	7,990	8,214	8,444	8,680	3.0	2.8	2.9
Bananas	20,666	21,328	22,010	22,715	23,351	24,004	24,677	25,367	26,078	26,808	27,558	28,330	29,123	29,939	3.0	2.8	2.9
Coconuts	4,990	5,150	5,314	5,485	5,637	5,795	5,958	6,125	6,297	6,473	6,654	6,840	7,031	7,228	3.0	2.8	2.9
Pulses	2,828	2,919	3,012	3,109	3,196	3,285	3,377	3,472	3,569	3,669	3,771	3,877	3,986	4,097	3.0	2.8	2.9
Yams	1,795	1,852	1,912	1,972	2,027	2,084	2,142	2,202	2,264	2,327	2,393	2,459	2,528	2,599	3.0	2.8	2.9

Table 5.15. *Gross Value of Crop Output According to NBS/NA (Cont'd)*

Crops	Gross value of agricultural output (millions of shillings at 1992 prices)														Growth rates (percent per year)		
	1985	1986	1987	1988	1989	1990	1991	1992	1993	1994	1995	1996	1997	1998	1985-90	1990-98	1985-98
Dry peas	2,633	2,716	2,804	2,892	2,975	3,058	3,144	3,232	3,322	3,415	3,511	3,609	3,710	3,814	3.0	2.8	2.9
Vegetables	16,033	16,546	17,075	17,622	18,116	18,623	19,144	19,680	20,231	20,798	21,380	21,978	22,594	23,226	3.0	2.8	2.9
Sunflower	109	112	116	120	123	126	130	134	137	141	145	149	153	158	2.9	2.9	2.9
Other crops	7,714	7,972	8,227	8,490	8,728	8,973	9,224	9,482	9,748	10,021	10,301	10,590	10,886	11,191	3.1	2.8	2.9
Copra	2	2	2	2	2	37	2	2	2	2	2	2	2	2	79.2	-30.6	0.0
Subtotal	103,692	107,013	110,438	113,979	117,165	120,484	123,817	127,288	130,851	134,519	138,282	142,151	146,131	150,221	3.0	2.8	2.9
Export crops																	
Seed cotton	13,020	15,236	11,503	6,752	8,887	8,462	16,017	18,491	8,937	7,454	15,070	15,173	12,060	6,405	-8.3	-3.4	-5.3
Green tea	3,069	2,852	2,588	2,545	2,934	3,715	3,329	3,593	3,878	4,096	4,712	3,895	3,637	4,822	3.9	3.3	3.5
Coffee	13,388	15,060	14,454	13,287	13,873	15,317	14,891	13,075	15,642	9,279	11,356	14,789	11,584	10,075	2.7	-5.1	-2.2
Sisal	3,962	3,962	4,075	4,087	4,291	4,420	3,776	4,423	2,986	3,637	3,551	3,074	3,686	3,686	2.2	-2.2	-0.6
Tobacco	7,244	9,507	7,230	6,503	6,318	6,317	8,621	12,831	14,319	12,417	15,566	16,635	19,236	28,650	-2.7	20.8	11.2
Pyrethrum	257	267	205	236	219	230	279	216	342	78	78	71	71	67	-2.2	-14.3	-9.8
Cashew nuts	7,075	7,075	3,749	5,688	4,249	3,739	6,632	9,163	8,737	10,354	14,088	18,160	14,887	16,665	-12.0	20.5	6.8
Cardamom	30	48	78	78	63	71	75	77	79	79	81	7	7	7	18.8	-25.1	-10.6
Cocoa	359	378	515	517	485	968	481	494	508	522	537	448	448	448	21.9	-9.2	1.7
Subtotal	48,404	54,385	44,397	39,693	41,319	43,239	54,098	62,361	55,426	47,916	65,039	72,252	65,616	70,825	-2.2	6.4	3.0
Total	373,936	391,762	394,829	403,431	420,377	438,639	460,596	477,443	484,150	483,675	520,901	544,183	556,434	572,469	3.2	3.4	3.3

Source: National Bureau of Statistics, National Accounts Section, compiled by Komba (1999).

Table 5.16. Agricultural GDP Using ASU/MAC Production Data and 1992 Prices

Crops	1985	1986	1987	1988	1989	1990	1991	1992	1993	1994	1995	1996	1997	1998	1985-90	1990-98	1985-98
						Gross value of agricultural output										Growth rates	
						(millions of shillings at 1992 prices)										(percent per year)	
Main food crops	224,844	285,850	242,549	288,438	292,484	277,236	267,716	258,848	300,848	281,274	314,465	323,093	269,890	350,267	4.3	3.0	3.5
Other food crops	99,544	102,732	106,020	109,420	112,478	115,665	118,864	122,196	125,617	129,138	132,751	136,465	140,286	144,212	3.0	2.8	2.9
Export crops	39,139	43,572	41,878	41,926	41,907	42,740	51,619	56,068	60,261	45,962	52,564	67,236	64,180	77,422	1.8	7.7	5.4
Livestock	70,137	72,074	74,760	76,832	78,893	81,261	83,487	85,773	88,122	89,343	91,789	94,307	96,820	98,680	3.0	2.5	2.7
Forestry & hunting	33,891	34,812	35,750	36,720	37,710	38,758	39,820	40,909	42,077	43,223	44,404	45,615	46,846	47,429	2.7	2.6	2.6
Fishing	28,572	29,441	30,336	31,257	32,217	33,141	34,108	35,119	36,668	38,106	39,633	41,240	42,764	44,262	3.0	3.7	3.4
Agricultural GDP	498,112	570,468	533,280	586,581	597,678	590,790	597,605	600,906	655,585	629,040	677,600	709,952	662,782	764,270	3.5	3.3	3.3

Source: Calculated from Table 5.17. GDP is calculated as 96 percent of the gross value of crop output.

Table 5.17. Gross Value of Agricultural Output According to ASU/MAC

Crops	Gross value of agricultural output (millions of shillings at 1992 prices)														Growth rates (percent per year)		
	1985	1986	1987	1988	1989	1990	1991	1992	1993	1994	1995	1996	1997	1998	1985-90	1990-98	1985-98
Main food crops																	
Maize	123,423	163,767	137,586	148,561	154,999	136,544	142,921	136,483	138,997	134,153	176,275	173,025	146,354	168,611	2.0	2.7	2.4
Paddy	21,660	32,805	40,103	61,371	60,194	57,761	31,863	30,764	50,306	56,035	48,815	63,333	43,164	81,619	21.7	4.4	10.7
Wheat	4,566	6,679	4,907	5,111	5,520	7,224	5,725	4,362	5,725	4,089	5,111	5,725	5,384	7,565	9.6	0.6	4.0
Millet/Sorg.	35,793	34,339	30,730	31,181	31,432	26,920	37,598	42,611	57,299	45,518	33,336	31,532	32,334	40,054	-5.5	5.1	0.9
Cassava	18,674	25,775	19,344	24,056	21,872	29,765	26,927	30,573	29,369	30,985	34,252	25,758	24,520	30,229	9.8	0.2	3.8
Beans	30,096	34,395	19,984	30,176	30,653	30,574	33,838	24,841	31,688	22,214	29,778	37,182	29,379	36,784	0.3	2.3	1.6
Subtotal	234,212	297,760	252,655	300,457	304,671	288,788	278,871	269,633	313,383	292,994	327,567	336,555	281,136	364,862	4.3	3.0	3.5
Other food crops																	
Oth starches	2,638	2,722	2,809	2,899	2,980	3,064	3,150	3,238	3,328	3,422	3,517	3,616	3,717	3,821	3.0	2.8	2.9
Groundnuts	6,506	6,716	6,930	7,152	7,352	7,558	7,770	7,986	8,211	8,440	8,677	8,920	9,170	9,426	3.0	2.8	2.9
Onions	2,637	2,721	2,808	2,898	2,979	3,063	3,147	3,237	3,327	3,420	3,516	3,615	3,716	3,820	3.0	2.8	2.9
Tomatoes	7,753	7,994	8,250	8,521	8,754	9,002	9,250	9,513	9,777	10,056	10,335	10,622	10,920	11,225	3.0	2.8	2.9
Potatoes	2,406	2,483	2,563	2,645	2,719	2,795	2,873	2,954	3,036	3,121	3,209	3,299	3,391	3,486	3.0	2.8	2.9
Sw. potatoes	10,596	10,935	11,285	11,646	11,972	12,308	12,652	13,006	13,371	13,745	14,130	14,525	14,932	15,350	3.0	2.8	2.9
Fruits	8,394	8,662	8,939	9,225	9,484	9,749	10,022	10,303	10,592	10,888	11,193	11,506	11,828	12,159	3.0	2.8	2.9
Barley etc.	5,992	6,183	6,382	6,586	6,770	6,960	7,155	7,355	7,561	7,773	7,990	8,214	8,444	8,680	3.0	2.8	2.9
Bananas	20,666	21,328	22,010	22,715	23,351	24,004	24,677	25,367	26,078	26,808	27,558	28,330	29,123	29,939	3.0	2.8	2.9
Coconuts	4,990	5,150	5,314	5,485	5,637	5,795	5,958	6,125	6,297	6,473	6,654	6,840	7,031	7,228	3.0	2.8	2.9
Pulses	2,828	2,919	3,012	3,109	3,196	3,285	3,377	3,472	3,569	3,669	3,771	3,877	3,986	4,097	3.0	2.8	2.9
Yams	1,795	1,852	1,912	1,972	2,027	2,084	2,142	2,202	2,264	2,327	2,393	2,459	2,528	2,599	3.0	2.8	2.9

Table 5.17. Gross Value of Agricultural Output According to ASU/MAC (Cont'd)

Crops	Gross value of agricultural output (millions of shillings at 1992 prices)														Growth rates (percent per year)		
	1985	1986	1987	1988	1989	1990	1991	1992	1993	1994	1995	1996	1997	1998	1985-90	1990-98	1985-98
Dry peas	2,633	2,716	2,804	2,892	2,975	3,058	3,144	3,232	3,322	3,415	3,511	3,609	3,710	3,814	3.0	2.8	2.9
Vegetables	16,033	16,546	17,075	17,622	18,116	18,623	19,144	19,680	20,231	20,798	21,380	21,978	22,594	23,226	3.0	2.8	2.9
Sunflower	109	112	116	120	123	126	130	134	137	141	145	149	153	158	2.9	2.9	2.9
Other crops	7,714	7,972	8,227	8,490	8,728	8,973	9,224	9,482	9,748	10,021	10,301	10,590	10,886	11,191	3.1	2.8	2.9
Copra	2	2	2	2	2	37	2	2	2	2	2	2	2	2	79.2	-30.6	0.0
Subtotal	103,692	107,013	110,438	113,979	117,165	120,484	123,817	127,288	130,851	134,519	138,282	142,151	146,131	150,221	3.0	2.8	2.9
Seed cotton	6,210	9,156	13,884	12,858	12,456	10,740	15,300	14,418	16,428	7,878	6,786	13,602	13,752	12,465	11.6	1.9	5.5
Green tea	3,080	2,840	2,600	2,560	2,920	3,720	3,320	3,600	3,880	4,080	4,720	3,880	3,640	4,840	3.8	3.3	3.5
Coffee	12,531	14,933	11,193	12,394	13,159	15,397	15,124	13,077	15,588	9,309	9,719	14,606	11,794	8,422	4.2	-7.3	-3.0
Sisal	3,931	3,931	4,054	4,054	4,300	4,423	3,808	4,423	2,948	3,686	3,563	3,071	3,686	3,686	2.4	-2.3	-0.5
Tobacco	7,007	9,583	7,247	6,251	5,907	5,907	8,895	13,155	14,494	12,159	15,490	16,314	19,062	28,645	-3.4	21.8	11.4
Pyrethrum	334	334	167	167	167	167	334	167	334	0	0	0	0	0	-12.9	-100.0	-100.0
Cashew nuts	7,288	4,222	4,088	4,999	4,355	3,777	6,599	9,177	8,710	10,376	14,087	18,175	14,531	22,202	-12.3	24.8	8.9
Cardamom	30	30	30	30	30	30	30	30	30	30	30	30	30	30	0.0	0.0	0.0
Cocoa	359	359	359	359	359	359	359	359	359	359	359	359	359	359	0.0	0.0	0.0
Subtotal	40,770	45,388	43,623	43,673	43,653	44,521	53,770	58,405	62,772	47,877	54,754	70,038	66,854	80,648	1.8	7.7	5.4
Total	378,674	450,161	406,716	458,108	465,488	453,792	456,458	455,326	507,006	475,390	520,603	548,744	494,120	591,746	3.7	3.5	3.5

Source: Production of main food crops, cotton, coffee, and cashew nut from MAC/ASU. Other crops production from NBS/National Accounts Section.

Table 5.18. *Gross Value of Fisheries Exports From Tanzania 1986-88 and 1996-98*

	Fresh water			Marine			Total		
	Metric tons	Export unit value US $/MT	FOB value US $ mil.	Metric tons	Export unit value US $/MT	FOB value US $ mil.	Volume MT	Value US $ mil.	Percent freshwater by value
1986-88	19	$2,700	$0.14	3,668	$2,230	$3.32	3,687	$3.46	4.0%
1996-98	28,956	$1,750	$51.14	4,282	$2,540	$10.89	33,238	$62.03	82.4%

Source: Computed from data in World Bank COD (1999).

6. RURAL POVERTY AND FOOD SECURITY

6.1 Rural Poverty in Tanzania

Definition and Measurement

Poverty is generally understood to be a state of not being able to obtain the goods or services necessary to meet some minimum standard of living. Measuring poverty thus involves two steps: 1) defining a measure of access to goods and services and 2) setting a threshold below which a household is considered poor. Access to goods and services may be measured by income or by consumption expenditure, although most poverty studies adopt the latter because it is a more direct measure of living standards and it is less subject to measurement error[1]. In either case, the value of subsistence food production must be included for the results to be meaningful. Adjustments are made for the household size and for regional differences in the cost of living. Some studies add the rental equivalent of owner-occupied housing and consumer durables.

Setting a threshold below which a household is considered poor (a poverty line) also involves a number of methodological options. The poverty line may be relative, such as the 40th percentile of per capita consumption expenditure, or absolute, such as US$1.00 per person per day, or some mixture, such as 50 percent of the average per capita income. Often absolute poverty lines are based on the cost of a "minimal" set of goods and services. Various approaches have been used to define the minimum basket, one of the more widely used ones being that of Ravallion (1994) which yields upper and lower poverty lines. Given the variety of methods and analytical approaches, measuring poverty rates is somewhat subjective in the sense that two researchers could use the same data to obtain different results. Thus, it is generally not valid to compare poverty rates from two studies unless they have deliberately adopted the same definitions, sample coverage, and poverty lines.

An alternative way of measuring poverty is to look at non-monetary indicators of the quality of life, such as health, education, access to water, housing characteristics, and ownership of consumer goods. These variables are easier to measure than income or consumption expenditure, but they generally focus on just one dimension of well being. The United Nations Human Development Index (HDI) is an attempt to construct a non-monetary indicator that covers various aspects of well-being. The HDI incorporates information on literacy, life expectancy, and income per capita.

Evolution of Poverty in Tanzania

Several national household surveys have collected income and/or expenditure data in Tanzania (see Table 6.1). Comparing the results, however, is complicated by the use of different measures (income and consumption expenditure), different coverage, and different poverty lines. In addition, it is necessary to adjust for price changes between studies.

---

[1] Consumption expenditure is less subject to measurement error for three reasons. First, it is less volatile over time because households attempt to smooth consumption in the face of fluctuating income. Second, households are less likely to underreport expenditure than income because expenditure is less sensitive and has no tax implications. Third, in developing countries a large share of income comes from self-employment in farm and non-farm activities, and calculating enterprise profit is a complex and difficult task.

A poverty profile prepared by the World Bank compares the HBS of 1969 and 1976 with two smaller rural surveys in 1979-80 and 1982-83 and the 1991 Cornell-ERB survey (World Bank PHRD 1993). They conclude that:

- Rural income stagnated from 1969 to 1976, rose somewhat until 1982-83, and increased more than three-fold in between that year and 1991.

- Urban income fell significantly between 1969 and 1976-77 but then more than recovered by 1991.

- Income inequality worsened between 1969 and 1991. Although urban inequality did not change, rural inequality became greater, particularly during the reform period (1976-77 to 1991).

These results must be interpreted with caution since the rural surveys in 1979-80 and 1982-83 covered only a few rural regions. In addition, the Cornell-ERB sample is relatively small (1,046 households in mainland Tanzania, of which 477 were in rural areas). Nonetheless, it suggests that the economic reforms initiated in 1984 had a strongly positive impact on rural living standards.

Another evaluation of trends in income and inequality was carried out by Sarris and Tinios (1994). They compared the 1976-77 Household Budget Survey with the 1991 Cornell-ERB survey, using per capita consumption expenditure as their measure of well-being. Using three methods of adjusting for inflation, they find that both rural and urban incomes probably rose between 1976-77 and 1991, but urban incomes rose more quickly (Table 6.2). Since the period 1976-1984 was characterized by a gradually worsening economic crisis, Sarris and Tinios argue that incomes must have risen substantially in the second half of the 1980s when the reforms were implemented.

Sarris and Tinios (1994) also compare poverty rates using three different poverty lines and three methods of adjusting for inflation, yielding nine results. In seven of the nine combinations, the proportion of households below the poverty line decreases from 1976-77 to 1991. Finally, they find unambiguous evidence that the distribution of consumption expenditure improved between 1976 and 1991.

Both the World Bank PHRD (1993) and Sarris and Tinios (1994) conclude that average incomes probably increased substantially in the reform period 1984-1991. They differ, however, on whether urban or rural households gained more and on whether or not income equality improved. Part of the explanation is that the comparisons in World Bank PHRD (1993) focus on income per capita, while Sarris and Tinios (1994) compare consumption expenditure. In addition, as discussed below, even the two calculations of per capita consumption expenditure from the Cornell-ERB survey differ substantially.

The 1993 Human Resource Development Survey (HRDS 1996) also provides information on household expenditure patterns. The survey was carried out from September 1993 to January 1994 and included a sample of 5,184 Tanzanian households including 2,262 rural households. Most of the questionnaire concentrated on access to health and education services, but an expenditure module was also included. Table 6.3 compares two estimates of per capita expenditure from the 1991 Cornell-ERB survey with the 1993 HRDS result, while Table 6.4 compares poverty rates. The estimate of per capita consumption expenditure from the 1993 HRDS is much higher (64 percent) than that of Sarris and Tinios using the 1991 Cornell-ERB survey, even after adjusting for inflation. On the other hand, the 1993 HRDS estimate is "just" 20 percent higher than the calculation found in the World Bank poverty profile.

There are several possible explanations for these differences, but we would argue that 1) the World Bank poverty profile calculations are more credible in light of the results from the HRDS and 2) that per capita expenditure increased between 1991 and 1993, though not necessarily by the 20 percent suggested by comparing the HRDS and poverty profile estimates. To the extent that the 1993 HRDS results imply that the 1991 Cornell-ERB survey underestimates consumption expenditure, particularly in rural areas, the improvements in living standards between 1976 and 1991 found by Sarris and Tinios (1993) and World Bank (1994) are also underestimated. In any case, the large discrepancy between two analyses of the 1991 survey and the large difference between the results of the 1991 and 1993 surveys are a manifestation of the weak empirical basis we have for identifying changes in poverty over time.

Characteristics of Rural Poverty

What are the characteristics of poor households in Tanzania? The most recent poverty profiles based on national household data are World Bank PHRD (1993) and Sarris and Tinios (1993), both of which use the 1991 Cornell-ERB survey[2]. In this section, we review those results and present new analysis of the 1993 Human Resource Development Survey.

The poverty profile prepared by the World Bank PHRD (1993) used two poverty lines, a lower line based on the cost of a minimum bundle of goods and services (US$ 152) and an upper one set at 75 percent of the average per capita expenditure (US$ 227 per capita). Using these poverty lines, 51 percent of Tanzanians were defined as poor and 36 percent as very poor.

Sarris and Tinios (1993) adopted three poverty lines based on the expenditure levels associated with 1,900, 2,000, and 2,100 calories per person per day. Using the middle poverty line, they estimate that 54 percent of rural households and 48 percent of all households are poor. Because of the similarity of these two results, it has become the conventional wisdom that about half of Tanzanian households are poor. The similarity of the two results is almost coincidental, however, since Sarris and Tinios calculated much lower per capita consumption expenditure but adopted a lower poverty line.

The World Bank PHRD (1993) identified some of the characteristics of poor households using the Cornell-ERB survey. One of the main conclusions of the study is that poverty is overwhelmingly a rural phenomenon. The incidence of poverty is 59 percent in rural areas but just 39 percent in small urban areas and 9 percent in Dar-es-Salaam (see Table 6.5). The depth and severity of poverty are also greatest in rural areas and least in Dar-es-Salaam[3]. For example, the severity of poverty in rural areas is twice as great as in smaller urban areas and more than 10 times greater than in Dar-es-Salaam.

The study also found that poverty is associated with less education, lower rates of literacy, and larger household sizes, none of which is surprising. Somewhat unexpected is the finding that female-headed households are no poorer than male-headed households. Also unexpected was the

---

[2] Narayan (1997) presents the results from a qualitative study of poverty, but the study does not estimate poverty rates or income levels.

[3] The depth and severity of poverty are measured using the P_1 and P_2 poverty measures proposed by Foster, Greer, and Thorbecke (1984).

lack of relationship between poverty and farm size. There are two probable explanations for the latter result. First, higher-income households with a non-farm source of income may have smaller-than-average farms. Second, in a land surplus region, it may be access to high-quality land rather than large areas of land that determines the potential for agricultural production.

The regional distribution of poverty is of great interest for policy purposes. The World Bank PHRD (1993) reports regional poverty rates based on the Cornell-ERB survey, but the results are unreliable because of the sample size is too small[4]. Although the sample of the 1993 Human Resource Development Survey (5,184 households) was not designed to generate regional estimates, the data should provide at least a rough estimate of the poverty rate since there are an average of 250 households per region.

The regional variation in poverty is shown in Table 6.6, based on the HRDS and a poverty line equal to the 40th percentile of per capita consumption expenditure. The results suggest that the highest incidence of poverty is found in the regions of Rukwa, Kigoma, Dodoma, Mtwara, and Singida. These regions are either remote (Rukwa, Kigoma, and Mtwara[5]) or semi-arid (Dodoma and Singida). The areas with the lowest incidence of poverty are Dar-es-Salaam, Pemba, and Zanzibar. The rankings do not change noticeably if we consider the depth or severity of poverty.

Table 6.7 presents the poverty rates for urban and rural areas. In order to maintain a sufficient sample size, we have aggregated the regions into six zones. The highest levels of *rural* poverty are found in the Central Zone (Dodoma and Singida) and the Southern Zone (Mtwara, Lindi, and Ruvuma). Overall, the incidence of poverty is twice as high in rural areas as in urban areas. Furthermore, the depth and severity of poverty are around three times as great in rural areas compared to urban areas.

The gender dimension of poverty has received considerably attention in recent years. Female-headed households represent 12-15 percent of rural households. According to the 1994 Human Resource Development Survey, the poverty rate among female-headed households is actually lower than among male-headed households, where poverty is defined according to consumption expenditure per capita. At the same time, according to the 1995 Participatory Poverty Assessment, female-headed households are generally considered poorer by rural households themselves (Narayan, 1997). There are two explanations for this discrepancy. One is that rural households define poverty more broadly to include access to land, ownership of assets, education, and purchase of agricultural inputs. By these measures, both the PPA and the HRDS agree that female-headed households are at a disadvantage. The second is that female-headed households are somewhat more common in urban areas where incomes are higher.

In order to examine more systematically the characteristics of poor households, we use the HRDS data and regression analysis to estimate the determinants of per capita consumption expenditure. The results, presented in Tables 6.8 and 6.9, suggest that poor households are large families in rural areas with an older head of household. They are likely to be farmers who grow maize but do not earn income from livestock, wages, or self-employment. A particularly interesting result is that households that grow cash crops are less likely to be poor, holding other variables such as

---

[4] The Cornell-ERB survey had a sample size of 1,046 households. This implies an average of just 50 households per region. Furthermore, rural households accounted for less than half the sample. Finally, the clustering of household samples means that a region might be represented by households in just 2-4 villages, making regional estimates of poverty meaningless.

[5] Although Mtwara is on the coast and relatively close to Dar-es-Salaam, it may be considered remote because of the poor road connection to Dar.

education and farm size constant[6]. Female-headed households may be poorer but statistical significance of this variable is weak, perhaps because we are controlling for education, farm size, and other variables. The effect of education is also weak, perhaps because we are controlling for different income sources.

The Participatory Poverty Assessment (PPA) was carried out in 1995 using a sample of 1367 households in 87 villages (Narayan, 1997). Unlike previous household surveys, the PPA used a wide range of qualitative questions on poverty, social capital, and gender issues, as well as a variety of techniques such as focus groups, community mapping, and diagramming social organizations[7]. Some of the main findings are as follows:

- In general, the poor considered themselves better off than in the mid-1980s, while the rich considered themselves worse off. Overall, more people reported an improvement (47 percent) than a deterioration (39 percent). This pattern was reversed when asked to compare their situation to that of the early 1990s.

- When asked about the causes of poverty, 47 percent cited constraints on farm income, such as lack of inputs, drought, or marketing problems.

- Female-headed households are poorer than male-headed households according to subjective community ranking. Although they are no poorer than male-headed household according to expenditure data, their low subjective ranking appears to be related to the fact that they have less land and fewer household assets.

- Social capital, measured as an index of the number and types of formal and informal associations that exist in a village, has a strong positive effect on household income. The authors speculate that associations raise income by facilitating 1) pressure to improve government services, 2) the dissemination of information, 3) the management of common property, and 4) the provision of credit.

The PPA also asked about constraints on agricultural productivity. Lack of credit, pests, availability of implements, and the price and availability of inputs were cited by more than 80 percent of the villages.

The most recent information on Tanzania living conditions based on a national survey comes from the 1996 Tanzanian Demographic and Health Survey (TDHS). Although the TDHA did not collect information on household expenditure, it provides information on a number of social indicators. The results, shown in Table 6.10, highlight the wide gap between urban and rural living conditions. Urban households are better off than rural households in virtually every category: electrification, source of water, housing construction, and ownership of various consumer goods.

---

[6] This result is largely because coffee farmers are better off than other farmers. The relationship is less clear with other cash crops.

[7] The PPA also included a standard expenditure module based on the HRDS, although due to a communication problem, this module was administered only to a subsample of about 800 households. Narayan (1997) presents only one table of expenditure data (Table 4.4), giving the per capita expenditure of male- and female-headed households.

6.2   Food Security

Definition and Measurement

Food security is generally defined as the condition in which all people at all times have enough food for a healthy and productive life. Food security involves three components: food availability, food access, and food utilization. Food availability implies sufficient production or imports to meet the food needs of the population. Food access refers to the ability of people to obtain food, either through their own production or by purchasing it with money earned from other activities. And food utilization means that the nutrient intake associated with food consumption is not impeded by inadequate nutritional information, poor sanitations, or problems in intrahousehold distribution (Haddad 1997).

Food security does not necessarily imply food self-sufficiency, since a household can be food secure if its income is high enough (and stable enough) to purchase its food requirements. In remote areas with poor transportation infrastructure, households may be forced, however, to produce most or all of their food requirements.
Food security can be defined at the national, regional, or household level. Due to data limitations, we focus here on national food security. Regional food security cannot be measured directly in the absence of data on regional flows of food, and household food security can only be measured using detailed surveys of food consumption.

Evolution of Food Security

A crude measure of national food security is the apparent per capita consumption of food, defined as production plus net imports divided by the population. At the national level, food security is sometimes measured by per capita availability of food, where availability is defined as production plus net imports. This is a very imperfect measure since it does not take into account the use of food as animal feed, variations in the caloric content of commodities, and changes in stocks. Figure 6.1 shows the composition and level of apparent food consumption from 1970 to 1997 according to the Food and Agriculture Organization (FAO). The large increase in per capita food production over 1971-75 is probably related to data collection problems, as argued by Sarris and van den Brink (1994). The figure shows a decline in apparent food consumption from 450 kg/person in 1983 to 330 kg/person in 1997. Most of the decline is due to a decline in apparent per capita consumption of cassava.

The FAO data used for this analysis are suspect for several reasons. First, the overall level of per capita food consumption is implausibly high, since 330-450 kg of staple foods corresponds to about 2,700-3,700 calories per person per day[8]. Second, the per capita consumption of cassava is roughly double the per capita production of cassava according to the Agricultural Statistics Unit (ASU) of the Ministry of Agriculture and Cooperatives. Third, the decline in food production since 1983 seems unlikely. If per capita food production were falling, we would expect the real price of food to rise reflecting the scarcity. In fact, however, the real price of staple foods has declined since the mid-1980s.

---

[8] This is a rough calculation based on the assumption that the staple foods provide about 3,000 calories per kilogram.

In Figure 6.2, we present alternative estimates of apparent per capita food consumption based on ASU production statistics and net imports[9]. The figures also show food consumption falling from 300 kg/person in 1986 to 250 kg/person in 1991 and stabilizing at that level except for a short-fall in 1997. The current quantity of 250 kg per capita corresponds to about 2,050 calories per person per day. Given that this figure excludes non-staple foods, this figure indicates that on average, the caloric needs of the Tanzanian population are being met.

Regarding the apparent decline in food consumption over 1986-91, three hypotheses may be proposed:

- Given that real incomes have risen since the mid-1980s, the decline in staple food consumption may be the result of consumers switching from staple foods to higher value foods such as animal products.

- Food production may have been overestimated in the late 1980s. It is notable that since 1992, when survey-based estimates of food production became institutionalized, per capita food consumption appears stable.

- If the data are accurate and consumers have not switched to higher value food commodities, the data reflect a decline in food security and nutritional intake since the mid-1980s.

The third hypothesis seems the least likely in light of increasing household income (see Section 6.1), declining real prices of food (see Section 4), and stable or improving nutrition indicators (see Section 6.3).

It is not possible to calculate trends in apparent food consumption at the regional level. In the absence of reliable data on the movement of food among regions, such calculations would over-estimate food security in food surplus regions and under-estimate it in deficit regions.

Patterns in Food Security

Food security at the household level is influenced by a variety of factors including food production, cash crop income, non-farm income, household size and composition, access to markets, and food prices. Food production and income are in turn influenced by farm size and land quality, availability of labor, equipment, access to credit, and management skills.

The link between income and food security is indicated by the analysis of the Cornell-ERB household data. Sarris and Tinios (1994) found that caloric intake is strongly affected by consumption expenditure, particularly in rural areas. As shown in Table 6.11, the relationship is statistically significant with a high degree of confidence. The income elasticity of caloric intake is estimated to be 0.66, indicating that a 10 percent increase in consumption expenditure is associated with a 6.6 percent increase in caloric intake of household members. Furthermore, in rural areas per capita consumption expenditure "explains" over half of the variation in caloric intake across households. Similar results were obtained in Dar-es-Salaam and other urban areas, although the elasticity is lower in "other urban" areas.

---

[9] These data do not take into account net changes in stocks. The only data available on changes in stocks refer to government stocks which have historically been quite small relative to annual production.

102

A crude measure of household-level food security is the value of food consumption per capita[10]. We estimate the value of food consumption as a function of various household characteristics using the 5,184 households in the Human Resource Development Survey. Table 6.8 provides the descriptive statistics of the variables used in the analysis while Table 6.12 presents the regression results. This analysis indicates that the per capita value of food consumption is significantly greater in urban areas, on larger farms, and among households that have some livestock income. In addition, wage earning households and those with self-employment income have higher values of food consumption. Interestingly, the value of food consumption is higher in households that grow at least one cash crop. On the other hand, the per capita value of food consumption is significantly lower in households where the head is older or a woman and households that grow crops. There are also some regional differences. The value of food consumption is higher on the Coast than in the Northern Highlands, and higher in the latter region than elsewhere.

Food Demand Patterns

What are the patterns in Tanzanian food demand and how are they changing over time? The answers to these questions are useful in interpreting food price and output trends, particularly for non-tradable foods whose price is determined by domestic supply and demand. The answers are also useful in anticipating rapid growth in certain food and agro-industrial sectors. The main factors influencing long-run shifts in food demand are population growth, income growth, and urbanization[11]. The effect of population growth on food demand is relatively predicable because population growth rates do not change quickly. In this section, we focus the effect of income and urbanization on per capita food demand.

We use data from the 1993 Human Resource Development Survey (HRDS 1996) to examine food demand across Tanzanian households. Food demand is estimated as part of a demand system consisting of nine food categories and nine non-food categories. We use a Working-Leser demand function of the following form:

$$s_i = a_i + b_i \ln(x) + \sum_j c_{ij} Z_j$$

where s_i is the share of total expenditure allocated to good i, x is per capita consumption expenditure, and the Z_j represent a set of household characteristics (a, b, and c are parameters to be estimated econometrically with the data). Consumption expenditure is defined as the value of cash purchases plus the value of home production plus the rental equivalent of owner-occupied housing[12]. The household characteristics include household size, sex of head of household, the age of the head of household, and level of education of the head of household. Although this

---

[10] It was not possible to estimate the caloric intake of households in the HRDS. Because the HRDS collected information on the value of food consumption but not the quantity, estimating caloric intake would require making use of the HRDS price data, something that was not possible in the time available.

[11] Price have an effect on short-run shifts in food consumption, but real prices generally do not rise or fall consistently over time, so their effect on long-term trends is less than that of population, urbanization, and income.

[12] The HRDS questionnaire does not appear to include any question regarding the value of home production. Nonetheless, enumerators were reportedly told to include home production in counting the value of expenditure. The high food share and the size of per capita expenditure in rural areas suggests that most or all home production was recorded.

analysis is somewhat limited[13], it sheds light on the effect of income and urbanization on food demand. The analysis was carried out separately for urban households, rural households, and all households.

The estimated coefficients for the national model are shown in Tables 6.13 and 6.14. They show that per capita expenditure and household characteristics have a statistically significant effect on the budget shares of many items, although the explanatory power of the model is weak. The "urban" coefficient, for example, reveals that hold income and other characteristics constant, urban households consume more rice, wheat, animal products, and fruits and vegetables than rural households, even after controlling for income and other household characteristics. At the same time, urban household consume less maize and "other starches" (mainly cassava and sweet potato).

Table 6.15 gives the average expenditure share and the income elasticity[14] of each budget category. Urban households allocate 60 percent of their budgets to food, the most important of which are animal products (14 percent) and "other food" (13 percent). In contrast, rural households allocate 68 percent of their expenditures to food, the most important items being animal products and maize. The higher food share in rural areas compared to urban is not surprising since rural households are poorer and Engel's Law states that food shares tend to decline with income. Maize and "other starches" (mainly cassava and sweet potatoes) constitute 23 percent of the budget of rural households, almost double the share of these goods in the budget of urban households. Somewhat surprisingly, animal products are as important in rural budgets as they are in urban budgets, though expenditure on animal products is higher in absolute terms in urban areas.

In both urban and rural area, maize has the lowest income elasticity among the categories listed. The urban income elasticity of 0.38 implies that a 10 percent increase in per capita income is associated with an increase in maize purchases of less than 4 percent. In rural areas, the maize elasticity is higher (0.63), but still less than one, indicating that the share of expenditure allocated to maize declines as incomes rise.

The highest income elasticities among the food categories are those of wheat products, potatoes, and animal products. Since the elasticities are above one, they are "luxuries" in the sense that demand rises more quickly than income. Rice is a luxury good in rural areas, but not among urban consumers.

Overall, the highest income elasticities are those of transportation and communication, demand for which is expected to rise at twice the rate of per capita income growth. Another non-food category with a very elastic demand is "other non-food", covering recreation and personal services.

These results have several implications for trends in Tanzanian food demand. First, as per capita income rises, demand for maize will increase but only slowly. Urban demand in particular is not very sensitive to income. Second, as per capita income rises, the demand for wheat, rice, potatoes,

---

[13] One limitation is that prices are not included in the demand equation. Although the HRDS includes price data, time constraints prevented us from including them in the econometric analysis. For similar reasons, we were not able to calculate a regional price index to adjust income for regional differences in the cost of living.

[14] The income elasticity is the percentage change in demand for the good associated with a 1 percent increase in per capita income (or, to be more precise in this context, per capita consumption expenditure).

and animal products will rise quickly. Third, urbanization will result in an increase in the per capita demand for wheat, rice, animal products, and fruits and vegetables, while reducing demand for maize, cassava, and sweet potatoes.

6.3 Nutrition

Definition and Measurement

Whereas food security is generally defined in terms of food consumption, nutrition refers to the adequacy of the diet as measured by body size and shape and the mortality rate. For children under 5 years of age, nutritional status is often measured by the height-for-age, weight-for-height, and weight-for-age. Moderate malnutrition is commonly defined as the share of children more than 2 standard deviations below the median level of a reference population. Thus, moderate stunting refers to children more than 2 standard deviations below the median in height-for-age. Stunting is considered a measure of the cumulative effect of chronic malnutrition. Similarly, moderate wasting refers to children more than 2 standard deviations below the median weight-for-height. Wasting is interpreted as reflecting acute or recent malnutrition. Children are considered underweight is they are more than 2 standard deviations below the median weight-for-age. Underweight is considered a composite measure of acute and chronic malnutrition. Child nutrition and health are also measured using the infant and under-5 mortality rates.

Adult nutrition is often measured using the body-mass index (BMI), calculated as the weight divided by the height squared. Maternal nutrition can be measured by the proportion of infants born less than 2.5 kilograms or by the maternal mortality rate, although these measures are also influenced by access to maternal health care.

Evolution of Nutritional Status

Tanzania has shown dramatic improvements in health and nutrition since independence. The infant mortality rate has fallen from 138 per 1,000 births in 1965 to 85 in 1997. Similarly, life expectancy rose from 42 years in 1960 to 50 years in 1990 (World Bank 1994). And maternal mortality has declined from 453 to 215 per 100,000 births over the period 1961-1991 (Bategeki and Magambo 1994).

Of particular interest, however, is the trend in nutrition since the initiation of the economic reforms in the mid-1980s. The Ministry of Health collects information from its clinics and hospitals, but these data are subject biases since patients are probably not a random sample of the population. Measures of child nutrition were collected in nine regions over 1984-1993 as part of the Child Survival, Protection, and Development (CSPD) project. These data show dramatic reduction in the proportions of underweight children[15] in the project area, though it does not tell us about trends elsewhere (Bategeki and Magambo 1994).

The best recent information on recent nutritional trends comes from the Tanzanian Demographic and Health Survey, carried out in 1991 and 1996. These surveys use large samples[16] and random selection procedures to ensure that the results are nationally representative. Table 6.16 compares

---

[15] Underweight children were defined as those less than 80 percent of the mean weight-for-height for the reference population.

[16] The 1991 TDHS had a sample of 6,097 children under five years of age, while the 1996 TDHS had a sample of 5,344 children under five.

the incidence of stunting, wasting, and underweight children according to the two surveys. The incidence of stunting declined overall and for every sub-category of child. The incidence of wasting and underweight children rose slightly between the two surveys. Since wasting is a measure of short-term nutrition, it is more sensitive to differences in season between the two surveys and differences related to the harvest that year. This table suggests that the long-term nutritional status of children either improved or remained relatively stable over the period 1991-1996.

The two DHS surveys also asked about the birth weight of children born with the previous five years. In the 1991 survey, 16.9 percent of the children were born less than 2.5 kilograms, whereas the corresponding figure in the 1996 survey was 10.7 percent[17].
Finally, the two surveys calculated the body-mass index (BMI) of women giving birth over the previous five years. In both surveys, 9.2 percent of Tanzanian mothers had a BMI less than 18.5 kg/m^2. These figures suggest that maternal health and nutrition has not fallen and may have improved between the late 1980s and the mid 1990s.

Patterns in Nutritional Status

According to the 1996 Tanzanian Demographic and Health Survey, child nutrition varies significantly with the characteristics of the household. Table 6.17 shows the rate of child malnutrition according to place of residence, region, and education of the head of household. Although we show the rates of moderate stunting, wasting, and underweight children, we concentrate on the moderate stunting because this measure is less affected by seasonal and annual variation.

Moderate stunting among children under 5 years of age is almost 40 percent more common in rural mainland Tanzania than in urban mainland Tanzania. The rate for Zanzibar lies between the two. This difference suggests that, in terms of child nutrition, the advantages of urban living including higher income and better access to health services outweighs any disadvantages in terms of higher food costs or a less sanitary environment. Children in urban areas are also less likely to be underweight, although there is little difference between urban and rural areas in terms of wasting.

The regional pattern in moderate stunting indicates that malnutrition is highest in Iringa, Lindi, Mtwara, and Tanga, Ruvuma, followed by Ruvuma, Morogoro, Coast, and Kigoma. It is interesting to note that two of the "big four" maize producing regions are included in this list. This result highlights the fact that per capita food production or per capita food availability is not a good measure of food security or nutritional status. The lowest rates of stunting are found in Tabora and Dar-es-Salaam. The proportion of underweight children shows a similar pattern. The rate of wasting, however, is quite different, possibly reflecting regional differences in recent harvests.

Children in Zanzibar are more likely to be underweight and suffer from wasting compared to children on the mainland (Table 6.17). About 50 percent of Zanzibar children under 5 years old suffer from malnutrition and 20 percent of children in rural areas are severely malnourished (MALNR FAO 1999). Zanzibar has no food security policy of its own. Infant mortality in

---

[17] These figures must be used with caution given that a large share of the respondents (51 percent in the 1996 TDHS) could not recall the birth weight. Since rural women were more likely to not know the birth weight, the actual figure is probably higher. Unless the degree of bias changed between 1991 and 1996, however, the figures imply that the rate has fallen.

Zanzibar has declined by 14 percent in the last 14 years (Mabele 1999a). This may be due to the fact that pre-natal, delivery and post-natal care has increased, albeit from a low base. In the last 5 years before the 1991-92 DHS, more than two-thirds of births in Zanzibar took place at home, compared to 48 percent on the mainland, and 12 percent in Dar es Salaam.

Over all parts of the country, the third section of Table 6.17 illustrates the strong relationship between the nutritional status of children and the level of education of the head of household. Although the table shows the relationship in highly aggregate form, it has also been shown elsewhere to be true households, especially if the educational levels of women in the household are taken into account (Smith and Haddad, forthcoming). In Table 6.17, the rates of moderate stunting are twice as high on average in households where the head has no education compared to those in which the head has at least some secondary education. In part, this relationship reflects the direct effect of education on feeding patterns. Another factor is that more educated parents earn higher incomes and higher incomes are associated with more quantity and better quality food.

Figure 6.1. *Food Availability According to FAO*
(kg/capita)

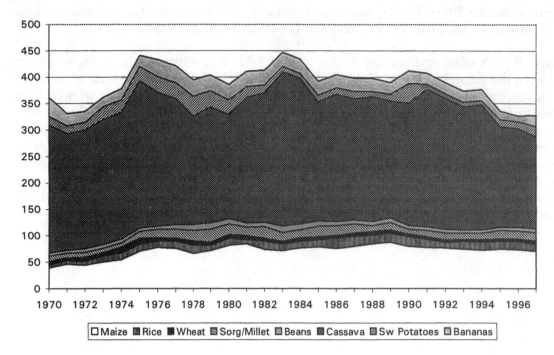

Source: FAO 1999.

Figure 6.2. *Food Availability According to ASU*
(kg/capita)

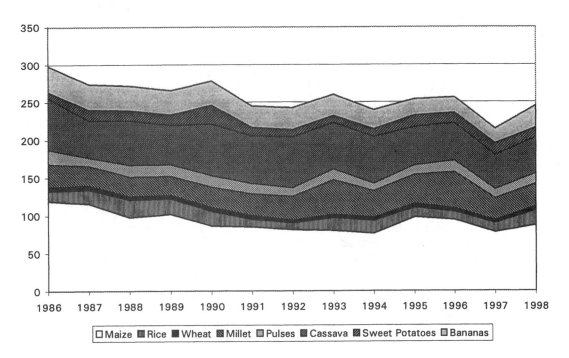

Source: Agricultural Statistics Unit of MAC.

Table 6.1. *Characteristics of Selected Household Surveys*

Name of survey	Year	Institution	Coverage	Sample size	Comments
Household Budget Survey	1969	Bureau of Statistics			First comprehensive budget survey. Generated zonal estimates.
Household Budget Survey	1976	Bureau of Statistics		5,000	Data collection over one year. Used for constructing National Accounts.
Cornell-ERB Survey	1991	Cornell U. & Economic Research Bureau of UDSM	Mainland Tanzania	1,046	Used for World Bank poverty profile and Cornell reports.
Household Budget Survey	1991-92	Bureau of Statistics	Mainland Tanzania	5,328	Used for constructing national accounts. Results published.
Human Resource Development Survey	1993	World Bank	URT (mainland and Zanzibar)	5,000	Used for Social Sector Analysis. Expenditure module but no income data.
Participatory Poverty Assessment	1995	World Bank	Mainland Tanzania	1,367	Focus on perceptions and qualitative aspects of poverty. Expenditure data collected but not published.

Source: World Bank PHRD (1993), Sarris and Tinios (1994).

Table 6.2. Comparison of Consumption Expenditure in 1976 and 1991

Method used to adjust for inflation	Percentage increase in per capita consumption expenditure from 1976-77 to 1991		
	Rural	Urban	Tanzania
Inflate 1976-77 expenditure with National Consumer Price Index	35%	125%	61%
Re-value 1976-77 expenditure quantities using 1991 prices for each good	-3%	67%	18%
Re-value 1991 expenditure quantities using 1976-77 prices for each good	15%	90%	36%

Source: Sarris and Tinios (1994), based on the 1976-77 Household Budget Survey and the 1991 Cornell-ERB survey.

Table 6.3. Comparison of Consumption Expenditure in 1991 and 1993

Variable and study	Consumption expenditure per capita (Tsh/person/year)		
	Rural	Urban	Total
At current prices			
1991 Cornell-ERB (Sarris and Tinios calculation)	32,365	92,262	44,984
1991 Cornell-ERB (World Bank calculation)	49,620	89,686	61,564
1993 Human Resource Development Survey	91,075	172,315	116,517
At constant (Dec 1994) prices			
1991 Cornell-ERB (Sarris and Tinios calculation)	72,082	205,483	100,187
1991 Cornell-ERB (World Bank calculation)	110,512	199,746	137,114
1993 Human Resource Development Survey	128,455	243,039	164,340
Percent change from 1991 (ST) to 1993	78.2%	18.3%	64.0%
Percent change from 1991 (WB) to 1993	16.2%	21.7%	20.0%

Note: Price adjustments using National Consumer Price Index. The September 1991 NCPI (44.9) was used to inflate the Cornell-ERB results, while the November 1993 NCPI (70.9) was used to inflate the HRDS results.

Source: Cornell-ERB results from Sarris and Tinios (1994), Table 3 and World Bank PHRD (1993) Table 3.1. HRDS results calculated by the authors from HRDS data files (HRDS 1996).

Table 6.4. Comparison of Poverty Estimates in 1991 and 1993

Study and variable	Rural	Dar-es-Salaam	Other urban	Total
1991 Cornell-ERB survey				
Poverty line (Tsh/person/year)	27,721	54,950	33,186	--
Poverty rate (percent of households)	54.1%	18.3	26.4	47.6%
1993 Human Resource Development Survey				
Poverty line (Tsh/person/year)	43,773	86,770	52,403	--
Poverty rate (percent of households)	20.5%	5.9%	12.9%	17.7%

Note: Sarris and Tinios (1994) calculated the poverty line by regressing caloric intake as a function of expenditure per capita and choosing the expenditure per capita that corresponded to an estimated caloric intake of 2000 calories per person per day.

Source: Cornell-ERB results from Sarris and Tinios (1994), Table 12, using the 2,000 calorie poverty line. Poverty line for 1993 calculated by inflating the 1991 poverty lines by the ratio of NCPI values for November 1993 and September 1991 (1.58). Poverty rates for 1993 calculated from HRDS data files (HRDS 1996).

Table 6.5. Measures of Poverty by Location of Household (1991)

Household category	Incidence of poverty (P0)	Depth of poverty (P1)	Severity of poverty (P2)
Location			
Rural areas	59.1	29.9	19.2
Small urban areas	39.3	15.1	7.8
Dar-es-Salaam	9.3	3.1	1.4
Agro-climatic zone			
North and west	40.2	18.0	11.3
Coast	61.1	31.7	20.9
Central-west	61.2	28.9	17.8
Southern highlands	57.6	30.0	19.0
Central-east	58.5	27.4	16.2
Dar-es-Salaam	9.3	3.1	1.4
Tanzania	51.1	35.9	15.6

Note: The North and west includes Kigoma, Kagera, Kilimanjaro, and Arusha. The Coast includes Lindi, Mtwara, Coast, and Tanga. Central-west includes Tabora, Mwanza, and Shinyanga. The Southern Highlands includes Rukwa, Ruvuma, Mbeya, and Iringa. And the Central-east includes Morogoro, Dodoma, and Singida.
Source: World Bank PHRD (1993).

Table 6.6. Measures of Poverty by Region (1993)

Region	Incidence of poverty P0	Index of the poverty gap P1	Index of the severity of poverty P2
Dodoma	.70	.26	.12
Arusha	.41	.15	.08
Kilimanjaro	.25	.06	.02
Tanga	.41	.15	.07
Morogoro	.38	.11	.05
Coast	.22	.06	.02
Dar-es-Salaam	.03	.00	.00
Lindi	.52	.19	.09
Mtwara	.69	.21	.09
Ruvuma	.55	.19	.09
Iringa	.42	.12	.05
Mbeya	.25	.07	.03
Singida	.64	.20	.08
Tabora	.48	.13	.05
Rukwa	.72	.30	.15
Kigoma	.71	.28	.15
Shinyanga	.43	.11	.04
Kagera	.22	.05	.02
Mwanza	.33	.09	.03
Mara	.25	.05	.01
Zanzibar	.18	.04	.02
Pemba	.10	.02	.01
Total	.40	.13	.06

Source: Calculated from the HRDS (1996) data using a relative poverty line of 40 percent. Note: P0 is the percentage of households with per capita expenditure below the poverty line, defined at the 40th percentile nationally. P1 is the poverty gap measure which takes into account both the incidence of poverty and the average expenditure of poor households. P2 is an index of the severity of poverty that takes into account the incidence of poverty, the average income of poor households, and the distribution of expenditure among those households. See Foster, Greer, and Thorbecke (1984).

Table 6.7. Measures of Poverty by Zone (1993)

Location	Zone	Incidence of poverty P0	Index of the poverty gap P1	Index of the severity of poverty P2
Rural	Coastal Zone	.40	.13	.06
	Northern Highlands	.39	.13	.06
	Lake Zone	.43	.12	.05
	Central Zone	.72	.25	.11
	Southern Highlands	.48	.15	.07
	Southern Zone	.65	.22	.10
	Total	.49	.16	.07
Urban	Coastal Zone	.08	.02	.01
	Northern Highlands	.15	.02	.01
	Lake Zone	.23	.05	.02
	Central Zone	.27	.06	.02
	Southern Highlands	.28	.10	.05
	Southern Zone	.45	.11	.04
	Total	.20	.06	.02
Average	Coastal Zone	.24	.08	.03
	Northern Highlands	.33	.11	.05
	Lake Zone	.39	.11	.04
	Central Zone	.68	.23	.10
	Southern Highlands	.39	.13	.06
	Southern Zone	.60	.20	.09
	Total	.40	.13	.06

Note: The Coastal Zone includes Tanga, Morogoro, Coast, Dar-es-Salaam, and Zanzibar. The Northern Highlands includes Arusha and Kilimanjaro. The Lake Zone includes Tabora, Kigoma, Shinyanga, Kagera, Mwanza, and Mara. The Central Zone includes Dodoma and Singida. The Southern Highlands includes Iringa, Mbeya, and Rukwa. The Southern Zone includes Lindi, Mtwara, and Ruvuma. P0 is the percentage of households with per capita expenditure below the poverty line, defined at the 40th percentile nationally. P1 is the poverty gap measure that takes into account both the incidence of poverty and the average expenditure of poor households. P2 is an index of the severity of poverty that takes into account the incidence of poverty, the average income of poor households, and the distribution of expenditure among those households. See Foster, Greer, and Thorbecke (1984).

Source: Calculated from the HRDS (1996) data using a relative poverty line of 40 percent.

Table 6.8. Descriptive Statistics From the HRDS

Variable	Description	N	Mean	Standard deviation
EXPPC	Expenditure per capita (Tsh/person/year)	5,184	171,559	206,318
FOODPC	Food expenditure per capita (Tsh/year)	5,183	120,260	177,677
URBAN	Binary variable for urban households	5,184	.5637	.4960
HHSIZE	Household size (persons)	5,184	5.77	2.98
FEMHEAD	Binary variable for female headed household	5,177	.14	.35
AGEHEAD	Age of head of household	5,177	42.8	13.6
FARMSIZE	Size of farm (hectares)	5,184	1.36	2.42
EDHEAD	Education of head (years)	5,177	5.91	5.10
FARMER	Binary variable for households with crop income	5,164	.61	.49
LIVEST	Binary variable for households with livestock income	5,164	.18	.39
WAGE	Binary variable for households with wage income	5,164	.22	.41
SELFEMP	Binary variable for household with non-ag. self-employment income	5,164	.06	.23
MZPROD	Binary variable for maize producers	5,184	.49	.50
CASHCROP	Binary variable for cash crop producers	5,164	.19	.39
COAST	Binary variable for households in Coastal Zone	5,184	.39	.49
LAKE	Binary variable for households in Lake Zone	5,184	.24	.43
CENTRAL	Binary variable for households in Central Zone	5,184	.06	.23
SHIGH	Binary variable for households in Southern Highlands	5,184	.13	.34
SOUTH	Binary variable for households in South	5,184	.07	.27

Note: Figures in this table represent the means and standard deviations of unweighted data and should not be interpreted as reflecting the means in the population. For example, the HRDS oversampled urban households so the mean of the "urban" dummy variable is 0.56, higher than the proportion of urban households in Tanzania.

Source: HRDS 1996.

Table 6.9. *Determinants of Per Capita Expenditure*

Model Summary:

R	.461
R Square	.213
Adjusted R Square	.210
Std. Error of the Est.	183617.7517

Variable	Unstandardized coefficients		Standardized coefficients		Statistical significance
	B	Std. error	Beta	t-statistic	
(Constant)	295,684.28	14,766.84		20.024	.000
URBAN	59,700.25	7,008.82	.143	8.518	.000
HHSIZE	-17,963.19	953.77	-.259	-18.834	.000
FEMHEAD	-12,775.09	7,526.67	-.022	-1.697	.090
AGEHEAD	-503.81	206.34	-.033	-2.442	.015
FARMSIZE	5,159.43	1,216.17	.061	4.242	.000
EDHEAD	836.56	527.44	.021	1.586	.113
FARMER	-33,547.15	8,307.50	-.079	-4.038	.000
LIVEST	28,057.50	7,456.78	.052	3.763	.000
WAGE	37,116.95	6,557.60	.074	5.660	.000
SELFEMP	83,680.22	11,332.58	.094	7.384	.000
MZPROD	-25,104.49	8,151.22	-.061	-3.080	.002
CASHCROP	15,629.60	7,458.65	.030	2.096	.036
COAST	1,683.23	9,588.88	.004	.176	.861
LAKE	-50,461.80	9,897.39	-.104	-5.098	.000
CENTRAL	-93,765.24	13,641.39	-.107	-6.874	.000
SHIGH	-60,390.39	11,001.05	-.100	-5.490	.000
SOUTH	-72,891.80	12,475.58	-.095	-5.843	.000

Source: Regression analysis of data from the 1993 Human Resource Development Survey (HRDS 1996).

Table 6.10. Urban-rural Differences in Social Indicators (1996)

Social indicator	Urban	Rural	Total
Percent with electricity in house	35.5	1.8	9.4
Source of drinking water (percent of households)			
Piped into residence	31.5	2.0	8.6
Public tap	46.3	23.1	28.3
Public well	13.6	31.6	27.6
Other	8.6	43.3	35.5
Total	100.0	100.0	100.0
Median time to water source (minutes)	6.0	20.8	16.0
Floor material (percent of households)			
Earth/sand	35.4	90.6	78.2
Cement	63.4	8.5	20.8
Other	1.2	0.9	1.0
Total	100.0	100.0	100.0
Percent owning a radio	65.4	33.8	40.9
Percent owning a television	6.0	0.4	1.6
Percent owning a refrigerator	7.5	0.4	2.0
Percent owning a bicycle	25.0	33.8	31.9
Percent owning a motorcycle	1.7	0.6	0.8
Percent owning a private car	4.3	0.6	1.4

Source: 1996 Demographic and Health Survey (Bureau of Statistics (Tanzania) and Macro International Inc. 1997a: 17-18).

Table 6.11. Relationship Between Income and Caloric Intake

Region	Intercept		Coefficient on log expenditure per capita		R-squared
	Coefficient	t-statistic	Coefficient	t-statistic	
Rural	0.89	3.00	0.66	22.72	0.52
Dar-es-Salaam	0.35	0.91	0.66	19.47	0.60
Other urban	3.68	11.07	0.38	12.50	0.34

Source: Table 11 in Sarris and Tinios (1994).

Table 6.12. Determinants of Food Expenditure

Model Summary:

R	.419
R Square	.176
Adjusted R Square	.173
Std. Error of the Est.	161785.8

Variable	Unstandardized coefficients		Standardized coefficients		Statistical significance
	B	Std. error	Beta	t-statistic	
(Constant)	223,545.861	13,011.075		17.181	.000
URBAN	32,679.898	6,175.478	.091	5.292	.000
HHSIZE	-14,416.550	840.368	-.242	-17.155	.000
FEMHEAD	-16,095.339	6,631.760	-.032	-2.427	.015
AGEHEAD	-716.228	181.805	-.055	-3.940	.000
FARMSIZE	3,290.242	1,071.571	.045	3.070	.002
EDHEAD	706.235	464.727	.020	1.520	.129
FARMER	-36,210.813	7,319.746	-.099	-4.947	.000
LIVEST	26,430.984	6,570.179	.057	4.023	.000
WAGE	34,444.671	5,777.910	.080	5.961	.000
SELFEMP	62,754.666	9,985.147	.082	6.285	.000
MZPROD	-9,148.544	7,182.045	-.026	-1.274	.203
CASHCROP	13,617.279	6,571.820	.030	2.072	.038
COAST	25,945.853	8,448.775	.071	3.071	.002
LAKE	-25,337.700	8,720.595	-.061	-2.906	.004
CENTRAL	-44,521.096	12,019.444	-.059	-3.704	.000
SHIGH	-30,841.699	9,693.039	-.059	-3.182	.001
SOUTH	-41,966.867	10,992.248	-.064	-3.818	.000

Source: Regression analysis of data from the 1993 Human Resource Development Survey (HRDS 1996).

Table 6.13. Determinants of Per Capita Food Expenditure

Parameter	Maize	Rice	Wheat	Potatoes	Other starch	Legumes	Fruit and vegetables	Animal products.	Other food
Number of observations	5,026	5,026	5,026	5,026	5,026	5,026	5,026	5,026	5,026
Adjusted R^2	0.29	0.01	0.09	0.03	0.16	0.18	0.06	0.02	0.06
INTERCEP	0.6188	0.0681	-0.0694	-0.0053*	0.1310	0.3236	0.1514	-0.0012*	-0.0999
LNPCTOTE	-0.0437	-0.0019*	0.0064	0.0012	-0.0038	-0.0196	-0.0068	0.0123	0.0220
URBAN	-0.0204	0.0124	0.0111	0.0049	-0.0593	-0.0266	0.0158	0.0071	0.0014*
HHSIZE	-0.0022	0.0006	0.0011	0.0000*	0.0005*	-0.0027	-0.0025	0.0008	-0.0022
FEMHEAD	0.0017*	0.0042	0.0007*	0.0013	0.0038*	0.0017*	0.0020*	-0.0007*	-0.0178
AGEHEAD	0.0004	0.0000*	0.0000*	-0.0001	0.0005	0.0001*	-0.0002	-0.0004	-0.0004
EDHEAD	-0.0011	0.0003*	0.0001*	0.0001*	-0.0005	-0.0005	0.0002*	0.0000*	-0.0005
PLOTSIZE	0.0003*	0.0004*	-0.0008	-0.0001*	-0.0018	0.0014	-0.0008	0.0017	-0.0013

* indicates that coefficient is not significant at 10 percent.
INTERCEP is intercept.
LNPCTOTE log per person total expenditure.
URBAN a dummy that is 1 for urban households.
HHSIZE household size.
FEMHEAD a dummy that is 1 for households with a female head.
AGEHEAD age of head of household.
EDHEAD education level of head of household.
PLOTSIZE size of household garden.
Source: Regression analysis of HRDS (1996) data.

Table 6.14. Determinants of Per Capita Non-food Expenditure

Parameter	Clothing	Personal care	Health	Education	Household items	Housing	Transport and communications	Energy	Other non-food
Number of observations	5,026	5,026	5,026	5,026	5,026	5,026	5,026	5,026	5,026
Adjusted R^2	0.03	0.06	0.03	0.09	0.08	0.06	0.16	0.09	0.10
INTERCEP	-0.0024*	0.0413	-0.0415	-0.0126	-0.0815	-0.0552	-0.3714	0.5857	-0.1795
LNPCTOTE	0.0030	-0.0005*	0.0039	0.0001*	0.0085	0.0038	0.0334	-0.0362	0.0178
URBAN	0.0064	0.0106	0.0048	0.0047	0.0001*	-0.0020*	0.0049	0.0174	0.0069
HHSIZE	0.0013	-0.0002*	0.0016	0.0017	0.0007	0.0036	0.0029	-0.0060	0.0009
FEMHEAD	0.0021*	0.0048	0.0015*	0.0028	-0.0023	0.0053	-0.0070	0.0046*	-0.0088
AGEHEAD	-0.0002	-0.0002	0.0000*	0.0001	-0.0002	0.0007	-0.0002	0.0003	-0.0001*
EDHEAD	0.0006	0.0002	0.0001*	0.0003	0.0002	0.0003*	0.0003	-0.0004*	0.0004
PLOTSIZE	0.0008	-0.0001*	-0.0007	0.0001*	0.0003	0.0019	0.0004*	-0.0017	0.0001*

INTERCEP intercept.
LNPCTOTE log per person total expenditure.
URBAN a dummy that is 1 for urban households.
HHSIZE household size.
FEMHEAD a dummy that is 1 for households with a female head.
AGEHEAD age of head of household.
EDHEAD education level of head of household.
PLOTSIZE size of household garden.
Source: Regression analysis of HRDS (1996) data.

Table 6.15. *Expenditure Share, Marginal Budget Share, and Income Elasticity by Budget Category*

Budget category	Urban households		Rural households		All households	
	Expenditure share	Income elasticity	Expenditure share	Income elasticity	Expenditure share	Income elasticity
Maize	0.07	0.38	0.12	0.63	0.09	0.53
Rice	0.06	0.84	0.05	1.25	0.06	0.97
Wheat	0.02	1.25	0.01	1.92	0.02	1.37
Potatoes	0.01	1.09	0.01	1.22	0.01	1.13
Other starch	0.05	0.69	0.11	1.13	0.07	0.95
Legumes	0.05	0.58	0.09	0.80	0.07	0.70
Fruit & vegetables	0.07	0.89	0.05	0.87	0.06	0.89
Animal products	0.14	1.01	0.13	1.23	0.14	1.09
Other food	0.13	1.25	0.11	0.99	0.12	1.18
Clothing	0.04	1.10	0.03	1.01	0.04	1.08
Personal care	0.04	1.04	0.03	0.80	0.03	0.99
Health	0.02	1.17	0.01	1.35	0.02	1.22
Education	0.01	1.11	0.01	0.85	0.01	1.01
Household items	0.02	1.66	0.01	1.37	0.01	1.61
Housing	0.04	1.21	0.05	1.02	0.04	1.09
Transport & com.	0.04	1.98	0.02	1.98	0.03	2.05
Energy	0.14	0.73	0.14	0.80	0.14	0.75
Other non-food	0.04	1.46	0.03	1.51	0.04	1.49

Note: See Tables 6.13 and 6.14 for the regression results of the national model.
Source: Expenditure shares calculated from HRDS 1996. Income elasticities estimated from HRDS data using regression analysis.

Table 6.16. Child Malnutrition in 1991-92 and 1996

Study	Category of child	Incidence of moderate malnutrition (percentage of children)		
		Stunting (height-for-age)	Wasting (weight-for-age)	Underweight (weight-for-age)
1991-92 Tanzania Demographic and Health Survey	Child's age			
	0-6 months	12.0	2.1	5.4
	48-59 months	56.8	4.4	27.6
	Child's sex			
	Male	48.1	6.2	28.7
	Female	45.3	5.1	28.9
	All children	46.7	5.6	28.8
1996 Tanzania Demographic and Health Survey	Child's age			
	0-6 months	10.7	5.5	7.0
	48-59 months	46.9	4.2	26.3
	Child's sex			
	Male	44.9	8.1	30.8
	Female	41.9	6.4	30.4
	All children	43.4	7.2	30.6

Note: Moderate malnutrition is defined as 2 standard deviations below the median of the NCHS/CDC/WHO international reference population.
Source: 1991-92 Tanzanian Demographic and Health Survey, cited in World Bank (1995) and 1996 Tanzanian Demographic and Health Survey (Bureau of Statistics (Tanzania) and Macro International Inc. 1997a).

Table 6.17. Nutritional Status of Children by Background Characteristics

Background characteristic	Moderate stunting (percent below −2.5 s.d. the median height for age)	Moderate wasting (percent below −2.5 s.d. the median weight for height)	Moderate underweight (percent below −2.5 s.d. the median weight for age)
Residence			
Mainland	43.6	7.1	30.5
Total urban	32.9	7.6	19.5
Total rural	45.9	7.0	32.9
Zanzibar	37.1	11.0	33.8
Region			
Dodoma	48.1	8.0	34.2
Arusha	43.7	7.2	35.1
Kilimanjaro	33.5	5.6	21.0
Tanga	55.3	4.9	36.2
Morogoro	52.7	4.1	25.5
Coast	51.7	11.2	34.3
Dar-es-Salaam	30.6	8.1	22.2
Lindi	58.6	7.0	41.4
Mtwara	58.0	5.9	35.6
Ruvuma	53.5	5.2	29.4
Iringa	70.5	6.2	48.2
Mbeya	46.9	6.2	20.8
Singida	38.6	7.0	28.4
Tabora	25.7	4.4	14.2
Rukwa	42.0	9.7	30.5
Kigoma	52.5	7.6	43.1
Shinyanga	31.3	6.8	27.8
Kagera	41.6	10.8	36.0
Mwanza	33.8	7.6	27.0
Mara	32.6	8.4	18.9
Education			
No education	49.4	8.5	36.9
Primary incomplete	44.0	7.4	32.9
Primary complete	41.2	6.6	27.7
Secondary+	24.1	5.2	11.9
Total	43.4	7.2	30.6

Source: Bureau of Statistics (Tanzania) and Macro International Inc. (1997a).

7. LINKS BETWEEN AGRICULTURE AND THE REST OF THE ECONOMY

Addressing the issues in this section involves defining whether agriculture is the leader of growth, in the sense that it comes first and provides the necessary stimulus to the creation of other economic activities, or whether it is the follower of growth, as discussed in Section 1. Recalling that discussion, agriculture as a follower of growth benefits from growth originating outside the farm sector, and possibly assists in extending industrial growth through input supply and funding consumer purchases of local industrial output. However, it is not growth's necessary precursor. For agriculture to be an engine of growth in a small, largely open economy, at least some of its major products must lie within the comparative advantage in production of the country.

Comparative advantage activities are the only economically sustainable way bring in new resource inflows into the country[1]. Comparative advantage is a relative concept; it matters not only what the efficiency of the individual activity is, but also what the alternatives are[2].

7.1   Whither Agricultural Comparative Advantage?

The usual partial equilibrium indicator of comparative advantage is the Domestic Resource Cost Ratio (DRC), or some derivative of it (Monke and Pearson 1989). This measure boils down a large number of partial equilibrium assumptions and parameters into a single number that indicates comparative advantage or not. While such measures are hardly infallible, they do serve to organize inquiry into sources of comparative advantage and to make the necessary assumptions explicit.

Estimation of a DRC involves defining a production activity, specifying: a given technology, location of production, end market for output, source of inputs, alternative uses of the primary factors of production used (land, labor, capital, etc.), and the real (or "shadow") value of foreign exchange in terms of domestic currency. The essence of DRC is to compare the best alternative use of the factors of production used to produce one unit of the good in question in terms of foreign exchange (the numerator), to actual net returns in terms of foreign exchange from using the same factors in the activity in question (the denominator). DRCs of less than one are conventionally interpreted to mean that the activity is within the country's comparative advantage.

Because of the myriad assumptions made, generally it is difficult to compare DRCs estimated by different authors at different time periods, except for the most broad-brush purposes. However, sets of DRCs using similar assumptions can be used to rank activities vis-a-vis each other with a fair degree of confidence, because of uniformity in underlying assumptions.

Two independent sets of agricultural DRCs for Tanzania are analyzed here. The first relates to 1991/92 data, on the eve of effective liberalization for most traditional exports. It comes from the 1994 Agricultural Sector Memorandum (World Bank AEOD 1994b). The second consists of a series of detailed calculations by the Netherlands Economic Institute Crop Performance Agricultural Sector Memorandum Team (MAC NEI 1999a-e), using 1997/98 data, supplied to the

---

[1] As compared to foreign aid inflows or short term mineral extraction.

[2] In the old textbook example, even if the permanent secretary is a faster typist than the clerical secretary, society is better off if the former hires the latter, both because the latter might be without work otherwise, and because of the presumption that permanent secretaries contribute more to the social good by governing than by typing.

authors of the present report by the Government of Tanzania, Planning Commission. To the extent possible, comparable activities are identified in terms of item, location, and technology.

DRCs for the earlier and later periods for a selection of agricultural export activities are displayed in Table 7.1, along with rates of change for both DRC and world prices over the period. DRCs in the earlier period indicated stronger comparative advantage (DRC less than 0.5) in cashew, tobacco and paddy rice, and two less traditional export crops: sesame and estate tea. Smallholder beverage crops had lower comparative advantage (i.e. higher DRCs) because of low world prices; cotton was in the doldrums for the same reason. Since DRC as a practical matter is a complex random variable, it is sometimes hard to say with a high degree of confidence that a given activity is less than one in an absolute sense, and thus adds more foreign exchange than producing it forgoes. However, only robusta coffee in Kagera was even close to one (at 0.84). It seems clear that many crops were in Tanzania's comparative advantage to produce and export in 1991/92.

Between the earlier and later periods, real world prices for coffee and tea improved very substantially, leading to higher rankings for smallholder arabica, robusta, and tea. Cotton prices also improved. Thus DRC fell (i.e. improved) substantially for arabica coffee and cotton. It improved marginally for cashew. Otherwise, DRC rose substantially (got less competitive) vis-a-vis the earlier period, principally because of higher labor costs, and not because of world prices, which mostly increased in real terms over the period. The role of labor costs in rising DRC was especially large for estate-produced items such as formal sector tea.

Two main points come out of Table 7.1 and its underlying calculations. First, in 1997/98, the national comparative advantage of Tanzania for the crop activities listed in Table 7.1 was quite robust, with the possible exceptions of estate tea and robusta coffee. Shifting resources into export crops in an undistorted environment would increase the country's access to foreign exchange. Second, the main danger to the competitiveness of Tanzania's export crops comes not from medium-term fluctuations in world prices (which affect the denominator), but from labor costs that seem to be rising faster than output prices (which affect the numerator). The flip-side of a depreciating RER is a cost of non-tradable inputs rising relative to prices of tradable outputs. Given this trend and the fact that labor and purchased inputs are the two main cost elements for export cropping, more labor-intensive crops (tobacco, cotton, and coffee) may continue to lose competitiveness over time, unless the conditions producing an appreciating RER cease.

Beyond the traditional export crops, Tanzania has successful export experience in a number of minor and non-traditional export crops, such as: sesame, groundnuts, pyrethrum, cut flowers, spices, coconut, and oil palm. Despite the hope held out for these items in the early 1990s (World Bank AEOD 1994a), their success by 1997/98 is still to be established. The failure to evolve a regulatory and tax environment capable of attracting large private sector investment in these activities may be a factor.

Non-traditional exports of animal products may yet provide a big source of growth. To date, the main success has been freshwater fish exports from Lake Victoria, as discussed in Section 5. Yet although they grew at a very high rate over the 1990s, they were completely disrupted by the unilateral imposition by the European Union of a health ban on fish imports from East Africa in January 1998. The latter was temporarily lifted and then re-imposed in March 1999 following instances of fish poisoning from pesticides, leading to claims in the press of high net losses to Tanzania, Kenya, and Uganda. Uganda's loss alone was estimated at US$5 million per month in hard currency (Mutaumba-Lule 1999). Tanzania's loss may have been of the order of U.S.$4 million per month, judging from the data in section 5.

128

The fisheries example suggests three reasons for caution: 1) the danger of over-dependence on an export item subject in a very thin market to arbitrary market closure by one external agency, 2) the experience with Lake Victoria fisheries suggests that the environmental sustainability of the resource may have been sacrificed to expediency (Jansen 1996), and 3) despite large foreign exchange earnings, the employment and consumption linkage impact may have been relatively small.

In conclusion, non-traditional and minor export crops and fishery exports may have some promise in the future, but they cannot compete for importance in terms of income or breadth of participation with the traditional export crops. If development of traditional export crops seems necessary to pursue comparative advantage on a broad scale, what are the implications for overall development strategy? The answer will depend on the nature of linkages between agriculture and the rest of the economy.

7.2   Agricultural Linkages to the Rest of the Economy

An intersectoral linkage is a stimulus to one sector from events in another. If it leads to net additional production it is a (real) growth linkage. If it only leads to a re-distribution of income, it is a pecuniary linkage. Traditionally, intersectoral linkages are thought of as being synonymous with increased demand for intermediate goods when production of the base good increases (backwards linkages), or cheapening of production when events in the sector in question cheapen another's inputs (forwards linkages). As pointed out by Hirschman, traditional smallholder agriculture typically does not have many backwards or forwards production linkages to the rest of the economy, at least not on the scale that a manufacturing facility would where the use of intermediate products is high and output might be used as an input to some other good (Hirschman 1958).

Hirschman's view side-steps the point that in an economy that is primarily rural and where people are very poor, and rural areas are relatively isolated, the primary intersectoral linkages occur on the consumption side, based on how poor rural people spend increments to income. In a detailed household-level modeling study of agricultural growth linkages in four African countries, Delgado et al. (1998) recently found that from 80 to 95 percent of total linkages (excluding negligible forward linkages) stemmed from consumption patterns.

Consumption growth linkages occur when increased consumer demand for an item stimulates net new production of the item. As discussed in section 3, this can only occur where consumer incomes are spent on non-tradable items. Otherwise, the increased demand for the tradable will either be met by decreased exports from the local zone (if it is an exportable), or increased imports (if it is an importable). If the good in question is a service or other non-tradable, and if they are elastic in supply, the new demand leads to new local production of the good in question (Delgado et al. 1998). This is because by definition the new demand cannot be fully met by imports to the local zone, nor by decreased exports of the consumption good.

The new demand for the non-tradable either stimulates new production (if supply is price responsive) or drives local prices up (if they are not). If there are under-used local resources that can be brought into production--likely to be the case in rural Tanzania--then such stimulus is likely to lead to real increases in production and incomes. In poor areas such as rural Tanzania, increments to income are largely consumed; even a small additional amount of income can produce a large stimulus if it is replicated many times. One of the attractions of traditional export crops is that they tend to boost the incomes of large numbers of rural people, leading in the aggregate to a major surge in demand for items that often can be (and can only be) produced in the local area concerned.

In sum, whether or not new income in rural areas leads to additional income creation beyond the initial stimulus in an economically sustainable manner depends on four things. First, the additional income must be from the tradable sector, in the sense that new resources are flowing into local rural areas. Second, the initial income stimulus must be widely spread to produce a large aggregate impact. Third, some of the additional items purchased with the additional income must be non-tradables. Fourth, the non-tradable items whose production is stimulated by increased demand must be forthcoming in price-responsive supply.

Conditions one and two are met by traditional export crops produced by smallholders, and could also be met by export crops sold from estates, but only if the extra profits are passed on to workers through increased employment or bonuses. Condition three and four need to be established empirically.

7.3   Consumption Patterns and Non-tradability

Section 6 above established in some detail the responsiveness of rural and urban household consumption patterns to increments in income, using the Household and Rural Development Survey 1993/94 (see Table 6.12). The key parameter for consumption linkages is the "marginal expenditure share" (MES) of each category of goods.[3] This is the percent of increments to income spent on the good. The expenditure (or "income") elasticities in Table 6.12 were in fact the quotient of the MES divided by the average expenditure share for each good. Unlike elasticities, MES convey the absolute amount that consumption of the good in question is likely to increase. Elasticities can be small if average expenditure shares are high (such as for starchy staples), yet the MES can be relatively high, as will be demand pressures on existing supplies if incomes increase. To find out how much of increments to incomes are spent on non-tradables, we need to define the latter in some detail.

Short of carrying out for each good the elaborate exercise given in Section 3 above for maize, rice, and cassava, defining goods as non-tradables is partly a matter of common sense and partly a maintained hypothesis about local markets. Following the discussion in Section 3, all services are non-tradables, since they are by definition produced only at the point of service. Perishable items and items with high bulk-to-value ratios are typically non-tradables in many rural markets. Housing is a non-tradable as are transportation services (but not tradable inputs to transportation, such as petroleum products.)

The detailed commodities enumerated by HRDS 1993/94 (HRDS 1996) were classified by the present research team as tradable or non-tradable. In some cases, a good could be judged tradable in one form (raw wheat and flour) and non-tradable in another (bread), leading to imperfect tradability for the aggregate good called "wheat" consumption. For maize, following Section 3, 25 percent of consumption is judged to be in markets where maize is a non-tradable. Results are shown in Table 7.2. Once detailed sub-items are defined as non-tradable or tradable, increments to consumption of these items can be assigned to either tradable or non-tradable shares of increments to consumption. The latter can be further aggregated, as in Table 7.3, for clarity of presentation.

---

[3] Also known as the "marginal budget share" or the "marginal propensity to consume".

The table shows that urban households in the survey allocated 65 percent of their average expenditure and 70 percent of increments to expenditure on non-tradables. The equivalent figures for rural households were 63 percent of average expenditures and 64 percent of marginal expenditure. Contrary to usual assumptions, we see that both rural and urban households in Tanzania allocate large shares of increments to non-tradable items: 41 percent of total increments to expenditure went to non-tradable food items and 28 percent to non-tradable non-food. The remaining 31 percent of increments to expenditure went to tradable food and non-food items. The results are startling: injecting small amounts of income widely spread in rural and urban areas has the potential to stimulate additional production of a wide variety of imperfectly tradable items.

7.4   Intersectoral Growth Linkages in Tanzania

The marginal expenditure data in the previous sub-section allows a very simple quantification cf the additional income generated by stimulating the agricultural export sector (or any other sector that puts small amounts of additional incomes in the hands of lots of people). The first step is to quantify the maximum increase achievable, or maximum multiplier. The basic idea is that initial income shocks are in part re-spent by receiving households; the households selling consumer items to the shocked households then spend some of their new income on consumer items, and the cycle repeats itself over and over. The limit on this re-spending comes from "leakages" that remove funds from the spending cycle. These notions are formalized as:

Total new spending (TNS) after k periods equals

$$TNS=SUM_k [INITIAL(1-MES_t -s)^k],$$

where SUM is a summation operation, INITIAL is the initial stimulus in money terms, MES_t is the aggregate marginal expenditure share of non-tradables, and s is the share of expenditure going to savings and taxes (in percent).

MES_t and s together represent leakages from the spending cycle: any saving, tax payments, or spending on tradables does not stimulate net new production. The solution to the expression above, as k tends to infinity, is the maximum amount that the initial stimulus can provoke new production.

Assuming that s=0, for simplicity, that k tends to infinity and $MES_t<1$ (by definition), the expression above is an infinite series that converges to

$$1/(1-MES_{nt}),$$

because $MES_{nt}=1-MES_t$. Furthermore, since MES are additive, they can be broken into their component parts to calculate the share of the total multiplier contributed by incremental spending on each sub-sector.

The final step is to take into account the likely fact that few consumer items in Tanzania are likely to be perfectly price responsive (elastic) in supply. Maize, for example, was estimated to have a supply price elasticity of 0.25 in Section 5, implying that a 1 percent price increase would increase production by 0.25 percent. Many non-tradable goods that account for much smaller shares of economic activity than maize may have higher supply elasticities, but still less that infinity. Haggblade, Hammer, and Hazell (1991) estimate that in East African circumstances, simple multipliers of the type given above over-estimate the true multiplier by about 30 percent because of the assumption about perfect elasticity of supply for non-tradables. Therefore the expedient adopted here is to reduce all multiplier estimates by 30 percent across the board. This was done for the HRDS (1996) data in Table 7.4.

The resulting adjusted multiplier is 2.78 for rural households and 3.32 for urban households (Table 7.4). At face value, it implies that every 1,000 shillings of additional household income from a tradable sector leads to an additional 1,780 to 2,320 shillings of income from new production in the non-tradable sectors. These figures have already been scaled down appropriately to adjust from over-optimism in the assumptions. However, even if they were cut in half again, they would still support the view that additions to household income from exportables that are widely spread will stimulate very substantial additional production in the demand-constrained non-tradable sectors.

The findings from the Tanzanian HRDS are in fact quite close to the multipliers of 2 to 2.9 found in Senegal, Burkina Faso, Niger, and Zambia by Delgado *et al.* (1998). They can also be compared to the multipliers of 2 to 2.7 found by Dorosh and Haggblade (1993) in Madagascar, using a Social Accounting Matrix, and 1.4 to 3.1 found in Malawi by Simler (1994).

Further evidence supporting this view can be found for Tanzania using a macroeconomic approach. Wobst (1999) recently completed a CGE model of Tanzania built around a Social Accounting Matrix (SAM) for 1992. The SAM has 56 sectors, of which 21 are agricultural. Wobst performed several new policy experiments for the present study using the 1992 SAM to assess the level of intersectoral multipliers in Tanzania. Results for four experiments are given in the columns of Table 7.5. Each experiment consists of increasing final demand in the sector named at the top of each column, with the effects percolating through the overall economy via the supply and demand relationships specified in the SAM.

In the first experiment, an increase in final demand equivalent in magnitude to 1.0 percent of GDP is administered to the demand for food; the overall impact on the economy is to increase GDP by 2.2 percent. This suggests a multiplier of 2.2. However, it is not clear where in the real world such a stimulus would come from, nor how it would be repeated. This is easier to see in the next two columns, where traditional exports have a multiplier of 1.8. The initial shock could come from something as un-dramatic as a significant rise in world prices, or from increased productivity in the sector that would increase demand for the product. Every 1,000 shillings of additional household income from increased sales of traditional exports leads to 800 shillings of extra income from the non-tradable sectors. If a large number of households are involved, the overall growth effect could be significant.

Non-traditional exports have the highest multiplier, at 2.4, while light manufacturing has the lowest, at 1.2. However, there are still major problems to work out on the institutional side of non-traditional exports, and if only a small number of households are involved, it is not easy to see how the overall effect in this sector would be big, even if the marginal effect is relatively large. The poor showing of light manufacturing illustrates the low overall level of linkages of this sector with the rest of the economy. Furthermore, there is little evidence that Tanzania currently has a comparative advantage in light manufacturing outside its own borders, so even this small multiplier may not be economically sustainable.

In sum, the macroeconomic simulations support the view that significant extra income can be achieved through successful stimulation of export industries that involve lots of people. The macroeconomic multipliers were slightly less optimistic than the simple multipliers using MES, but they still suggest that viable exports can be a productive engine of new growth.

132

7.5   Rural-urban Linkages

The second row in Table 7.5 gives the exact amount in millions of shillings that a one billion shilling sectoral shock is expected to produce, using the 1992 SAM. These additions are broken down into four household sectors receiving income (plus other recipients such as government, not shown). Overall, both the non-traditional export and food sectors would channel more additional income to rural households than would traditional agricultural exports. However, the long run viability of strategies built solely on these sectors is in doubt.

In an absolute sense, development of the agricultural export and food sectors provides a greater stimulus to urban household incomes (508 to 646 million per billion stimulus, depending on the column) than does direct investing in light manufacturing, which is preponderantly urban (378 per billion stimulus). Furthermore, growth linkages between all sectors and the rural non-farm sector are weak (41 to 62 million). Both these findings arise because rural-urban linkages in the model are better developed that urban-urban links, as they probably are in real life.

Empirical work on rural-urban linkages is scarce in Tanzania. The new six-city, Peri-Urban Study by the World Bank (World Bank AFR2M 1999) is an attempt to remedy this. It gathered single-visit data from a total of 598 households interviewed over a six-week period in the Spring of 1998, in peri-urban areas of Dar-es-Salaam, Arusha, Moshi (Kilimanjaro), Mbeya, Mwanza, and Lindi. Interestingly, on the basis of results for all six towns, the authors find no evidence to indicate that farming in peri-urban areas is more commercialized or more intensive than elsewhere in the country. Yet they do note that proximity to the perimeter of the city was strongly correlated with the production and marketing of perishable items such as fruit and vegetables.

Non-farm activities contributed only a modest share of peri-urban household income. Unlike Asia and Latin America, but like most of Africa (Delgado 1997), the share of non-farm income increased sharply and monotonically while going up the income distribution (from 6 percent in the lowest income quintile to 37 percent in the highest income quintile) (World Bank AFR2M 1999). This has been interpreted elsewhere in Africa as evidence that access to capital (or credit) is the binding constraint on income growth (Reardon *et al.* 1994; Delgado 1997). Interestingly, the study shows that access to credit was the main perception by sample members of what was holding them back from increased economic activity.

The finding of lack of agricultural intensification in peri-urban areas is especially surprising, given a seeming abundance of local milk, poultry and pork in Dar-es-Salaam and Arusha. Part of the explanation may lie in the fact that the Peri-Urban Study did not sample inside town limits, which for Dar and Arusha are quite extensive. As discussed in Section 5 above, a recent rapid appraisal of the dairy sector in Tanzania pinpointed the rapid expansion of production in recent years inside the city limits of Dar-es-Salaam and Arusha, noting that the patterns of development depended on proximity of infrastructure, and also the lack of development around the other cities surveyed (MAC Sokoine ILRI 1998). Dar-es-Salaam alone was estimated to have at least 20,000 dairy cows kept within city limits. Combined with the casual observation reported above that livestock feed outlets proliferate immediate upon entering the city limits suggests that poor infrastructure and possible taxation costs of bringing perishables into town (MAC 1999b) may be a hindrance to the agricultural development of the peri-urban areas of the bigger towns. These factors may instead encourage inappropriate and unsustainable development of concentrated livestock production within urban areas.

Another interpretation of the World Bank Peri-Urban Study results, discounted here, is that per capita incomes are in fact not rising in Tanzanian cities, in which case there are not likely to be many growth linkages to observe between urban and peri-urban/rural areas. Intensive high value agricultural items such as milk, eggs, chicken, fruits, and vegetables tend to be non-tradables in peri-urban markets. At best, they compete against imports, and imperfectly so. They typically have higher income elasticities of demand than other agricultural items. If income is growing broadly in urban areas, for whatever reason, animal products and horticulture will be in high demand, with rising prices and local production. Presumably the reverse is true as well. Peri-urban agriculture almost always develops as a follower of urban development, and not as a leader of urban growth.

Another interpretation of the results of the Peri-Urban Study is the possibility that incomes are only growing in urban areas where either structural adjustment reforms in industry or spin-offs from higher spending by foreign aid agencies are having a favorable impact on non-agricultural service and manufacturing incomes, such as in Dar, Arusha, and possibly, Tanga. Towns dependent on agriculture as the motor of growth--such as Dodoma, Tabora, Iringa, Mwanza, and Lindi--may not be doing well in the current climate of dis-incentives to agricultural production. If so, there is no reason why their peri-urban areas would be doing better.

Table 7.6 provides some circumstantial evidence to support the previous points. The cells of the table are ratios of retail milk prices between the major urban center listed and an associated peri-urban supply market. These ratios have increased steadily over the 1987/90 to 1995/98 period in Dar and Arusha, and only in the second half of the period in Tanga. For the other pairs of markets listed, the urban market has become progressively cheaper relative to the peri-urban market.

Thus the peri-urban to urban market relationship may be different in the cities that are growing compared to those that are not. We hypothesize that Dar, Arusha, and Tanga prices are growing faster than their affiliated markets because demand is increasingly more rapidly than milk transport from peri-urban areas (not milk production) can keep up. The reverse is true in the other towns, where lack of demand and increasing local production are keeping urban prices low relative to outlying markets. In the first case, the issue is to reduce marketing costs. In the second case, the issue is to find an economically sustainable engine of growth that will fuel increased consumption of high-value non-tradable agricultural items that peri-urban areas typically produce.

Resolving the competing explanations of the empirical findings of the survey underlying the Peri-Urban Study requires further investigation in the absence of hard evidence one way or the other. Peri-urban agriculture is rarely a lead sector in economic growth; given the higher opportunity cost of labor and land close to big cities, the production involved is typically high-value non-tradables stimulated by urban demand growth. This is different from exportables, which are capable of breaking demand constraints in semi-open economies. The empirical work underlying the Peri-Urban Study did not explore these issues and cannot be used either to support or condemn economic growth strategies based on agricultural tradables.

Table 7.1. Domestic Resource Cost Ratios (DRC) and World Prices for Major Tradable Crops

Crop	Location	Technology	1991-92 DRC	1991-92 Rank (1 is best)	1997-98 DRC	1997-98 Rank (1 is best)	World price 1997-98 $/ton	Percent change in DRC (- is good) 1991-92 to 1997-98	Percent change in deflated world prices (+ is good) 1991-92 to 1997-98
Sesame	Dodoma	Medium input	0.23	1	0.31	2	800	+35	+28
Cashew	Mtwara	Medium input, raw	0.27	2	0.26	1	530	-1	-2
Tea	Iringa	Medium input, estate	0.37	3	0.55	5	1,310	+49	+82
Tobacco	Tabora	Medium input, flue-cured	0.40	4	0.56	6	2,300	+40	+7
Paddy	Shinyanga	Medium input, lowland	0.45	5	0.78	8	213	+73	+5
Maize	Iringa	Medium input	0.59	6	0.72	7	104	+22	0
Coffee	Arusha	Arabica, improved	0.66	7	0.32	3	2,700	-52	+213
Tea	Iringa	Medium input, smallholder	0.67	8	0.92	10	1,310	+37	+82
Cotton (lint)	Shinyanga	Medium input, mixed soils, oxen	0.68	9	0.50	4	1,390	-26	-3
Coffee	Kagera	Robusta, no fungicide	0.84	10	0.86	9	1,900	+2	+54

Note: The DRCs quoted above were prepared by different teams at different times. The earlier set includes little data on the underlying assumptions and they were matched as carefully as possible with the very detailed and elaborately documented second set, which was used to specify the location and technology used. Comparisons between the two sets are therefore only indicative. The changes in relative rankings within years are robust, however, and support the rest of the analysis. These figures are identical to those using the same assumptions in World Bank COD (1999) except for coffee, where World Bank COD (1999) reports DRCs of 0.27 for Arabica coffee and 0.56 for Robusta under medium technology assumptions.

Source: 1991-92: World Bank AEOD (1994b-c). 1997-98: MAC NEI (1999d-e). Results and underlying calculations provided courtesy of the Planning Commission, Government of Tanzania.

Table 7.2. Share of Expenditure on Non-tradable Commodities

Aggregate commodity groups	Commodity groups	Share of non-tradables in category
Staples		72
	Maize	25
	Rice	0
	Wheat	54
	Potatoes	100
	Other starch	100
	Legumes	83
Animal products		82
Other food		90
	Fruit and vegetables	100
	Other food	85
Non-food items		58
	Clothing	0
	Personal care	16
	Health	38
	Education	91
	Household items	7
	Housing	100
	Transportation and Communication	74
	Energy	66
	Other non-food	79

Source: Aggregations of average household expenditure on individual non- tradable items, with household averages weighted by quantity consumed by that household in total sample consumption.

Table 7.3. Household Average and Marginal Expenditure Shares by Major Sector, 1993-94
(percent)

Commodity groups	Urban households	Rural households	All households
Average expenditure shares			
Tradables			
Staples	13	17	15
Animal products	3	2	2
Other food	2	2	2
Non-food products	16	17	16
Non-tradables			
Staples	13	22	17
Animal products	11	11	11
Other food	17	14	16
Non-food products	24	16	20
Marginal expenditure shares			
Tradables			
Staples	9	15	11
Animal products	2	3	3
Other food	2	2	2
Non-food products	17	16	16
Non-tradables			
Staples	9	21	14
Animal products	12	13	12
Other food	20	13	18
Non-food products	28	17	24
MBS of non-tradables	70	64	68

Source: Average expenditure shares calculated from HRDS 1996. Marginal expenditure shares calculated from the coefficients of a Working-Leser semi-log regression.

Table 7.4. Potential Additional Income to Households From Re-spending of an Extra Tsh 1,000 of Household Income From Tradables

	Urban households	Rural households	All households
Overall multiplier[a]	3.32	2.78	3.09
Net increments to income[b]	1,627	1,248	1,462
Sources of growth in income[c]			
Staples	219	405	306
Animal products	275	246	263
Other food	474	260	384
Non-food	659	338	509

a Consumption growth multipliers estimated as the solution to an infinite series $1/(1\text{-leakage})^t$ where leakages from savings are assumed to be zero, where additional consumption of tradables is assumed either to decrease exports or to increase imports, where non-tradables are assumed to be infinitely price elastic, and where non-tradable intermediate inputs are ignored.

b The initial income stimulus is netted out and results are decreased by 30 percent to allow for the unrealistic assumption of a perfectly elastic supply of non-tradables.

c The major sector whose non-tradables are stimulated by new spending and their total potential contributions to household income as a result of the initial stimulus.

Source: Calculated from the coefficients of a Working-Leser semi-log regression.

Table 7.5. Differential Economy-wide Effects of an Initial Increase in Sectoral Final Demand

Economy-wide effects		Food	Traditional agricultural exports	Non-traditional exports	Light manufacturing
		(elasticities)			
Percent final increase in GDP at factor cost stemming from an initial sectoral stimulus equivalent to 1 percent of GDP		2.2	1.8	2.4	1.2
		(million 1992 Tsh)			
Increments to income per initial 1 billion Tsh stimulus	GDP	2,225	1,779	2,431	1,209
	Households, urban, agriculture	366	247	371	151
	Households, urban, non-farm	267	261	275	227
	Households, rural, agriculture	1,236	893	1,380	522
	Households, rural, non-farm	62	55	62	41

Note: Results are from separate experiments by sector using a 1992 social accounting matrix (SAM) for Tanzania. The SAM has 56 sectors, of which 21 are agricultural, and four household types. The sectors above are aggregated from the sectors of the model.
Source: Calculations kindly performed by Peter Wobst of IFPRI using a social accounting matrix (SAM) for Tanzania contained in his Ph.D. dissertation for the University of Hohenheim, Germany. For details of the underlying model, see Wobst (1999).

Table 7.6. Milk (Maziwa) Prices in Associated Urban and Rural Feeder Markets 1987-98

Ratio	1987-90	1991-94	1995-98
Urban price increase relative to feeder market price			
Dar-es-Salaam/Kisarawe	0.9	1.0	1.2
Arusha/Mbulu	1.3	1.7	1.9
Tanga/Lushoto	1.5	1.3	1.9
Urban price decrease relative to feeder market price			
Dodoma/Mpwapwa	2.1	2.1	1.8
Tabora/Urambo	1.9	1.6	1.3
Iringa/Mafinga	1.1	1.4	0.8
Mwanza/Geita	1.9	1.9	1.5
Lindi/Newala	1.2	0.8	0.8

Source: Calculated from annual ratios of retail milk prices collected by MAC, Market Development Bureau.

8. SUMMARY, CONCLUSIONS, AND RECOMMENDATIONS

This final Section summarizes insights derived from each Section above, to answer the four questions of Section 1: the net impact of policy on agricultural incentives since 1986, agricultural performance since 1986 in the light of those incentives, the impact of agricultural performance on poverty and food security, and the links between agricultural performance and overall economic development. It then builds an overall conclusion about the role of agriculture in economic growth and poverty alleviation in Tanzania at the present time. Key elements of a workable, long-term, agriculture-led growth strategy for Tanzania are reviewed, leading to a list of urgent nearer-term priorities for action.

8.1   Impact of Policy Reforms on Agricultural Incentives Since 1986

The task of identifying the net effect of policy changes on the agricultural sector is not easy. In addition to data limitations and discrepancies, it is necessary to separate the influences of macroeconomic and sectoral policies, which are not necessarily compatible. Then there are the influences of weather, world prices, and other exogenous events. Finally, the data mostly permit to comparing the situation before and after reforms were implemented, while the real issue is what would have happened in the absence of those policies.

What are the Policy Changes That Have Affected Agriculture?

- From 1986 to 1993, the real exchange rate depreciated significantly, stimulating the production and dampening the consumption of tradable goods such as export crops.

The depreciation of the RER occurred through rapid devaluation of the nominal exchange rate by more than the difference in inflation rates between Tanzania and its trading partners. By the early 1990s, the official rate was on par with the market rate. As will be discussed later, agricultural exports did not respond until export marketing was liberalized in the early 1990s.

- Since 1993, currency depreciation has failed to keep pace with the excess of domestic over world inflation, reducing the incentives to produce tradable goods including export crops, rice, and wheat.

Speculating about the cause of this reversal is outside the scope of this report. Yet it must be noted that as a consequence much of the realignment of prices of tradable and non-tradable goods achieved over the period 1986-1993 has been lost. The appreciating RER makes imported foodstuffs more attractive and affordable to domestic consumers. It makes Tanzanian agricultural exports (50 to 70 percent of total merchandise exports) less attractive to foreign buyers, with the result that real prices paid to producers need to fall to very low levels in order to be able to sell internationally.

- Food crop marketing was largely deregulated in the second half of the 1980s.

Tanzania moved from a marketing system controlled by crop authorities and cooperatives to a liberalized market in which traders and cooperatives compete to provide marketing services. Movement controls were relaxed in 1984 and abolished in 1987. Private traders were first allowed to buy from cooperatives and later allowed to purchase food crops from farmers. Fixed pan-territorial prices were abandoned, replaced by floor prices, references prices, and finally market prices.

- In the first half of the 1990s, Tanzanian liberalized input distribution and export marketing.

Fertilizer subsidies were removed in phases from 1991 to 1995, as private traders were allowed to import and distribute fertilizer. Private traders began to purchase export crops, eventually replacing the marketing boards.

- Central government expenditure on agriculture has fallen both in absolute real terms and as a percentage of total expenditure, although recent as yet un-funded budget projections show planned improvement.

The fiscal savings associated with the elimination of inputs subsidies and the end of loss-making commercial activities by the National Milling Corporation have not been redirected to vital public support for the agricultural sector such as research, extension, quality control, and price information. Rather the savings appear to have been dedicated to reducing overall expenditure.

How Have the Policy Reforms Affected Crop Prices?

- The market-determined prices of food crops in the early 1990s were substantially higher in real terms than the official procurement prices of the 1980s, but data do not exist on the black market prices many farmers obtained in the 1980s. Real producer prices of food fell sharply in the mid-1990s.

Market prices in the 1980s were 50-200 percent higher than the official procurement prices of the 1980s, any many farmers in the 1980's sold their harvest outside the official system. Real producer prices of maize, paddy, wheat, and sorghum/millet fell substantially in 1995-1997. First, international commodity prices have fallen substantially in the 1990s. Second, prices in the early 1990s were affected by the drought in southern Africa and associated Tanzanian maize exports. Third, since 1993 the real exchange rate has appreciated making imports of maize, wheat, and rice less costly relative to domestic goods. As a result, net imports of maize, wheat, and rice (including food aid) have increased to over 100 thousand tons per annum since 1993.

- The behavior of agricultural prices depends on whether food is tradable or non-tradable.

The prices of tradable goods are largely determined by world prices, the exchange rate, and trade policy, while the prices of non-tradables are driven primarily by changes in domestic supply and, to a lesser extent, demand. Furthermore, tradability is a characteristic of markets, not of goods. The tradability of the same good may vary within a country, being greater near the ports and along major transport routes.

- Econometric analysis of food prices suggests that rice is largely tradable, cassava is largely non-tradable, and maize is highly tradable, but only in the more accessible regions of the country.

Using monthly data for 44 markets and 15 years, we test whether retail prices are influenced more by world prices and the exchange rate or by the size of the most recent harvest. Rice prices are strongly influenced by world prices throughout Tanzania. Cassava prices are unaffected by world prices but strongly affected by domestic supply. Maize prices are affected by world prices in

142

regions that are more accessible, but in isolated regions only domestic supply shows a significant effect.

- The non-tradability of a number of major food items has implications for Tanzanian agricultural strategy.

In a pure open economy, national income is greatest when resources are devoted to sectors with a comparative advantage, i.e. export sectors. In a closed economy, production must adapt to local demand. But Tanzania is best classified as a semi-open economy, defined as one in which a significant part of the food sector is non-tradable. In such an economy, it is necessary to maintain a balance between the tradable and non-tradable sectors. A policy of food self-sufficiency would reduce income by producing goods that would be cheaper to import. At the same time, stagnation in the non-tradable food sector would result in higher wages and choke off the expansion of tradable production.

- Export crops were implicitly taxed by the overvaluation of the Tanzanian shilling in the 1970s and 1980s.

Between 1970 and 1985, inflation raised the price of non-tradables by a factor of 12, while depreciation barely doubled the shilling price of tradable goods. The result was to drastically reduce the incentives to produce and sell export crops through official channels. Foreign exchange rationing was necessary to limit the importation of artificially cheap rice and wheat. And restrictions on imported consumer goods further reduced the incentives of farmers to produce for sale.

- During the late 1980s and early 1990s, successive devaluations reduced the implicit taxation of export crops and livestock.

From 1986 to 1993, the nominal exchange rate increased by a factor of 18, far outpacing the six-fold increase in domestic prices. The net effect was a five-fold depreciation of the real exchange rate. The devaluations were successful in eliminating the black market and alleviating balance of payment pressures.

- The devaluations of the late 1980s increased real producer prices but less than would be expected given the size of the devaluations.

Between 1986 and 1993, the real producer prices of six of the eight main export crops rose 24 to 68 percent (cotton and robusta prices fell). This was less than would be expected given the size of the devaluations for two reasons. First, the real FOB prices fell for five of the crops. In the case of coffee, world prices fell by about 65 percent, largely offsetting the potential benefits of the devaluations for producers. Second, the crop authorities increased their marketing margins for seven of the eight, absorbing part of the benefits of the devaluation. In the case of cotton and flue-cured tobacco, the parastatal went from paying farmers 50 percent more than the FOB price in 1986 to paying them less than half the FOB price in 1993.

- Since 1993, real producer prices for all the major export crops have fallen between 25 and 70 percent

Since this is the period that private traders began to purchase and export, it is tempting to think that they have conspired to increase marketing margins. In fact, marketing margins have fallen for

143

five of the six commodities that have been liberalized (tea and pyrethrum are not yet fully liberalized). Nor have world prices fallen during this period. Rather the explanation for the falling producer prices is the appreciation of the real exchange rate since 1993.

How Have These Policy Reforms Affected the Costs of Marketing and Production?

- Econometric analysis reveals that food marketing margins have fallen since 1986.

Using monthly data on retail prices in 44 markets in Tanzania, we show that that marketing margins for maize, rice, and wheat between Dar and other cities have fallen over 1986-1998, a trend that is statistically significant. For example, since 1986 maize marketing margins have decreased 40 percent in real terms, while rice margins have fallen by 11 percent. These changes presumably reflect the increased efficiency and lower cost of private traders in a competitive market compared to the previous three-tiered government regulated markets for food crops.

- The analysis also indicates that food crop marketing margins are affected by the distance between markets, transportation infrastructure, and seasonality.

Marketing margins rise with distance but the per kilometer cost falls with distance. Although not surprising, these results confirm that marketing margins are roughly proportional to transportation costs, consistent with the hypothesis of competitive markets. Margins are also lower in towns that are ports or on the line-of-rail. These results confirm the value of investments in transportation infrastructure as a means of reducing margins and promoting market integration. Seasonality has a significant effect on marketing margins, implying that transport rates rise during periods of peak demand.

- Devaluation and input subsidy removal have significantly increased the price of fertilizer, which, combined with lower producer prices, has adversely affected the incentive for fertilizer use.

The fertilizer subsidy was reduced from 78 percent in 1990-91 to zero in 1994-95.

- Fertilizer use has fallen sharply, particularly on maize, although the impact on maize production may not be very large.

National fertilizer use has fallen from around 120 thousand tons in 1990 to about 65 thousand tons in 1996. Given the physical return to fertilizer use, we argue that even if all the reduction were from applications to maize, maize output should have fallen by less than 5 percent. The small impact of fertilizer prices is confirmed by the supply response analysis in which the impact of fertilizer prices was statistically insignificant. Finally, it is worth noting that average maize yields have not declined since the late 1980s when fertilizer subsidies were in effect.

- Purchased agricultural inputs are not widely used by Tanzanian farmers: only 15 percent use fertilizer, 19 percent use pesticides, and 27 percent use improved seed.

This has adverse effects on yields and quality, particularly in the case of coffee and cotton.

- An important unresolved issue is whether input demand is constrained because the returns do not justify the cost and risk or because of the scarcity of input credit

The answer will vary from one crop to another and from one region to another. In general, we expect the profitability of inputs and thus input demand to decline in more remote areas, both due to both lower farm-gate producer prices and higher farm-gate input costs.

- Crop budget analysis suggests that at current prices, fertilizer use on maize is simply not profitable in many situations, though the result depends on soils, rainfall, and proximity to markets.

If fertilizer is not profitable, then credit is not the problem. Strategies to expand input use must instead focus on reducing marketing and transportation costs. The goal should be to achieve optimal use of inputs rather than maximum use of inputs.

- In the case of export crops, particularly those grown in accessible regions, the constraint is more likely to be credit. The promotion of institutions that can provide inputs on credit, particularly to producers of high-value crops (including export crops), is a key avenue to stimulating the agricultural sector.

Just 5 percent of Tanzanian farmers obtain credit in a given year. A variety of experiments are underway to develop an institutional framework to facilitate input credit for export crop producers. The central problem is how to ensure those providing inputs on credit that they will be able to recover the loans at harvest. This is more difficult in a liberalized output marketing system because farmers can avoid repayment by selling to another buyer.

8.2   Performance of the agricultural Sector Since 1986

Some controversy has arisen over the performance of the Tanzanian agricultural sector. In particular, a recent study identified an apparent discrepancy between food production data that stagnation and agricultural GDP data that showed strong growth. Resolving this data discrepancy has implications for our understanding of how the reforms have affected the agricultural sector.

What is the Source of the Discrepancies in the Agricultural Data?

- Agricultural production statistics in Tanzania have suffered from inconsistency among the three main sources of data, but they have improved in recent years.

The three sources are the National Accounts section of the National Bureau of Statistics (NBS), the Agricultural Statistics Unit (ASU) of the Ministry of Agriculture and Cooperatives (MAC), and the Crop Monitoring and Early Warning Unit (CMEWU) of the MAC. The capacity for survey-based production estimates has increased over time, and production estimates since 1993 have been largely based on national sample surveys.

- We concur with the conclusions of Kiregyera et al (1999), Mlay (1999), and Komba (1999) that the food production data used by the NBS in calculating agricultural GDP are seriously flawed and that the data generated by the ASU are more accurate.

The NBS production estimates are based on simple extrapolations forward and backward from the 1991-92 Household Budget Survey and are highly implausible. The CMEWU estimates are pre-harvest forecasts useful for anticipating shortages but not for evaluating the long-term performance of the agricultural sector. The ASU estimates are the most reliable figures of the three. Nonetheless, it should be noted that before 1993 even ASU estimates were based on the subjective reporting of village extension officers.

- Replacing the NBS food production data with ASU food production data does not substantially alter the trends in agricultural GDP since 1986.

The NBS estimates show the six main food crops growing 3.6 percent per year over 1986-1998, while the ASU estimates yield a growth rate of 3.5 percent.

- Replacing NBS data for three traditional export crops with data from the ASU, however, results in an upward revision in agricultural GDP growth.

The NBS data suggest that the value of export crops has grown just 3.0 percent per year since 1986, while the ASU data indicate a more respectable 5.4 percent annual growth rate.

What Has Been the Performance of Agriculture Since 1985?

- Maize production has grown an annual rate of 2.4 percent over 1985-1998, somewhat less than the population growth rate of 2.8 percent.

On the one hand, it is a matter of concern that maize production has fallen (slightly) in per capita terms since 1985. On the other hand, this growth rate is fairly respectable given the declining real producer price and the large increase in fertilizer prices. The removal of fertilizer subsidies does not seem to a major factor in the slow growth: maize production actually grew faster (2.7 percent) in the 1990s when the subsidy was being phased out. Effective demand constraints linked to high marketing costs probably play an important role in preventing maize output from growing more quickly than population.

- Rice and wheat production have grown rapidly since the pre-reform period, presumably reflecting demand growth.

Since 1985, rice output has expanded three-fold and wheat production has grown by 60 percent. Both commodities have high income elasticities of demand, and both are consumed in greater quantities by urban households. Thus, income growth and urbanization led to higher demand for rice and wheat. In addition, devaluation has made imported wheat and rice more expensive, raising the producer price of both crops, at least until 1994.

- Most of the other staple crops have grown at the rate of population growth, albeit with considerable fluctuation from year to year.

The growth rates of sorghum/millet, beans, cassava, sweet potatoes, and bananas tend to track population growth, aside from weather-related fluctuations. As staple foods, limited demand prevents them from expanding any more rapidly.

- In general, food crop production grew rapidly in the late 1980s, before slowing to the rate of population growth in the 1990s

During the late 1980s, staple food crops grew 4.3 percent annually while other food crops grew at 3.0 percent. Since 1990, the annual growth rates have fallen to 3.0 and 2.8 percent, respectively. One interpretation is that food crop production responded to the liberalization of domestic food markets in the late 1980s, but have now reached a saturation point, with the exception of wheat and rice.

- Export crop production was stagnant in the late 1980s but has grown dramatically in the 1990s.

Export crop production expanded just 1.8 percent per year over the late 1980s. In contrast, the growth rate in the 1990s has been 7.7 percent per year. Strong growth in cashew nuts and tobacco have offset declines in coffee.

- Small-scale dairy production has clearly grown rapidly since 1986, mostly within urban areas, and the same is thought to be the case for eggs, poultry meat, and swine production, although the statistics on these sub-sectors are very uncertain.

The circumstantial evidence confirming direct but scanty evidence of this growth (other than dairy), most of which comes from single-period household surveys, includes evidence of population growth, urbanization, and measured high propensities for urban people to consume these items. On the other hand, most of the additional production seems to come from within the towns themselves and from rural areas. The observed lack of this sort of activity in peri-urban areas suggests that infrastructure problems and other barriers to local trade such as district-level taxation may be a serious constraint to peri-urban agricultural development.

- Using ASU data on production of the six main food crops and three traditional export crops, and without modifying current livestock estimates, we calculate that agricultural GDP has grown 3.5 percent per year since 1986.

This calculation uses the NBS figures for minor food crops and livestock activity, both of which are subject to modification in light of ASU statistics. Thus, this figure should be considered highly tentative until the NBS fully re-estimates agricultural GDP, including a review of the underlying livestock assumptions.

What Factors Affect Agricultural Supply?

- Econometric analysis of price and production data confirm that farmers respond to price incentives, adjusting production of both food and cash crop according to relative prices.

Using annual-regional panel data, we estimated the supply response to price for five crops: maize, paddy, coffee, cotton, and cashew nut. The short-term supply elasticities of maize and paddy were 0.25 and 0.61, respectively. The estimated supply elasticity of cotton was 1.0, while that for cashew nut was 0.84. The fact that the production of cashew nut, a tree crop, responds within one year of a price change probably reflects farmer response in sulfur application and harvesting intensity. Coffee supply responds to price changes only after three years does not respond to price changes until the third year, as expected for a tree crop with a three-year gap between planting and the first harvest.

- In the analysis of the supply response of maize, paddy, coffee, cotton, and cashew nut, the fertilizer price does not have a statistically significant effect for any of the five commodities.

This is somewhat surprising given the large increase in fertilizer prices in the early 1990s. One possible explanation is that fertilizer use is determined by factors other than price, such as availability or access to credit. Alternatively, the use of fertilizer may be so low that fertilizer price changes have negligible effects on output.

8.3   Poverty, Food Security, and Nutrition

The government of Tanzania places a high priority on reducing poverty and food insecurity. Achieving these objectives is closely linked to the performance of the agricultural sector because most of the poor earn most of their income from agriculture and because Tanzanian farmers supply the overwhelming majority of food consumed in the country. Thus, trends in poverty and nutrition are important indirect measures of the performance of the agricultural sector and, more broadly, the success of the reforms. In addition, the patterns in poverty and malnutrition provide useful information for the design of policy, including agricultural policy.

Who is Poor and Has the Poverty Rate Changed Over Time?

- Although it is difficult to compare household income and expenditure data across time, the evidence indicates that between mid-1970s and the early 1990s incomes have risen and poverty rates have fallen.

This conclusion is based on the comparison of the 1976 Household Budget Survey and the 1991 Cornell-ERB survey analyzed by Sarris and Tinios (1994) and the World Bank (1994), as well as our own analysis of the 1993 HRDS data. Since the period 1976-1984 was one of ever deepening economic crisis, it is safe to assume that any progress made between the two surveys occurred since the reforms were launched in the mid-1980s. The two studies cited above differ in whether urban or rural incomes grew more quickly and even in their estimates of per capita expenditure in the Cornell-ERB survey. These discrepancies highlight the extreme caution that must be exercised in comparing poverty rates across time.

- Poverty is primarily a rural phenomenon in Tanzania.

The incidence of poverty is twice as great in rural areas as in urban area, while the severity of poverty is three times greater. Furthermore, urban incomes are 2-3 times greater than rural incomes. Finally, rural households lag behind urban households in almost every physical indicator of living standard: housing type, electrification, access to clean water, ownership of consumer durables, and incidence of child malnutrition.

- After controlling for education, farm size, place of residence, and other household characteristics, farmers that grow cash crops have higher incomes than those that do not.

This conclusion is based on econometric analysis of 5,184 households in the 1993 HRDS data. The result was driven mainly by the higher incomes of coffee farmers, holding other factors constant. It is interesting to note that coffee farmers tend to be poorer than the average Tanzanian, but they are better off than other rural farm households with similar education, farm size, and other characteristics.

What is the Food Security Situation in Tanzania?

- According to FAO data, apparent per capita food consumption has declined since 1986, but a number of factors suggest that the data are not reliable.

The data are suspect because they imply an implausibly high level of per capita caloric intake. In addition, such a dramatic fall in food consumption should be reflected in household survey data and/or nutrition indicators. In fact, household survey data show rising incomes over this period (see above), food prices have fallen since the late 1980s (see above), and nutrition indicators show either improvement or no change since 1986 (see below).

- According to data from the Agricultural Statistics Unit of the MAC, apparent per capita food consumption has been relatively stable since the early 1990s when survey-based production estimates began.

According to the data, apparent per capita food consumption was higher in the 1980s than in the 1990s. This finding contradicts indirect measures of food security including estimates of household income, real food prices, and nutrition indicators, as discussed above.

- Household food security, measured by the per capita value of food consumption, varies significantly as a function of place of residence, household size, farm size, occupation, and whether or not the household grows cash crops.

This finding is based on econometric analysis of the household data in the HRDS. Food security (as defined here) is lower in large, rural, female-headed households that grow crops on a small farm and do not earn income from livestock, wages, or non-farm self-employment. Food security appears to be better in households that grow cash crops. These results should be interpreted with some caution, however, given the fact that the per capita value of food consumption is a crude measure of household food security.

- Demand analysis using the HRDS reveals that income elasticity for maize is relatively low, while those of wheat, potatoes, animal products, and rice are relatively high.

The low income elasticity for maize implies that maize demand will grow much more slowly than the growth in per capita income, particularly in urban areas. The higher income elasticities for the other food items is not surprising, given that they are more costly sources of calories. As households become richer, they begin to shift from low-cost sources of calories, such as maize and starchy tubers, toward more expensive sources of calories.

- The demand analysis also suggests that urbanization is likely to shift food demand toward preferred staples and high-value foods.

According to our analysis of the HRDS data, after holding income, household size, education, and other variables constant, urban households spend more on wheat, rice, white potatoes, and animal products than do rural households. At the same time, urban households spend less on maize, cassava, and sweet potatoes.

Has Nutrition Improved or Worsened?

- Various nutrition and health indicators have shown considerable improvement in the decades following independence.

The rates of infant mortality and maternal mortality have fallen dramatically since independence, while life expectancy has risen. The specter of HIV/AIDS, however, threatens to reverse some of these gains.

- Available evidence indicates that nutrition has either improved or has remained unchanged since the mid-1980s when the reforms were implemented.

The most important source of information about changes in nutritional status is the comparison of the 1991 Tanzanian Demographic and Health Survey (TDHS) and the 1996 TDHS. The rate of stunting (a measure of chronic malnutrition) among children under five years fell between the two surveys, while the rate of wasting (a measure of recent or acute malnutrition) rose slightly.

8.4   The Role of Agriculture in Overall Economic Development

To finally answer the question: "follower or leader of growth?" it is necessary to see if agriculture is still capable of leading economic development in Tanzania. The sector is clearly large enough to have an aggregate impact on national growth. The next question is what has happened to the sector's comparative advantage after all the changes over the 1990's. In small, open economies, lead sectors must either produce directly exportable items or through their output lower the costs of production of tradables. Given an affirmative response to the last question, then a further element desirable in a lead sector is that it creates large spin-off effects, in the form of intersectoral linkages. Growing agriculture, for example, would have to be clearly linked to helping other sectors growing through cheaper inputs or higher demand for output. Finally, "lead" is a relative term, so there is always the question of what are the alternatives, and are they better?

8.5   Tanzania's Comparative Advantage in Agriculture

The report did not investigate Tanzania's comparative advantage in sectors other than agriculture, but it did find:

- Traditional export crops still remain within Tanzania's comparative advantage, but rising living costs since 1994 (and not falling world prices) are beginning to reduce the clear advantage once held.

Comparative advantage is important because it is the basis of competitiveness of local production on both internal and external markets. Competitiveness is the requirement for staying in business on a sustained basis. The impact of rising living costs is to raise wages relative to the value of output, without raising the standard of living of workers. It is the microeconomic manifestation of an appreciating real exchange rate. The direction of change since 1994 is reminiscent of the period before 1986. Looking at alternatives to traditional export crops, the report found:

- Most non-traditional export crops may be useful as highly profitable niche activities, but cannot play the same widespread role as the traditional crops because of the much smaller number of people involved.

The same policy environment useful for promoting traditional exports will also be beneficial for promoting non-traditional export crops and fishery items. While these are useful activities, they tend to be restricted to a small number of actors and are not likely to have the widespread poverty alleviation impact of traditional export cropping by smallholders. Furthermore, the report emphasized that growth-leading sectors need to be able to produce widespread increments to incomes in rural areas, in order to take advantage of intersectoral growth linkages that stem from the effects of consumer spending.

- Other non-traditional but high value agricultural export activities may hold considerable promise for generating increased foreign exchange, although their direct employment impacts and associated demand linkages may be less than those of traditional and non-traditional export crops.

Exports of fishery items, seaweed, and live small animals tend to fall under this category. There is little doubt from past experience that Tanzania can do well in these items. However, the perishable (or disease-prone) and very quality-sensitive nature of the products requires a high degree of organization and is usually associated with capital-intensive production and transport methods. Furthermore, the use of common property resources such as Lake Victoria or brackish water in marine estuaries in fisheries production requires a high degree of environmental monitoring and enforcement that is not without cost.

Inter-sectoral Growth Linkages

The report established that transfer costs within Tanzania are very high (of the order of US$ 0.14 - 0.18 per ton/km). This means that many goods in inland markets are in effect de-linked from world trade. Analysis of survey data showed that consumers spend as much as two-thirds of their increments to income on non-tradable items. This high degree of non-tradability in purchases means that economic activity in rural areas is dependent on purchasing power coming in to local households from outside the local area, to stimulate demand for local products.

- Export agriculture has major growth linkages with the non-farm sector, but through the consumption side and not through the production side. Estimated expenditure multipliers are of the order of 2 to 3.

This means that Tsh 1,000 of new household income from sales of export crops in a remote area can lead to a further Tsh 2,000 in additional local employment in the production of non-tradable goods and services. The simple kinds of multipliers constructed in Section 7 to support this view are sometimes criticized as being too partial equilibrium in nature. Therefore a more aggregated experiment was run using a 56 sector Social Accounting Matrix for Tanzania based on 1992 prices and resource flows.

- Experiments with the 1992 SAM for Tanzania show that a one billion shilling stimulus to GDP generated in the traditional export crop sector leads to a total additional 1.8 billion shilling increase in overall GDP.

While this is slightly less optimistic than the partial equilibrium multiplier analysis, it leads to the same conclusions: there is a large extra return from the non-tradable sectors when export cropping takes off. Furthermore, export cropping has far more growth linkages than urban light manufacturing.

- A one billion stimulus to GDP generated in light manufacturing adds only 1.2 billion to GDP, or an additional return of 20 percent from spin-offs.

Thus export agriculture had additional spin-off effects of 80 percent, whereas urban light manufacturing had spin-offs of only 20 percent.

Even if the main constituency were purely urban, boosting export cropping is a more effective way of increasing urban incomes than investing in urban light manufacturing.

- Stimulus of the traditional export and food sectors in the SAM provide one to two thirds higher income increases for urban households after linkage effects than does direct stimulus of the light manufacturing sector.

This is because of the greater links of the export cropping sector to items produced by urban areas than the links of light manufacturing. Extra income in smallholder export cropping may be small, but it is widely spread, and goes for consumption of locally produced goods and services. Investment in light manufacturing benefits a small number of people whose aggregate impact through the consumption side is small, even if their incomes rise substantially. This is evidence of the consumption dependence of rural people on local urban goods and services. The reverse relationship is less evident.

- The absence of growth or intensification in peri-urban agriculture as recorded in a recent World Bank survey is not incompatible with a vision of export agriculture as a leading growth sector in Tanzania.

In Tanzania as in the rest of the developing world, widespread and rapid per capita urban income growth is likely to be quickly translated into soaring demand for animal and horticultural products. These perishable products are occasionally import substitutes, but rarely exportables from most countries. In Tanzania, they are mostly non-tradables, and incapable of being lead sectors in economic growth, although they can follow growth and extend its benefits. For at least four of the six peri-urban areas surveyed in the World Bank Peri-Urban Study, economic activity in the towns concerned depends on the health of tradable agriculture, which is in the doldrums. It is not surprising that few linkages were observed.

For the others, it seems implausible that income is not rising. Dar-es-Salaam has a large service sector with spending noticeably bolstered by government revenue, export receipts, and large foreign aid inflows. Arusha has both growing coffee sector income and substantial tourism income. Direct evidence on dairy and indirect evidence for poultry, eggs, and swine suggest that production response to income growth is occurring within city limits (at least 20,000 dairy cattle in Dar-es-Salaam alone), and thus in areas not surveyed. This suggests that infrastructural and institutional barriers to rural-urban trade need to be reviewed. It does not address what makes cities grow in the first place.

In sum, the links from agricultural development to overall development are strong, but those from urban manufacturing development to overall development have yet to be seen. Tanzania and its development partners should give careful consideration to the risks of embarking on a development strategy that once again side-lines export agriculture, one of the few proven sources of comparative advantage outside tourism and minerals. The proponents of a non-export-agriculture strategy need at a minimum to show how the vast mass of the population, living in areas made into largely non-tradable zones because of poor infrastructure, will be brought into a process of market-led development. This report has not argued against an urban manufacturing strategy per se, but has tried to lay out in detail the hard questions that need to be addressed in any strategy in Tanzania to promote widespread growth and improved equity on a sustained basis.

We have tried to show that export agriculture is the most likely engine of such a strategy at the present time.

8.6   The Need for a Workable Long-term Strategy for Agriculture-led Economic Growth

The single most worrying finding of this report for both agricultural growth and overall economic development is the renewed sharp appreciation of the real exchange rate, starting in 1994. This is probably the outcome of a series of unrelated decisions and events, the sum total of which is to reduce the rate of depreciation below the gap between Tanzanian and world inflation. Whatever the reason, the observed appreciation of the RER since 1993 has disastrous effects on the incentives to the tradable parts of agriculture, especially export crops.

Recognizing that such events are hard to control because of their complexity and because doing other-wise might bring to bear strong urban political pressures, it is nonetheless imperative to bring to the attention of decision-makers the consequences: loss of competitiveness of tradable agriculture, food shortages, and rural hardship as growth multipliers work in reverse. In Tanzania, an additional job is lost in the non-tradable sectors every time a job is lost in export agriculture.

Even within the context of a slightly appreciating RER, it is still possible to increase competitiveness and benefit from rural growth linkages through sectoral policies that lower the costs of production of agricultural tradables. This can be done at all stages from production through retail marketing. On the production side, focused adaptive agricultural research on maize, rice, cotton, coffee, cashew, and dairy can make great contributions in Tanzania. Production costs for export crops in rural areas are kept low--and welfare of workers raised--if the cost of the principal food items are lowered through technological change, extension thereof, and the availability of adapted purchased inputs. Marketing costs are very high, and can be lowered both by better roads (a primary necessity) and lower taxation on marketing services. Extension of telephone networks (either landline or wireless) in rural areas can serve a variety of purposes, as well as greatly improve arbitrage in agricultural trade.

The withdrawal of the state from Tanzanian agriculture has left a void in rural areas away from cities. This is a transitional problem in moving to a market-oriented system. Yet the growth of the institutional and legal environment necessary to nurture the growth of economic transactions under market principles has been slow. There is high need for greater progress in creating a reliable and enforceable regulatory environment for internal and external agricultural trade, including measures and standards. Clearer legal codes and better means of enforcement of contracts will be necessary to overcome high transactions costs that presently discourage the private sector from entering all but the most lucrative agricultural opportunities.

The decentralization of revenue generation and agricultural support services in Tanzania has led to very different tax regimes being applied in different districts, and also apparently to some arbitrary differences within districts. Maize farmers in remote areas such as Ruvuma can produce large maize surpluses, but have been hit several times in the last few years by the sudden imposition by regional authorities of arbitrary maize movement bans across the Malawi, Zambia and Mozambique borders, leading to great losses for producers and significant unpredictability of returns. Export crop taxation by local authorities is heavy and apparently somewhat arbitrary.

Two priority areas for rejuvenating agricultural performance in Tanzania are finding viable ways to stimulate the use of purchased inputs and developing suppliers' credit schemes that have a good record of reimbursement of loans. The necessity of higher input use is a fact of life for higher agricultural yields and for the maintenance of the resource base. Calculations in the report suggest that input use on food crops in not profitable in many situations, and that good returns to fertilizer are presently possible on only a few export crops such as fertilizer on coffee and sulphur on cashew nut. Input use has fallen substantially in food areas. The more densely settled among these are beginning to exhibit signs of fertility depletion. It is vital to find ways to get the real cost of inputs down.

While agricultural credit is always fraught with difficulties, experience in both Tanzania (Kilimanjaro Cooperative Bank) and elsewhere shows that provided a crop is profitable (such as Arabica coffee), suppliers' credits have a good chance of being reimbursed. The time frame should be relatively short (30 - 60 days), and the collective responsibility of a primary society should be involved.

Calculations in the report show that the real returns on food cropping rose after market liberalization and with the southern African drought in 1991, but have fallen steadily since 1994. Regular shipments of food aid since 1994 have helped temper food prices that would otherwise possibly have risen in real terms. Food aid has undoubtedly eased the pain of retrenchment for townspeople, but it also sends a very discouraging signal to farmers and traders. In bad agricultural years, rural people are hit with both low yields and low prices. Since the report also shows that the relatively and absolutely poor are primarily food farmers, it is questionable whether regular annual food aid is really serving the interests of equity. Food aid has also relieved the pressure on government to deal with an agricultural problem in the food sector that is getting worse every year.

Moving to do something about all this is a Tanzanian decision. The responsibility of this report is to make clear the view of the authors that it is not really a question of whether Tanzania needs to radically change its development focus in order to place priority on agriculture. Rather, the question is how long the politically difficult choices involved can be put off, and at what ultimate cost in terms of getting back on a sustainable growth track. Some specific actions that need to be implemented sooner rather than later are the subject of the next section.

8.7   Urgent Policy Action Issues in the Nearer Term

Send a Signal to Food Producers That Their Severely Depreciated Real Incentives to Produce Will Improve

- High-level government discussion of this issue in the media would be helpful if followed by concrete steps, such as those below.

- Re-centralize the authority currently exercised by the regions to impose export bans on food trade at short notice.

- Legislate a national ban on local taxation of food shipments across district boundaries.

- Develop a transparent national policy on food aid that links food aid acceptance to publicly available information showing need and lack of alternatives.

Increase Use Rates For Fertilizer and Other Needed Purchased Inputs in Intensive and High-value Cropping Situations

- Continue to avoid re-imposing direct fertilizer subsidies to producers, which cannot be sustained.

- Lower cost by importation of needed fertilizer and do not attempt to use high cost local plant.

- Encourage distribution of inputs by crop merchants through tax policy.

Reduce the Risks (and thus costs) in Internal Agricultural Trade

- Encourage a uniform fiscal treatment of export crops across all districts and avoid multiple taxation.
- Give priority to enforcement of contracts and the rule of law in rural trade.

- Improve governance.

Re-establish a Rural Financial System

- Explore alternative financial institutions for making loans to individuals guaranteed by collectivities.

- Provide fiscal incentives for rural banking facilities (Offices, ATM's--see South African experience).

- Develop an appropriate regulatory code and mechanism for overseeing rural banking.

- Explore legal options and financial incentives for linking private sector agents with collectivities of producers under contracts for export crop marketing.

Plan with Partners for Improved Basic Transportation Infrastructure

- There is no way around the need for much improved communications along the main inland-coast axes. Foreign assistance can best be employed to provide the needed asset transfer.

- Explore options for better telecommunications via private sector funded cell phone nodes in rural areas.

- Review possibility of contracting government shipments inland to private haulers to create additional demand for back-haulage during peak periods.

Develop Institutional Capacity of Government for Policy Analysis.

- Improve capacity to analyze interactions between agriculture and the overall economy.

- Separate the functions of policy analysis, policy data, and policy research.

- For policy analysis: this is vital both for MAC and for the Ministry of Finance and the Planning Commission. Agriculture is not just a sector-it is a leading sector, in fact the main engine of growth.

- For policy data: bolster the currently good but somewhat informal collaboration between the National Statistics Bureau, the Agricultural Statistics Unit, and the Market Development Bureau of MAC. Involve the Bank of Tanzania more in this partnership.

- For policy research: increase contracting out to the Economic Research Bureau of the University of Dar-es-Salaam, Sokoine University of Agriculture, and other competent local consultants.

Review Government and Development Partner Priorities Towards Agriculture

- Give higher priority in the national development budget to agriculture, to implement changes mentioned above.

- Development partners need to review aspects of their development assistance to ensure that interventions are targeted to promoting economic activity in tradable sectors, which can bring along non-tradable ones, whereas the reverse is not the case.

REFERENCES

Amani, H., and W. Maro. 1992. Stock management: Problems and policy under market liberalization for grains in Tanzania in J.B. Wyckoff and M. Rukuni. *Food security research in southern Africa: Policy implications.* Proceedings of the Sixth Annual Conference on Food Security Research in Southern Africa, October 28-30, 1991. Michigan State University/University of Zimbabwe, Harare.

Amani, H. K. R., and O. J. N. Mashindano. 1999. The Impact of agricultural performance on poverty alleviation, food security and nutrition in Tanzania since 1985. Collaborator study prepared for this report. Washington, D.C.: International Food Policy Research Institute.

Amani, H.K.R., S.M. Kapunda, N.H.I. Lipumba, and B.J. Ndulu. 1989. Impact of market liberalization on food security in Tanzania. In *Household and national food security in southern Africa,* ed. G. Mudimu and R. Bernsten. Proceedings of the Fourth Annual Conference on Food Security Research in Southern Africa, October 31-November 3, 1988. Michigan State University/University of Zimbabwe, Harare.

Bagachwa, M.S.D., and A. Naho. 1995. Estimating the second economy in Tanzania. *World Development* 23(August): 1387-1399.

Bank of Tanzania. 1999. *Monthly economic review*, February. Dar-es-Salaam, Tanzania.

Bank of Tanzania. Various issues. *Economic bulletin.* Dar-es-Salaam, Tanzania.

Bank of Tanzania and Kenyan Rural Enterprise Programme. 1997. Survey and analysis of rural/micro financial institutions in Tanzania. Nairobi, Kenya.

Bategeki, W. B., and F. W. Magambo. 1994. The Tanzania nutrition sector overview. A consultancy report for the World Bank. Washington, D.C.: World Bank. Mimeo.

Bitegeko, J.. 1999. Review of agriculture policy since 1985. Collaborator study prepared for this report. Washington, D.C.: International Food Policy Research Institute.

Bryceson, D. F. 1993. *Liberalizing Tanzania's food trade.* London: James Currey.

Bureau of Statistics (Tanzania). 1996. *1994 Indicator monitoring survey (IMS), volume 1: Preliminary report, Tanzania mainland.* Dar-es-Salaam, Tanzania.

Bureau of Statistics (Tanzania). 1997a. *Gender statistics and related issues newsletter.* Dar-es-Salaam, Tanzania.

Bureau of Statistics (Tanzania). 1997b. *Women and men in Tanzania.* Dar-es-Salaam, Tanzania.

Bureau of Statistics (Tanzania) and Macro International Inc. 1997a. *Tanzania demographic and health survey 1996.* Calverton, Maryland.

Bureau of Statistics (Tanzania) and Macro International Inc. 1997b. *Tanzania demographic and health survey 1996: Summary Report*. Calverton, Maryland.

Bureau of Statistics (Tanzania) and President's Office—Planning Commission. 1987. *Survey of industrial production*. Dar-es-Salaam, Tanzania.

Bureau of Statistics (Tanzania) and President's Office—Planning Commission. 1994a. *Collection of official statistics in Tanzania 1994*. Dar-es-Salaam, Tanzania.

Bureau of Statistics (Tanzania) and President's Office—Planning Commission. 1994b. *National accounts of Tanzania: 1976-1993*. Dar-es-Salaam, Tanzania.

Bureau of Statistics (Tanzania) and President's Office—Planning Commission. 1995a. *1994 (January to June) prices and price index numbers for twenty towns in mainland Tanzania*. Dar-es-Salaam, Tanzania.

Bureau of Statistics (Tanzania) and President's Office—Planning Commission. 1995b. *1994 (July to December) prices and price index numbers for twenty towns in mainland Tanzania*. Dar-es-Salaam, Tanzania.

Bureau of Statistics (Tanzania) and President's Office—Planning Commission. 1995c. *Central register of establishments technical and statistical report November, 1995*. Dar-es-Salaam, Tanzania.

Bureau of Statistics (Tanzania) and President's Office—Planning Commission. 1995d. *Selected statistical series: 1951-1994*. Dar-es-Salaam, Tanzania.

Bureau of Statistics (Tanzania) and President's Office—Planning Commission. 1995e. *Transport statistics 1993*. Dar-es-Salaam, Tanzania.

Bureau of Statistics (Tanzania) and President's Office—Planning Commission. 1996a. *Household budget survey 1991/92, volume II: Methodology, Tanzania mainland*. Dar-es-Salaam, Tanzania.

Bureau of Statistics (Tanzania) and President's Office—Planning Commission. 1996b. *Household budget survey 1991/92, volume IV: Household characteristics, Tanzania mainland*. Dar-es-Salaam, Tanzania.

Bureau of Statistics (Tanzania) and President's Office—Planning Commission. 1996c. *Industrial commodities quarterly report 1996:1*. Dar-es-Salaam, Tanzania.

Bureau of Statistics (Tanzania) and President's Office—Planning Commission. 1996d. *Statistical abstract: 1994*. Dar-es-Salaam, Tanzania.

Delgado, C. L.. 1992. Why domestic food prices matter to growth strategy in semi-open West African agriculture. *Journal of African Economies* 1(November): 446-471.

Delgado, C. L. 1997. The role of smallholder income generation from agriculture in Sub-Saharan Africa. In *Achieving food security in southern Africa: New challenges, new opportunities*, ed. L. Haddad. Washington, D.C.: International Food Policy Research Institute.

Delgado, C. L., J. Hopkins, V. A. Kelly, P. Hazell, A. A. McKenna, P. Gruhn, B. Hojjati, J. Sil, and C. Courbois. 1998. *Agricultural linkages in Sub-Saharan Africa*. Research Report 107. Washington, D.C.: International Food Policy Research Institute.

Department of Statistics, Ministry of State Planning and Investments (Zanzibar). 1996. *Zanzibar statistical abstract 1995*. Zanzibar, Tanzania.

Dercon, S. 1993. Peasant supply response and macroeconomic policies: Cotton in Tanzania. *Journal of African economies* 2(October): 157-194.

Dorosh, P. A., and S. Haggblade. 1993. Agricultural-led growth: foodgrains versus export crops in Madagascar. *Agricultural Economics* 9 (August): 165-180.

Edwards, S. 1989. *Real exchange rates, devaluation, and adjustment: Exchange rate policy in developing countries*. Cambridge, MA: The MIT Press.

Faber, M. 1995. Tea estate rehabilitation in Tanzania. *World Development* 23(August): 1335-1347.

FAO (Food and Agriculture Organization of the United Nations). Various issues. *Quarterly bulletin of statistics*. Rome.

FAO (Food and Agriculture Organization of the United Nations). 1999a. FAOSTAT database. <http://faostat.fao.org/default.htm>. Accessed April 16.

FAO (Food and Agriculture Organization of the United Nations). 1999b. Special report: FAO/WFP crop and food supply assessment mission to Tanzania. <http://www.fao.org/giews/english/alertes/1999/srtan299.htm>. Accessed May 13.

Ferreira, L. 1994. *Poverty and inequality during structural adjustment in rural Tanzania*. Policy Research Department, Transition Economics Division Research Paper Number 8. Washington, D.C.: World Bank.

Foster, J., J. Greer, and E. Thorbecke. 1984. A class of decomposable poverty measures. *Econometrica* 52(July): 761-765.

Gautam, M., and J. R. Anderson. 1999. Peri-urban agriculture, extension and rural development at the turn of the century. Draft report. Mimeo.

Government of Tanzania and The World Bank (Macroeconomics 2, Africa Region). 1998. *The United Republic of Tanzania public expenditure review, volume 1: Main report*. Washington, D.C.

Haddad, L. 1997. Overview of part I: Introduction. In *Achieving food security in southern Africa: New challenges, new opportunities*, ed. L. Haddad. Washington, D.C.: International Food Policy Research Institute.

Haggblade, S., J. Hammer, and P. B. R. Hazell. 1991. Modeling agricultural growth multipliers. *American Journal of Agricultural Economics* 73 (May): 361-364.

Havnevik, K. J. 1993. *Tanzania: The limits to development from above*. Uppsala, Sweden: The Scandinavian Institute of African Studies.

Havnevik, K. J., and M. Harsmar. 1999. The diversified future: An institutional approach to rural development in Tanzania. A study commissioned by the Expert Group on Development Issues, Swedish Ministry of Foreign Affairs. Stockholm, Sweden: Swedish Ministry of Foreign Affairs. Mimeo.

Heisey, P. W., and W. Mwangi. 1997. Fertilizer use and maize production. In *Africa's emerging maize revolution*, ed. D. Byerlee and C. K. Eicher. London: Lynne Rienner Publishers.

Hirschman, A. 1958. *The strategy of economic development*. New Haven, Conn., U.S.A.: Yale University Press.

HRDS (Human Resource Development Survey by The Population and Human Resources Division of the East Africa Department of the World Bank in collaboration with the University of Dar-es-Salaam and the Government of Tanzania's Planning Commission). 1996. <www.worldbank.org/lsms/country/tza/tanzhome.html>. Washington, D.C.: World Bank.

IMF (International Monetary Fund). 1999. *International financial statistics yearbook*. Washington, D.C.

International Bank for Reconstruction and Development. 1999. *Tanzania: Policy framework paper 1998/99-2000/01*. Washington, D.C.

Jansen, E. G. 1996. *Rich fisheries-poor fisherfolk: The effects of trade and aid in the Lake Victoria fisheries*. SUM Working Paper 1996.7. Oslo, Norway: Centre for Development and the Environment, University of Oslo.

Kahkonen, S. 1999. What influences the emergence and expansion of commercial activities in Tanzanian peri-urban areas? College Park, MD: Center for Institutional Reform and the Informal Sector, University of Maryland. Mimeo.

Kenny, C. and M. Syrquin. 1999. Growth and transformation in East Africa. In *Tanzania: Peri-urban development in the African mirror* (volume 2), ed. S. Yusuf. World Bank Report No. 19526TA. Washington, D.C.: World Bank. AFR2M.

Kiregyera, B. 1997. Data needs assessment for agricultural development in Tanzania, consultancy report. Dar-es-Salaam, Tanzania: Ministry of Agriculture and Cooperatives, Agricultural Sector Management Project. Mimeo.

Kiregyera, B. 1998. Tanzania donors' assistance committee meeting on food and agriculture statistics, mission report. Dar-es-Salaam, Tanzania: Food and Agriculture Organization of the United Nations. Mimeo.

Kiregyera, B., R. P. Katyal, A. Athmani, and R. S. Mlay. 1999. Examination of agricultural data and economic accounts for food and agriculture in Tanzania. FAO/World Bank Agricultural Statistics Assistance to Tanzania draft report.

Komba, J. 1999. Agricultural Statistics. Collaborator study prepared for this report. Washington, D.C.: International Food Policy Research Institute.

Kravis, I. B. 1970. Trade as a handmaiden of growth: Similarities between the nineteenth and twentieth centuries. *Economic Journal* 80(December): 850-872.

Kyle, S. C., and J. Swinnen. 1994. The theory of contested markets and the degree of tradedness of agricultural commodities: An empirical test in Zaire. *Journal of African Economies* 3(April): 93-113.

Mabele, R. 1999a. Agricultural policy and performance in Zanzibar. Economic Research Bureau, University of Dar-es-Salaam, Dar-es-Salaam. Mimeo.

Mabele, R. 1999b. Tanzania country economic memorandum Zanzibar section. Economic Research Bureau, University of Dar-es-Salaam, Dar- es-Salaam. Mimeo.

Maro, W. A. 1999. Agricultural marketing and transportation in Tanzania. Collaborator study prepared for this report. Washington, D.C.: International Food Policy Research Institute.

Mawalla, J., M. Munissi, N. Kimkanga, W. Mwaikambo, S. Wangwe, and M. Julien. 1999. Facilitating agribusiness development in Tanzania, what governments should do... Rotterdam, The Netherlands/Dar-es-Salaam, Tanzania: Netherlands Economic Institute. Mimeo.

Mfungahema, R. 1999. Impact of policy and world markets on the Tanzania agricultural sector since 1985. Collaborator study prepared for this report. Washington, D.C.: International Food Policy Research Institute.

MAC 1996. Ministry of Agriculture (Tanznaia). 1994/95 Market review of maize and rice. Dar-es-Salaam, Tanzania. Mimeo.

MAC 1997a. Ministry of Agriculture and Cooperatives (Tanzania). Agricultural inputs study. Dar-es-Salaam, Tanzania. Mimeo.

MAC 1997b. Ministry of Agriculture and Cooperatives (Tanzania). *Agricultural and livestock policy, 1997.* Dar-es-Salaam, Tanzania.

MAC 1998a. Ministry of Agriculture and Cooperatives (Tanzania). *Basic data: Agriculture and livestock sector 1991/92-1997/98.* Dar-es-Salaam, Tanzania.

MAC 1998b. Ministry of Agriculture and Cooperatives (Tanzania). Impact of taxes and levies on the agricultural sector. Dar-es-Salaam, Tanzania. Mimeo.

MAC 1998c. Ministry of Agriculture (Tanzania). 1996/97 Market review of sorghum, millets and cassava. Dar-es-Salaam, Tanzania. Mimeo.

MAC 1998d. Ministry of Agriculture (Tanzania). Review of the cashewnut marketing (1996/97). Dar-es-Salaam, Tanzania. Mimeo

MAC 1998e. Ministry of Agriculture and Cooperatives (Tanzania). 1996/97 Marketing review of coffee. Dar-es-Salaam, Tanzania. Mimeo.

MAC 1999a. Ministry of Agriculture and Cooperatives (Tanzania). Public expenditure review financial year 1999 for agriculture sector: A draft report. Dar-es-Salaam, Tanzania. Mimeo.

MAC 1999b. Ministry of Agriculture and Cooperatives (Tanzania). Review of the impact of taxes, levies and fees on the agricultural sector. draft report. Dar-es-Salaam, Tanzania. October. Mimeo.

MAC BS 1994. Ministry of Agriculture (Tanzania) and Bureau of Statistics (Tanzania). *National sample census of agriculture 1993/94 Tanzania mainland: Report volume II (Household characteristics, livestock count, implements, and storage)*. Dar-es-Salaam, Tanzania.

MAC BS 1995. Ministry of Agriculture (Tanzania) and Bureau of Statistics (Tanzania). *National sample census of agriculture 1993/94 Tanzania mainland: Highlights (Summary of findings of household characteristics, livestock count, implements and storage facilities)*. Dar-es-Salaam, Tanzania.

MAC BS 1996a. Ministry of Agriculture (Tanzania) and Bureau of Statistics (Tanzania). *National sample census of agriculture 1993/94 Tanzania mainland: Report volume III (Planted area, crop production, yield estimates, agricultural inputs and related characteristics)*. Dar-es-Salaam, Tanzania.

MAC BS 1996b. Ministry of Agriculture (Tanzania) and Bureau of Statistics (Tanzania). *National sample census of agriculture 1993/94-1994/95 Tanzania mainland: Report volume I (Technical and operational report)*. Dar-es-Salaam, Tanzania.

MAC BS 1996c. Ministry of Agriculture (Tanzania) and Bureau of Statistics (Tanzania). *National sample census of agriculture 1994/95 Tanzania mainland: Report volume II (Holdings characteristics, livestock poultry, agricultural practices, extension services and census evaluation)*. Dar-es-Salaam, Tanzania.

MAC BS 1996d. Ministry of Agriculture (Tanzania) and Bureau of Statistics (Tanzania). *National sample census of agriculture 1994/95 Tanzania mainland: Report volume III (Planted area, crop production, yield estimates, agricultural inputs and related characteristics)*. Dar-es-Salaam, Tanzania.

MAC BS 1997. Ministry of Agriculture (Tanzania) and Bureau of Statistics (Tanzania). 1997. *The census of large scale farming 1994/95 Tanzania mainland (Holding characteristics, temporary crops, permanent crops, livestock, agricultural workers, agricultural inputs and related characteristics)*. Dar-es-Salaam, Tanzania.

MAC FEWS 1999. (Ministry of Agriculture and Cooperatives (Tanzania) and Famine Early Warning System (USAID). Wholesale price meta data. Dar-es-Salaam, Tanzania.

MAC NEI 1999a. (Ministry of Agriculture and Cooperatives (Tanzania) and Netherlands Economic Institute). 1999a. *Final reports crop and food studies, volume 1: (a) National policies, sector performance and farming systems; (b) Food crop sub-sector report* (draft). Rotterdam, The Netherlands.

MAC NEI 1999b. (Ministry of Agriculture and Cooperatives (Tanzania) and Netherlands Economic Institute). *Final reports crop and food studies, volume 2: Food crops grains* (draft). Rotterdam, The Netherlands.

MAC NEI 1999c. (Ministry of Agriculture and Cooperatives (Tanzania) and Netherlands Economic Institute). *Final reports crop and food studies, volume 3: Food crops non-grains* (draft). Rotterdam, The Netherlands.

MAC NEI 1999d. (Ministry of Agriculture and Cooperatives (Tanzania) and Netherlands Economic Institute). *Final reports crop and food studies, volume 4: Traditional export crops* (draft). Rotterdam, The Netherlands.

MAC NEI 1999e (Ministry of Agriculture and Cooperatives (Tanzania) and Netherlands Economic Institute). *Final reports crop and food studies, volume 5: Minor and non-traditional export crops grains* (draft). Rotterdam, The Netherlands.

MAC NEI 1999f (Ministry of Agriculture and Cooperatives (Tanzania) and Netherlands Economic Institute). *Livestock sub-sector study-Tanzania Mainland.* Policy and Planning Dept., Dar-es-Salaam, September.

MAC Sokoine ILRI 1998. (Ministry of Agriculture and Cooperatives (Tanzania), Sokoine University of Agriculture (Morogoro, Tanzania), and International Livestock Research Institute). *The Tanzania dairy sub-sector: A rapid appraisal* (volumes 1, 2,3). Dar-es-Salaam, Tanzania.

MALNR FAO 1999. (Ministry of Agriculture, Livestock, and Natural Resources (Zanzibar) and Food and Agriculture Organization of the United Nations). Agricultural sector policy. Dar-es-Salaam. Mimeo.

Mlay, O. 1999. Agricultural statistics and performance. Collaborator study prepared for this report. Washington, D.C.: International Food Policy Research Institute.

Monke, E. A., and S. R. Pearson. 1989. *The policy matrix for agricultural development.* Ithaca, N.Y.: Cornell University Press.

Moshi, H. P. B. 1998. *Fiscal and monetary burden of Tanzania's corporate bodies: The case of public enterprises.* Nairobi, Kenya: African Economic Research Consortium.

Msambichaka, L. A., A. A. L. Kilindo, and G. D. Mjema. 1995. *Beyond structural adjustment programmes in Tanzania: Success, failures, and new perspectives.* Dar-es-Salaam, Tanzania: Economic Research Bureau, University of Dar-es-Salaam.

Msambichaka, L. A., H. P. B. Moshi, and F. P. Mtatifikolo. 1994. *Development challenges and strategies for Tanzania: An agenda for the 21st century.* Dar-es-Salaam, Tanzania: Dar-es-Salaam University Press.

Mutumba-Lule, A. 1999. EU wants list of pesticides before lifting fish ban. *The East African,* April 26-May 2.

Myint, H. 1975. Agriculture and economic development in the open economy. In *Agriculture in development theory*, ed. L. G. Reynolds. New Haven, Conn., U.S.A.: Yale University Press.

Narayan, D. 1997. *Voices of the poor, poverty and social capital in Tanzania*. Environmentally and Socially Sustainable Development Studies and Monographs Series 20. Washington, D.C.: World Bank.

Ngondo, A. 1999. Profile of the agricultural sector. Collaborator study prepared for this report. Washington, D.C.: International Food Policy Research Institute.

Nordas, H. K., and A. Angelsen. 1998. *Macmod, a macroeconomic model for the Tanzanian economy*. Bergen, Norway: Chr. Michelsen Institute.

Planning Commission (Tanzania). 1997. *The economic survey 1997*. Dar-es-Salaam, Tanzania.

Planning Commission (Tanzania) and the World Bank. 1995. *Workshop on socio-economic growth and poverty alleviation in Tanzania, proceedings, volume 1: Speeches and summary*. Dar-es-Salaam, Tanzania.

Poulton, C. 1997. *The cashew sector in Tanzania: Overcoming problems of input supply*. Paper submitted to the Policy Research Programme, Natural Resources Policy and Advisory Department, Overseas Development Administration. Kent, UK: Department of Agricultural Economics and Business Management, Wye College, University of London Wye.

Poulton, C., A. Dorward, and J. Kydd. 1998. The revival of smallholder cash crops in Africa: Public and private roles in the provision of finance. *Journal of International Development* 10(January-February): 85-103.

President's Office—Planning Commission (Tanzania). 1998. National population policy (draft, November). Dar-es-Salaam, Tanzania. Mimeo.

Putterman, L. 1995. Economic reform and smallholder agriculture in Tanzani: A discussion of recent market liberalization, road rehabilitation, and technology dissemination efforts. *World Development* 23(February): 311-326.

Rao, J. M. 1994. Agriculture in economic growth: Handmaiden or equal partner. In *Agrarian questions*, ed. K. Basu. Oxford, UK: Oxford University Press.

Ravallion, M. 1994. *Poverty comparisons*. Fundamentals of pure and applied economics, volume 56. Chur, Switzerland: Harwood Academic Press.

Reardon, T., A. A. Fall, V. Kelly, C. Delgado, P. Matlon, J. Hopkins, and O. Badiane. 1994. Is income diversification agriculture-led in the West African semi-arid tropics? The nature, causes, effects, distribution, and production linkages of off-farm activities. *In Economic policy experience in Africa: What have we learned?*, ed. A. Atsain, S. Wangwe, and A. G. Drabek. Nairobi, Kenya: African Economic Research Consortium.